LOVE'S REVOLUTION

LOVE'S REVOLUTION

INTERRACIAL

MARRIAGE

Maria P. P. Root

 Temple University Press
PHILADELPHIA

Temple University Press, Philadelphia 19122
Copyright © 2001 by Maria P. P. Root
Published 2001
Printed in the United States of America

⊗The paper used in this publication meets the requirements of
the American National Standard for Information Sciences—Permanence
of Paper for Printed Library Materials, ANSI Z39.48-1984

Library of Congress Cataloguing-in-Publication Data
Root, Maria P. P., 1955–
Love's revolution: interracial marriage / Maria P. P. Root
     p. cm.
   Includes bibliographical references and index.
   ISBN 1-56639-825-8 (cloth : alk. paper) — (ISBN 1-56639-826-6 (pbk.
   : alk. paper)
     1. Interracial marriage—United States.   2. Racially mixed children—
     United States—Family relationships.   I. Title.
HQ1031.R64 2001
306.84'6—dc21   00-032566
ISBN 13: 978-1-56639-826-8 (pbk. : alk. paper)
032310-P

Contents

Acknowledgments

This project took many twists and turns over six years, growing into a much larger study than I initially planned. Consequently, I am able to offer more analysis about interracial marriage than was possible even a few years ago—and with more confidence. I am grateful for all the work that has laid the foundation for my research and analysis.

One does not complete an endeavor such as this one without the generosity of many people. I am grateful to the approximately two hundred women and men who formally shared their experiences and insights on what continues to be an emotionally intense issue for this country—racial intermarriage and its offspring. It is an important subject because so much of this country's history was predicated on the fear of race mixing.

The last two phases of the book were completed with the help of two women with whom I have been fortunate to work. Jaslean LaTaillade and Valerie White made it possible to bring the Multiracial Families Project to completion. They assisted me for approximately one year in conducting focus groups, interviewing people, and transcribing tapes. Both doctoral students at the time, their advanced level of study and their understanding of race relations and human complexity were essential to the quality of the final interviews. Ms. White also contributed to the successful completion of the Biracial Sibling Project. Michele Stulken, Julie Warden, Elizabeth Erausquin, Darouny Syphachane, and Jason Thomas provided essential help in transcribing interview tapes.

Several friends and colleagues gave me honest criticism and feedback on an earlier version of this book. All of them gave an incredible gift of time by carefully reading the manuscript in draft form. Each person's published and unpublished work and life experience on this topic was very much appreciated. I especially thank Michael C. Thornton for providing specific suggestions for rearranging parts of the manuscript and for his critique of the content and linkages between chapters. G. Reginald Daniel generously allowed me to use him as a sounding board to further flesh out how I wanted to discuss notions of class versus caste and to develop my business models of family. Abby L. Ferber provided reminders and specific suggestions as to how and where I could tie race and gender together more effectively. Her recent book was very clarifying. Ronald C. Johnson made helpful suggestions about how to relate past data on intermarriage to my findings. His work on intermarriage in Hawaii was useful for thinking through intermarriage in the continental United States. His amazing breadth of knowledge also helped stimulate my thinking on other parts of the manuscript. Paul N. Spickard provided some fact checks; his historical research on intermarriage was particularly useful. Lory Y. Kitamura Tintor provided reflective comments that helped me make more effective use of examples. B. J. Winchester reassured me that my research on contemporary interracial marriage might be useful to the general public. Robin A. LaDue provided supportive comments and editing. Elizabeth Jenkins encouraged me to write this book in spite of some reservations I had. I also want to acknowledge the interracial family support groups and their representatives who helped support this work from Oregon, Los Angeles, Berkeley, Wisconsin, Minnesota, Chicago, Washington, D.C., New York, and Florida. I am grateful to my editor, Janet Francendese, who demonstrated much largesse, knowledge, and support.

Lastly, I thank my parents, Milagros Alejandra Pastor Newhouse and Robert Norman Newhouse, who gave me my first exposure to interracial marriage, cross-cultural living, and interclass differences.

LOVE'S REVOLUTION

1

Love and Revolution

ove promises happiness and wholeness. Contemporary marriage suggests that fulfillment of these promises is invaluable and worth sacrifices. With love as a beacon, a couple commits to a constructive and transformative phase of their life, believing that they—and the world—will be better off as a result. They believe they can become better human beings through marriage than they can by remaining single.[1]

Families support this ideology of love so long as their children uphold two conventions in their choice of partners. *Marry within your own race. Marry someone of the opposite sex.* Until quite recently, beloved sons and daughters who defied these rules were rejected and disowned. Fear and hate invaded homes that were previously full of love; racism rendered them loveless.

The pages that follow allow the reader a glimpse of the paths different families have taken through interracial marriage. While hate, fear, and anger are common responses to interracial marriage and have powerful short-term effects, love has proved a formidable opponent. With stealth, persistence, and a few legal twists, love carves a more hopeful path for future race relations through the sacrifices of many who have made and make their commitments to love for better or worse.

Carl, a twenty-year-old visionary and leader, noticed the girl in the crowd, fist stridently punched up through the

1

air, punctuating the fervor of the political rally. Catherine, twelve or thirteen years old, was with her parents, involved in a political campaign to reform institutions that have divided the world into haves and have-nots. By fate or coincidence, Carl and Catherine would meet several years later, in the 1940s, two young adults working for a mutual cause.

They were an unlikely pair. Catherine was an only and much-loved child. Carl, the youngest of eight children, was placed in foster care at an early age, only to be turned out with the rest of his siblings onto the streets of San Francisco when he was ten. His oldest sister was given $150 by the state of California to feed and house all eight of them.

Catherine's parents had taught her to appreciate persons from all walks of life. Specifically, they taught her not to judge a person by color. Carl's foster mother, in contrast, warned him, "Don't get yourself involved with some white woman. She will only make trouble for you."

Catherine knew stability, consistency, and comfort amidst political turmoil that anchored family life and values. Carl knew the struggle of finding the next meal, working small jobs, moving, and changing schools so many times that it was a miracle he finished high school. That Catherine would graduate was a given. And despite her parents' progressive racial ideology, they unconsciously assumed that she would marry a white man.

They liked Carl, Catherine remembers. They admired him when he was just a guest at the house. But when Catherine announced her intention to marry him, her parents turned their backs on her. It was years before Catherine and her parents were reconciled. Their opposition to her marriage was typical of the era, and their view of interracial marriage was widely held by both black and white Americans. The legal system supported their prejudices; interracial marriage was illegal in 1946 in California. Carl and Catherine took a train to Washington state to formalize their commitment to each other. Even there, however, they were met with threats of physical harm, intimidation, and name calling. They returned home quickly to the safety and support of friends, and spent the rest of their married life as part of a quiet revolution fueled by love.

Fast-forward several decades and the effects of this revolution are strikingly apparent. The Supreme Court's 1967 decision in *Loving v. Virginia*, the result of nearly twenty years of civil rights reform, lifted the ban on interracial marriage nationwide, which has gradually made a significant difference in people's thinking about race. Just before their fiftieth anniversary, Carl and Catherine renewed their marriage vows in San Francisco, as it was Catherine's wish to be legally married in California. This was the wedding they never had. Living family members came for the ceremony: Carl's brothers, Catherine's mother, and their three children and their families. Several other longtime friends, other married interracial couples, also attended.

Although not intended as a political tool, each interracial marriage helps to change long-held assumptions and social conventions. And as these assumptions gradually change, the ideology of love allows many families to stand strong as their children make a commitment to transform their lives and cross color lines in marriage. Interracial relationships, including interracial marriage, are natural consequences of increased social interaction between races. Familiarity leads people to challenge and eventually break down stereotypes. Love does not always stay within color lines even when people are determined to enforce racial apartheid.

On a beautiful June day in Akron, Ohio, in 1994, thirty-year-old Keith and twenty-nine-year-old Marcia committed themselves to each other before their beaming parents and 250 guests. Their brothers and sisters served as groomsmen and bridesmaids as these two clans vowed to support this couple's commitment to create a life together. Keith, a high school teacher, and Marcia, a bank teller, had met five years earlier at the local community college, where they were taking the same evening class. Marcia comes from a religious black family in a small town in Alabama. Her father owns a cabinet business and her mother had been a housekeeper, when she was younger, for more well-to-do families. Keith was raised in a white family that still celebrates its Irish heritage. His father owns a small appliance store and his mother has helped with various aspects of the business.

Marcia's parents described her as very independent. Initially surprised by her choice of a white husband, they worried that this might make her life harder, but they were able to appreciate Keith, whom they considered a fine young man. They hoped that the marriage would withstand the pressures that still burden interracial couples. Marcia had been married in her early twenties and divorced. Since then, her mother observed, she had matured, and her parents trusted her judgment. Keith possessed the values they had taught her to respect.

Keith's parents, who had met Marcia only once and were also worried about the social consequences of their son's choice, reluctantly gave the couple their blessing. By the time the wedding day arrived, however, Keith's parents sincerely welcomed Marcia into their family.

This country has fixated on black-white intermarriage since the days of slavery.[2] The prohibition on these marriages eliminated black economic competition and black competition for white women. Today, however, racial intermarriages cover a wide spectrum of racial mixing, particularly as the demographics of this country have changed. And, as with earlier patterns of economic motivation and competition for women, as men of Asian, Mexican, and Native American descent were used as laborers and isolated from access to women of their culture, white men began to prohibit mongoloids, Chinese, Filipinos, Hindus, Mexicans, and mulattos from intermarriage with the white population. And although black-white intermarriage still provokes the most hostile response among families, other types of intermarriage can also generate anger, fear, and divisiveness.

A summer wedding in Denver in 1996 was marred by parental disapproval, though friends of Jeff and Joy expressed great love and support. Members of their softball league, coworkers, and high school and college friends attended the wedding. Jeff's father, a second-generation Chinese American, refused to show up for the ceremony; his mother, torn between love for her son and loyalty to her husband, reluctantly attended. Jeff tried to persuade his mother to open her heart to Joy; he assured her that Joy was everything she wanted in a daughter-in-law—except Chinese. He reminded his mother that a Chinese American wife was no guarantee of cultural continuity and that his last Chinese girlfriend had not even liked rice.

Joy's Midwestern parents invoked the racial yardstick, telling her that she could have done better. Although they came to the wedding, their attendance had been in doubt until the last minute. Joy and Jeff had even considered eloping to avoid the tense, embarrassing scenes they envisioned. With the encouragement of friends, and after much strategizing, they decided to go forward with a public ceremony. They welcomed both sets of parents, but asked that they not attend if they planned to object publicly to the marriage or otherwise embarrass them. Joy arranged for a friend to give her away in case her father refused this ceremonial privilege.

Joy is a physical therapist and Jeff a nurse; they had met at work at the clinic. Joy's parents had always wanted her to "marry up," perhaps to a doctor; given Jeff's race and profession, her parents saw Joy's marriage as "marrying down." Since Jeff was their only son, Joy represented for his parents an end to the cultural line. They told him bluntly that he was contaminating their Chinese blood. They saw Jeff's decision to marry a non-Chinese as a personal affront and a disavowal of pride in his cultural heritage.

Joy and Jeff were in their early thirties when they married. Both had worked for years and had saved money. Able to finance their own wedding and support themselves, they were not dependent on parental approval in the way that earlier generations or younger couples might have been.

Another interracial couple, Linda and Charles, developed a friendship while attending the local community college. In spite of the usual assumptions that they would marry "among their kind," in 1993 twenty-three-year-old Linda and twenty-five-year-old Charles married in a quiet ceremony in Madison, Wisconsin, attended only by their immediate families and followed by a garden reception for friends and extended family. They and their parents and grandparents received their guests graciously and happily.

Charles had never considered marriage with a white woman desirable or even possible. In fact, as one of the student leaders of the Black Student Association on campus, he was accused of "selling out" and "dissing his black sisters" when he began dating Linda. Linda had never imagined marrying a black man either. In childhood fantasies enacted with her girlfriends, Prince Charming was always white.

Because of their families' initial opposition to their marriage, Charles and Linda were both practical and patient in introducing each other to their respective families. Linda's family, while acknowledging that Charles was a "great young man" so long as he was just a friend, opposed the engagement on the familiar grounds that "Marriage is hard enough; why make it more difficult?" "How will you raise children?" they asked. "You don't have enough life experience to know the difference between infatuation and love." Charles's family made fun of Linda's habits and naïveté about race, but they eventually accepted her. His sisters and aunts questioned his motives repeatedly, and one sister told him, "You insult me and all black sisters" and "You know, she's gonna use you up and leave you broke." After three years of dating and socializing with each family, they decided to go forward with marriage over these objections. When Linda's parents saw that they could not change her mind, they did "a 180-degree turn" and welcomed Charles into the family. She concludes they were testing the conviction of her love for Charles. Charles's family slowly warmed to Linda, though one sister still refuses to be in the same room with her when they visit. Linda has learned not to make this her problem. She realizes that she cannot make Charles's sister accept her and has resolved not to waste her time trying.

The stories go on and on. Black men with white women, Asian women with white men, white men with Indian women, Chicana women with white men. And, increasingly, black women with white men, Asian men with white women, black men with Asian women. Love alone motivated these women and men to cross the color line, despite a lifetime of cultural indoctrination. None of these or any of the other couples I interviewed entered into their marriage for the purpose of making a political or social statement. As a result of the hatred and fear they encountered, however, most of them developed a political outlook of mindful action and responsible reaction that became another means, along with their love, of withstanding the assaults of bigotry, fear, hate, and misunderstanding. These women and men have been the scouts on the front lines of a quiet revolution.

Trends in Interracial Marriage

Interracial marriage has grown at least 500 percent since 1970. Numerically, black-white intermarriages represent the greatest number of relationships, while the largest proportion of intermarriage occurs across various Asian American communities, where rates can be higher than 50 percent in some cities.[3] White people, however, intermarry in the greatest numbers. This fact does not escape the attention of white supremacist groups, who distribute hate-filled literature warning that intermarriage will be the end of the white race.

Historically, rates of intermarriage of whites with American Indians and persons of Mexican descent have been high but have met with less opposition and generated less legislation than white marriages to African and Asian Americans. The likely explanation is that American

Indians and persons of Mexican descent have been intermixed with the white population for more generations than have other groups. The longer history of intermixing has resulted in some light-skinned members of both these populations, which makes them less threatening to many whites. The phenotype of a person of Mexican or American Indian descent is apt to be more similar to that of a white person than is the phenotype of a person of Asian or African descent—and the children of these intermarriages are more likely to be phenotypically indistinguishable from the white population.

Intermarriage tends to be more acceptable—and has certainly become an established fact of life with each succeeding generation—within ethnic and racial minority communities, though it is not always welcome there. Historically, a general pattern has prevailed with all immigrant groups to the United States. The first generation has a very low rate of intermarriage. Second-generation immigrants are a bridge generation between the American and native cultures. They are still affected by certain cultural values and imperatives that may set them apart from their mainstream peers. Their children, however, the third generation, fluent in English and American popular culture, share much in common with their peers of the same socioeconomic standing. Several researchers have noted that intermarriage becomes significant by the third generation following immigration.[4]

Although Hawaii has the most intermarriage proportionally, five states account for the largest numbers of intermarriages: California, Florida, Oklahoma, Texas, and Washington.[5] With the exception of Washington, these states historically had anti-miscegenation laws that specifically outlawed black-white intermarriage.[6] California also forbade white and Asian (Mongolian) marriage. California, Florida, and Texas declared such marriages void. Florida, Oklahoma, and Texas had severe penalties for violating the anti-miscegenation laws, including a two-year prison term. Much has changed since the repeal of those laws more than thirty years ago.

The particular configurations of interracial marriage vary by state and region. In California, where more than a quarter of all interracial couples live, all mixtures are present.[7] With the numerically largest Asian American population in the United States, California is home to the largest proportion of interracial marriages involving Asian Americans. In Oklahoma, most intermarriages occur between American Indians and whites. In Texas, black-white and Chicano/Latino-white intermarriages prevail.

Appendix A provides a detailed discussion of intermarriage trends since 1960. For the purposes of this overview, a few summary statements will suffice. The civil rights movement prompted the repeal of anti-miscegenation laws and promoted greater social interaction among people of all races. Interracial dating became increasingly common and, once the legal barriers toppled, so did interracial marriage. Between 1960 and 1970 the number and rate of interracial marriages doubled; between 1970 and 1980 they tripled. After 1970 black men married white women in unprecedented numbers, reversing the pattern of black-white marriages.[8] By the 1980s Asia had become a more common source of foreign spouses than Europe; Mexico and the Philippines became the leading countries of origin for foreign spouses.[9] Even if interracial marriages represented less than 1.5% of all marriages, these rapid changes were significant and would continue into the 1990s.

Broad trends since 1960 can be summarized as follows:

1. Women (except for black women) intermarry more than their male counterparts;
2. Later generations have higher rates of intermarriage than the first generation;
3. High rates of intermarriage, as in the Hispanic and American Indian populations, yield more similar rates of intermarriage for women and men;
4. Later age of marriage is associated with intermarriage;
5. Uneven sex ratios influence patterns of intermarriage;
6. Similar size groups of different races and ethnicities in proximity are associated with intermarriage for younger persons, at least in Hawaii, California, and Arizona;
7. When first marriages for black partners are separated from all marriages for black partners, there is a significant trend toward substantially increasing rates of interracial marriage;
8. Variables influencing intermarriage differ by racial and ethnic group; and
9. Younger age is associated with greater acceptance of racial intermarriage.

Increasing rates of intermarriage with each generation and changing patterns of interracial marriage support the observation that we are in the midst of a quiet revolution. It started decades ago. Consider Debbie, who blends into the forty-something crowd in New York state. She is an ordinary middle-class white woman living an ordinary middle-class life. She has a loving husband, children, and family and can boast being married for twenty years, longer than many of her friends. The first phase of her marriage, however, challenged her family's intellectual and emotional values. Her marriage changed the way in which they experienced race in this country. They acquired black kin: a son-in-law and then grandchildren. She related her mother's reaction to her announcement that she was going to marry a black man:

> I know one of the things for my mom is how other people are going to view her. So I kinda felt for her, in that sense, when I heard her say, you know, "How am I gonna address what other people have to say to me?" She felt so much pressure on her. And in addition, you know, how's the child going to relate to the world? That concept. And then the other piece that she said to me was, she literally said, "We've grown up ten miles outside of New York, in a very white suburb that if it had a black family in there, it was because I think someone had come up and lived with the guidance counselor's family from the South," and went all through high school with us, and so that was, like, it. And then across the river from us, was Patterson, New Jersey, which in the sixties was going through riots, and so when, around the time when we were getting married, and maybe in the same conversation, my mother literally said to me, "You mean, you are actually acting on the values that we gave you?" because they espoused very liberal values. Of course I was acting on those values. I believed them. And she was like, "You really, really believe all this?" From my mom! And yes, I believed them!

Some very real structural changes imposed by legislation have allowed for increased opportunities to develop friendships, love relationships, and ultimately commitments to marriage between people of different races. Mariel, a twenty-four-year-old Chicana raised in a suburb of Los Angeles, reflected on what influenced her decision to marry her black husband:

> I was really active in La Raza [literally, the struggle, the Chicano movement] and feel committed to my people, so I always thought I would marry a Chicano guy. I love my older brothers and even thought

I would marry one of their friends. When I went away to college at Berkeley I was just exposed to so many people. My political ideals didn't change. But I met my husband in my second year. He was very supportive of my commitments. We just started doing things together, studying, talking, going to parties. He fit in well with my friends and I liked his friends. It was like we would go to parties and there were all sorts of people there and I'd find I always had more in common with him than with just about anyone in a room. We had really good talks. And music. We both loved music and movies. So one thing led to another. I tried to talk myself out of my feelings for him, thinking I should just keep it as good friends, but then I thought, "Shouldn't the man I marry be my best friend?" My family liked him. I mean, like, if my brothers didn't like him, this would have been real hard. They have a lot of influence on me even though I make up my own mind. We talked a lot about what it meant to marry someone different than your own cultural background. But I realized I didn't have to give up my commitment to my people. We believed in the same issues. Now it might have been different if he was white. I'm not sure how that would have gone over.

Mariel explained her attraction in terms of romantic theories of love. The man she married should be her best friend. They shared much in common; there were no significant objections from her family; and they had time to get to know each other away from the watchful eye of their families. She also grew up in an area of the country where interracial and interethnic interaction is common.

What people often fail to ask is why intermarriage rates have been so low for certain groups. Certain established demographic factors predict that intermarriage should occur at a faster pace than has actually been the case in the last quarter of the twentieth century. Imbalanced sex ratios,[10] the small numbers of racial minorities in some communities and in the nation at large,[11] and the age composition should have guaranteed a quicker mix even despite in-group prohibitions on inter-marriage.[12] But the caste connotations of race, particularly of blackness, slowed intermarriage trends. Across all groups, colorism makes darker skin a barrier to consideration of potential partners.

Despite some contemporary objections to Asian-white marriages, these marriages do not tend to provoke the same degree of antagonistic or fearful response that black-white relationships do. Nevertheless, Asian Americans were seen as similar to African Americans in being less desirable partners in a recent twenty-one-city survey of whites, blacks, and Latinos on the subject of openness to racial intermarriage.[13] Although it has taken approximately a century, Asian Americans seem to be moving from a group representing a caste to a group with class mobility. Racialized gender stereotypes of Asian American women weigh heavily in this transformation. Asian American women have been stereotyped as more traditionally feminine—more sacrificing, obedient, and domestic—even in the 1990s.[14] They also have been perceived as small and petite, one criterion of attractiveness by white male American standards. In contrast, while Asian American men might be stereotyped as highly intelligent or as good wage earners, stereotypes have emasculated them, removing them from competition with white men. Their attractiveness might be compromised by height and build, generally associated with masculine attractiveness. On average, white and black men are taller than Asian men, a physical feature that connotes status, power, and physical attractiveness.[15] In addition, whereas Asian American women have slowly achieved a presence in video media, Asian American men in media roles are few and far between. The high rates of intermarriage for Asian American women with white men have made Asian Americans acceptable partners in some situations. White male involvement in this transformation has been critical; their privilege had facilitated a subtle change in Asianness from a caste to a class. The same change has occurred with Latino and Indian women, but not with black women—blackness still has caste connotations.

The concepts of structural and dyadic power, which refer to the similarity in status between two people and between groups in a community, help make sense of the demographics and of how Debbie's marriage—and others like hers—take place. The structural power constructed by whiteness and maleness has ironically given rise to several of the patterns we see now. Black women have been rendered less desirable by both race and gender and are thus partnered in intermarriages proportionately less than any other group. As a group, they have historically been opposed to intermarriage, particularly when compared to white women and both white and black men.[16] Thus, when a black woman suggests that "white women are out to get any man they can" or "are trying to take all the good black men," her statements reflect a demographic fact. White women are not to blame, however; the construction of whiteness and its control by white men are responsible. While white women are second-class citizens by gender, ironically they have more room to search for other partners. The construction of whiteness, designed to provide white males advantages over everyone else, has backfired. White women are not that distant in power from men of color and thus can be expected to participate significantly in intermarriage. Moreover, male privilege still yields much structural power. Combined with institutional racism, which leaves fewer black men available for intermarriage—as we will see in Chapter 3, male privilege accounts for black men's ability to intermarry much more freely than black women can. Men are still in the position of choosing and women in the position of hoping to be chosen. If there were fewer black women, their mate choices would probably be more effectively guarded by black men. If black women are now marrying more frequently across racial lines, another surge in black female intermarriage will probably be revealed by the 2000 census.

Because they are already high, rates of intermarriage for women (except black women) and for Latino and American Indian groups are likely to stabilize. If families continue to produce more children who question race and gender stereotypes and who truly believe in the equality of all people, the structural barriers to interracial marriage will be further eroded. The grip of male power and white privilege on mainstream American culture will continue to weaken.

How we teach our children to think critically about equality, and to strive for it not only in thought but in deed, will make a difference in the world they pass on to their children. I am hopeful that the generation now coming of age will achieve more equity in relationships by gender, race, and sexual orientation than has any previous generation. I am confident that this nation will witness a noticeable increase in interracial marriage for white men, black women, and Asian American men. Intermarriage has ripple effects that touch many people's lives. It is a symbolic vehicle through which we can talk about race and gender and reexamine our ideas about race.

But the obstacles of culturally ingrained assumptions and prejudices remain to be overcome. One couple in an interracial marriage summed up both the difficulties and the hope when I first discussed this project with them years ago. In the privacy of their own homes, among friends, they relate to each other as people. They negotiate on chores, enjoy time with each other, pay bills, dream of a bigger house and a better life. They have their differences, but they treat each other with respect through it all, trying to be aware of differences in their personalities and backgrounds that stem from class values, regional culture, family culture, and gender differences. But when they go out into the world, even if only to run an errand on a Saturday afternoon, they are jolted back to reality by the taunts of neighbor children chanting "jungle fever, jungle fever, they've got jungle fever." Under ten years of age, these children, some black and some white, are already policing their interracial union. These children cannot possibly comprehend the depth of meaning and history that this taunt communicates. Living in an integrated neighborhood, who will these children date? Who will be their partners twenty years from now?

Though interracial marriage has expanded and taken on new meanings over the decades, mixed and hostile attitudes, held most pervasively by whites, still exist, especially toward black-white intermarriage. Many white people remain unaware that blacks also have mixed, hostile, and suspicious attitudes toward whites, based on centuries of a reign of terror simply because of the invention of their race.[17] A potent and parallel prejudice exists within many Asian American communities toward interracial marriage, particularly when the pairing is with a black partner.[18] Extreme hostile attitudes are less common but exist within all groups to some degree. Wednesday morning, July 8, 1998, provides me an extreme reminder. It is just past 6:00 A.M. and the clock radio gently nudges me to consciousness. A few minutes later, I am jolted out of my grogginess by the news of a hate crime in Massachusetts. A married couple celebrating their twentieth anniversary at a cookout is attacked, the black husband beaten to death, his white wife widowed. Will the problem of the color line consume the twenty-first century, too?

Research Aims and Methods

I began to formalize the research for this book in 1992. After publishing the first contemporary edited volume on children of interracial marriage, *Racially Mixed People in America*, I had the opportunity to talk with people at community conferences, most of them in California, dedicated to themes of multiracial families and people of mixed heritage.[19] These discussions established the direction of this research and helped clarify the questions I wanted to pursue. Several studies have documented trends, unique issues, and problems,[20] and additional books by people involved in intermarriages had begun to appear.[21] I wanted to add something to the small but growing body of literature on interracial families. As a psychologist, my interest was in the transformations these relationships catalyze in families, as families are a primary source of socialization on the issue of race. I wanted to explore how interracial relationships reflected changing norms of family, gender roles, and conceptions of race, three issues that I did not think could be separated.[22]

Since 1992 I have completed some six hundred hours of formal conversations and interviews with couples, individuals, and groups representing all regions of the country. All of these interviews were conducted in person by one of the researchers connected with the project.[23]

In the first phase of this research (from 1992 to 1996), I interviewed couples or partners of thirty-five past or present interracial marriages. I asked them to describe how they met; what issues they dealt with at different stages of their relationship; their support systems; how they were received by each other's families and whether the reception of them or their partner would have been different had they been of the other gender; and what they had learned about themselves and race through their relationships. If the marriage had ended, I asked them to explain why they thought it had not survived. Each interview took, cumulatively, between one and eight hours. The last few interviews offered little new information, so I moved on to the next phase of research.

Because I wanted to understand how whole families were affected by these marriages, I needed to interview family members as well as the couples themselves. In 1996 and 1997, I started the Multiracial Families Project at the University of Washington. This second phase of the research involved twenty more individual interviews, each approximately two hours in length, but this time with mothers, fathers, sisters, and brothers of persons who were interracially married. None of the interviewees were related. In addition, in 1997 approximately eighty-five people participated in seven focus groups, each two hours in length, in Seattle, Los Angeles, and Madison, Wisconsin. Although these groups were drawn from the local population, they included people from all regions of the country due to the mobility of the U.S. population.[24] The focus groups included interracially married people as well as mothers, fathers, sisters, and brothers of people who had married across racial lines. The people within each group were not related.[25] No further focus groups or interviews were conducted because new information had ceased to surface.

I did not originally envision the last phase of research, but because of families' concerns about the children of these marriages, enough data was collected to help provide some well-researched reflection on these concerns—from the standpoint of children who grew up in interracial families. I conducted the Biracial Sibling Project under the auspices of the University of Washington from 1997 to 1998. In this study, I recruited two siblings, eighteen years or older, from families who shared the same biological parents, though they might not have been raised together. I sought to represent every possible type of mixed marriage, but the combinations were primarily black-white and white-Asian, with a smaller proportion of black-Asian. More than sixty people aged eighteen to fifty-two completed an average of four hours of interviews through this project. The purpose of this study was to explore the factors that affect identity development. Both family history and phases of development over each person's life span were explored.

Several more hours have been donated by people willing to fill out questionnaires or talk by phone. On many occasions since I began this project, I have been fortunate to have enlightening conversations with taxi drivers, strangers in hotel lobbies, fellow passengers on airplanes. I also participated in two radio call-in shows that took place in Detroit and Washington, D.C., on the subject of interracial marriage. Almost all fifty states are represented by the participants in this study.[26]

Since completing the first draft of this book, I have had time to test my conclusions by presenting them in community settings, conversing with groups composed of members of interracial families, and speaking informally with individuals. I am heartened that the stories and experiences people have shared with me corroborate the findings and conclusions of my research.

My study differs from others on interracial relationships in both method and the type of data collected. Seeking multiple perspectives on interracial relationships—the couples, the extended families, and children of interracial marriages—I recruited people through newspaper ads, newspaper articles, conference workshops, and word of mouth.[27] Personal friends were not included in the formal research.

I did not systematically research the influence of interfaith marriages, although information about religion spontaneously emerged in some of the interviews. The first phase of this study included several interviews with lesbian and gay couples. These interviews were informative in terms of sorting out the construction of race and gender roles, but an analysis of interracial same-sex relationships is not offered in this book.[28]

Approximately 175 families contributed to my research. More women than men participated; of intermarried persons and their relatives, more white persons participated than any other single group, a fact I attributed to two circumstances. First, women tend to volunteer more frequently than men in studies soliciting personal information. Research requests for personal disclosure are still much more consonant with female than with male socialization. Secondly, more white women than any other group of participants had been disowned or traumatized by their family's reactions. For the first two phases of the study, participants ranged in age from the early twenties to the early seventies; for the third phase with biracial siblings the range was eighteen to fifty-two, with an average age in the late twenties. Although the overall sample was influenced primarily by Judeo-Christian perspectives, persons of Baha'is, Buddhist, Islamic, and other faiths were included.[29]

Previous studies on racial intermarriage provide statistical information on education, age, numbers of marriages, trends, and attitudes, while others describe the themes and experiences that engage these couple's lives. My study focuses on understanding family systems, social factors, and the interplay between race and gender. I did not seek information on problems or issues commonly confronting these couples, though of course this information surfaced spontaneously at times. The questions behind this study were, "What enables some families to expand their embrace to include a new member and their family? Why do other families refuse to do this?" At first I approached these questions obliquely, but in the middle stage of the study I posed them directly. "Racism" did not seem an adequate explanation of why some families were unable to embrace the love, hope and commitment that marriage symbolizes; I wanted to go beyond that simplistic answer to examine the motives and values behind it. Nor did I assume that because family members might embrace a racially different newcomer they were free of racial prejudices.

Overview

Marriage engages many psychological processes, challenging everyone involved to share and trust, to give of themselves and make sacrifices for each other. Despite the rise in divorce rates, marriage is still regarded as a long-term commitment. Dating, on the other hand, is driven by curiosity, experimentation, and temporary alliances. Interracial marriage must be regarded very differently than interracial dating because of its permanence and demands on extended families.

Marriage requires the couple's parents to balance a connection to their children with a letting go. They may have to resolve feelings of jealousy and insecurity that arise when their child develops new bonds with his or her in-laws. Marital partners must strike a new balance between dependence and independence.

In my interviews, some participants spoke about how the level of commitment intrinsic to marriage caused anxiety, when families suddenly included relatives of a different race and blood kin of mixed race. Racial differences blind many people to the other ways in which a marriage seems perfectly appropriate—for example, similarities between partners in education, income, and class.[30] For the vast majority, the heterosexual imperative and racial homogamy still prevail over all other considerations.

I wanted to understand how loving families could reject beloved daughters and sons, could even attempt to erase them from the family history, because of their choice of a partner. I was struck by the similarity between stories of rejection when a child chose a racially different partner and rejection when a child announced that he or she was gay or brought home a same-sex partner. Several people spontaneously recounted that parents whose children were late in marrying feared they were gay or lesbian; in these instances the parents were more open to intermarriage, being relieved that their child was heterosexual and seeing intermarriage as the lesser evil.

Both interracial and homosexual relationships have brought about legal consequences or the invocation of religion as a higher moral authority. Both were often dismissed as merely sexual, as a way to undermine their legitimacy and potential for success and happiness.[31] Some couples had to keep their relationship secret in order to maintain family ties. In both types of relationship, individuals of any age were treated as children and were told that their love was a passing phase, a sign of confusion, or a form of rebellion. Parents who had difficulty accepting their son's or daughter's choice of partner because of race or sexual orientation often blamed themselves or, conversely, saw their child's choice as an attempt to hurt or reject them.[32] Many family members, in their hurt and confusion, became angry; some defensively threatened to withdraw their love in the hope that this would force the child to change his or her mind. All of these reactions are based on a sense of injury to the parents' view of themselves and a feeling that they have been rejected.

A son's or daughter's choice of someone their parents would not have chosen for them does not mean the parents have failed. It simply means that integrated workplaces and social interactions increase the chances for interracial partnerships to form. Thanks to legal reforms, love can now venture into territory previously off limits. The law no longer sanctions irrational opposition, at least not to the degree that it did. Yet racism is still most prevalent and most pronounced when it comes to persons of African descent. Even in these allegedly progressive times, interracial marriages with black partners are still regarded more suspiciously and with more hostility in all communities than other interracial marriages are. The selection of white partners by black men and women is still regarded as an invitation to terrorism; it still evokes the sexual exploitation and rape of black women by white men and the lynching of black men by white mobs supposedly avenging the violation of white women.[33]

Family members may think that the motivation for an interracial marriage is a reprehensible desire to make a political or social statement. While such motives might underlie some dating of any kind, it did not drive *any* of the couples in this study. Although the septuagenarians, Catherine and Carl, introduced at the beginning of this chapter, felt that political inclinations allowed them to make their choice in the 1940s, their intention to marry was about love, not politics. They were among the most "political" of participants in this study, but they felt they could not live without one another.

More often than not, sons and daughters chose interracial partners with characteristics that would otherwise meet with parental approval. Their fiancées or spouses loved them, were willing to make a long-term commitment, were at similar levels of responsibility, and had shared goals and visions. These things were true of all the couples introduced so far in this study. If a child's partner fulfilled the stereotypical gender expectations that parents had, this helped soften the blow of the partner's racial difference. This meant daughters-in-law who were loving, able to put family needs before their own, even willing to sacrifice their own aspirations for the success of their husbands' careers. And it meant sons-in-law who were responsible, ambitious family men willing to make sacrifices to ensure the happiness and financial security of their wives and children.

The collision between racism and parental hopes and expectations was the subject of the 1967 film, *Guess Who's Coming to Dinner*. The only child of wealthy white parents, Joanna (Katherine Houghton) announces her intended engagement to John Prentice (Sidney Poitier), an internationally renowned physician active in humanitarian causes in impoverished areas. Sophisticated, worldly, and sensitive to their daughter's needs and naïveté, Prentice ought to be a dream come true as a son-in-law. In fact, however, his race unmasks the prejudices deeply imbued in Joanna's progressive white parents. Prentice's own parents are also prejudiced, but for different reasons, and Prentice tries to give them the news of his engagement without immediately revealing the race of his fiancée.

As in the film, otherwise loving, supportive parents may suddenly become irrational, cold-hearted, punitive authoritarians, quick to accuse their children of poor judgment. This dramatic change in behavior added significant tension—and necessitated significant strategizing—to the wedding plans of Jeff, the Chinese American, and Joy, the white Midwesterner. Such behavior emerges as the parent grieves over some perceived loss. Reasoning, begging, and soul searching ("What did I do wrong?") fail to resolve the tension because the negative reaction stems from social stereotypes of irreconcilable racial differences.

When parents grieve, what exactly do they perceive they have lost? The loss may appear imaginary to an impartial observer, though no less real to parents in despair or humiliation over their son's or daughter's choice. The parents' expectation of their children's happiness, fairy-tale marriage, happy family vacations together, proud boasts to friends of their daughter- or son-in-law are suddenly swept away. The cultural construction of race creates and fuels fears that lead to parents' grief over the imagined loss of social status and social mobility for themselves and their children. Their cultural beliefs tell them that interracial relationships bring tragedy, violence, grief, and heartache. These themes permeate popular culture, especially mainstream motion pictures made for white audiences—for example, *Birth of a Nation* (1915), *Pinky* (1949), *Show Boat* (1951), *Sayonara* (1957), *South Pacific* (1958), *Imitation of Life* (1959), *West Side Story* (1961), *Jungle Fever* (1991), *Zebrahead* (1992), *Mississippi Masala* (1992), and *Heaven and Earth* (1993), to name only a few. Portrayals of human intolerance and prejudice, films like these, geared to white audiences, foster propaganda that interracial romance is dangerous and doomed to tragedy.

At the same time, such films are less critical than they might be of the harassment, violence, and prejudice directed at interracial couples. Interestingly, a more positive look at interracial love can be found in movies featuring same-sex romance, for example, *The Incredibly True Adventures of Two Girls in Love* (1995) and *The Wedding Banquet* (1993).

For families of color who actively participate in ethnic communities and maintain cultural traditions, anticipated grief may be complicated by worries that intermarriage will dilute cultural tradition and "purity," as Jeff's parents feared. Parents fear that their daughters and sons will become strangers to them, at the least, or will turn against them and their culture, at worst. *The Wedding Banquet* (1993) is the gay interracial analogue to *Guess Who's Coming to Dinner*. A beloved Chinese American son plans to introduce his white American partner to his parents. The son first introduces the partner as a friend, which allows the parents to assess him as a person. He prepares an elaborate Chinese meal, speaks some Chinese, and is an attentive, respectful host—everything parents could want in a son-in-law. With his appreciation of Chinese culture, his respect for his partner's parents, he is perfect in every way, except, of course, gender and race. A complex set of maneuvers designed to hide his homosexuality is eventually foiled. The parents move through their shock and grief that their son is gay, and before long, like the parents in *Guess Who's Coming to Dinner*, they are able to realize that their son has chosen someone who has the qualities they value.

Parents' grief over the race of their child's partner seems to be grief more for what they themselves have lost than for their child. Resolving that grief means that they must reconcile their disappointed hopes with a reality they did not anticipate. They must be able to accept their child's autonomy. They must also honestly face the fact that they grieve not for their child but for themselves and for their assumption that racial sameness would guarantee both a happy marriage and an unbroken family line. Sometimes a parent's grief over the loss of an imagined future is expressed in anger. Such parents can became stuck in righteous anger at real or imaginary loss—loss of racial purity, loss of a son or daughter to "the other side," loss of standing among their peers for not having raised their child right. They may utilize psychological defenses such as denial (she is no daughter of ours; she was always different from the other children), or minimization (it is just a phase), or compartmentalization (excluding this child and his or her new partner from family gatherings), to avoid having to come to terms with the new situation. Their feelings of anger and rejection stem from a sense of profound betrayal that was not intended by their daughter or son. Whereas an interracial dating relationship may sometimes be an act of rebellion, interracial marriage is rarely about rebellion. When it is, it is a statement of profound anger toward parents and involves a radical loss of integrity because it uses an outsider to wage war on family members.

Often in this drama, parents are unable to see the costs of the anguish their child is experiencing. To be forced to choose between your family and the person you love is a no-win situation. The withdrawal of parental and family love leaves a gaping psychological wound, a wound that almost always leaves a permanent scar, a reminder of the happiness and wholeness that was taken away. As a result, unrealistic pressure may be placed on the marital love to make up for the loss, which is usually a recipe for marital failure.

Catherine paid dearly for her parents' inability to accept her choice and love her unconditionally. Fifty years later, people still face their parents' limitations because of ingrained racism and fear of the unknown. Jeannette, a woman from a white family in Lansing, Michigan, experienced her parents' fear when she began dating Jim, a black man who had been her friend for several years.

> I think they had a picture in their minds of what they expected me to be with as far as a partner and that person would be within my own race, within my religion. There were some personal characteristics. His personality—he's very outgoing, kind of aggressive type of personality, dominant. I think they thought he would just kind of run right over me and so that was one of their concerns. We finally made a decision that we were getting married and they changed. At first my dad said,

"I won't support you financially." They realized this was the way it was going to be and out of their love for me they had a change of heart and now they are really wonderful. They have opened up their hearts. . . . I was surprised how my husband let him in or kind of opened himself up 'cause I was afraid there'd been a lot of hurt.

Jeanette's father's threat to withdraw financial support was couched in terms of concern for his daughter that masked the racial prejudice reflected in his comments. It is almost impossible to imagine that he would have made the same threat if his daughter's fiancé had been white. Her father's reaction also provides a window into how gender plays out in the drama of opposition to interracial marriage. Jeannette told me that her mother's reaction was guided by her father's. When he came around, her mother was very ready to accept Jim. There is also the theme of competition and the fear of losing what is one's property or kin. Jeannette's father's concern that she would be dominated and lose herself in the marriage was probably a part of his fear of losing control over his daughter. Traditionally, in mainstream white American culture, a daughter becomes part of her husband's clan, a change symbolized by her adoption of her husband's surname. The fear of losing a white daughter to a black man predates the Civil War and was exploited by D. W. Griffith's landmark film, *The Birth of a Nation* (1915), which portrayed the Ku Klux Klan in a heroic role and was held responsible for the Klan's renewed popularity. Protests over a daughter's choice of a black husband are based in part on notions of people as property, whiteness as property, competition, and fear of losing members of one's racial clan.[34] Although Jeannette's father was not a white supremacist, his response exists along a continuum. In an article on women of the radical Right, the Southern Poverty Law Center reports, "A chief mission of the Reconstruction- and 1920s-era Klans was the protection of the 'honor' and chastity of white women. In more modern times, the 'Fourteen Words' penned by imprisoned terrorist David Lane in the 1980s has become a family-oriented mantra for the white supremacist right: 'We must secure the existence of our people and a future for white children.'"[35]

Jim, despite the harsh treatment he received from Jeanette's parents, was impressive in his ability to open his heart to her father. Where did he get this ability? Jim explained that his father died when he was young, leaving his mother to raise him and three siblings in a midsize town in Georgia. His mother had loved his father very much, and Jim had experienced his mother's capacity to love deeply. She had told him since he was a teenager that she would love whomever he chose. And although he knew that she assumed he would marry a black woman, he also had faith in her capacity for love and knew that she would welcome and love Jeanette. I asked Jim how she was able to know this about herself given that she had grown up in very segregated times in the South, experiencing maltreatment and harsh discrimination by white people. He answered, "My mother believes that our hearts know no color. Its only our eyes and brains that are so easily fooled. I think she felt strongly about this because my father died early in their marriage. He was the love of her life and still is. She wants us each to find someone to love in the way she loved him. I think she believes if I have this with Jeannette, I'll be the best person I can be."

As I conducted interviews and focus groups with interracially married persons and their extended families, it became clear that the responses to these marriages were politically and economically based, though their motives were not always conscious. Although we live in an age in which people marry for love, we also live in a country that has not resolved its racial wounds, and when race is a factor in marriage, it becomes apparent that marriage still has an aspect of a business transaction. In such transactions, daughters are often depicted as pawns rather than as free agents making their own choices.

More and more, however, increased female financial independence, access to birth control, and geographical mobility have changed women's roles in relationships, their choices of partners, and their dependence upon parental approval. Women, rather than being pawns, are central figures in the growth of interracial marriage and the raising of multiracial children. Interracial marriage provides a unique opportunity to examine how race and gender have interacted throughout the history of this country. In a recent twenty-one-city survey of attitudes toward racial marriage, Taylor and her colleagues found some interesting general trends that show some interaction of gender with race or ethnicity (black, white, Latino/Hispanic) in respondents' willingness to intermarry. In general, they found that perceived similarity of demographic variables of race, class, and ethnicity was not considered essential for a good marriage; previous experiences with interracial dating increased the willingness to intermarry; men of all three groups were more willing than women to intermarry, though the percentage was 45 percent or higher for all groups; and the groups toward which both men and women had the greatest reservations were Asians and blacks. More detailed analyses revealed that whereas higher education overrode prejudices and increased the willingness among both white women and white men to intermarry a black or Latino, education did not similarly affect African American men's attitudes. Education did, however, increase the willingness to intermarry a Latino among African American men and women both.

For both black and white women, loneliness was associated with increased willingness to consider interracial marriage—and an increased pool of potential partners was associated with all women's willingness to marry interracially. More religious white men were willing to consider intermarriage with black and Latino women. And lower income for both white and black men was associated with willingness to marry with lower-status groups, blacks and Latino, which Taylor et al. explained by the likelihood of increased opportunity for equal status among groups at lower socioeconomic levels.[36]

The civil rights movement had a significant impact on the generation that came of age during that era and their progeny—so significant that it often seems to outweigh the influence of family. Although they might be disowned by their families, interracial couples will find support among friends who have been similarly influenced by history. In a span of less than twenty-five years, several civil rights reforms set the stage for the quiet revolution that began in the 1950s. In 1954, the Supreme Court decision in *Brown v. Board of Education* formally repealed the Jim Crow laws of separatism in public places. *Brown* laid the foundation for race mixing and for future efforts to repeal the legal barriers between the black and white races. In the next decade, the Civil Rights Act of 1964 prohibited discrimination on the basis of race, color, religion, sex, age, ethnicity, or national origin; the Fair Housing Law of 1968 prohibited discrimination against people seeking housing on the basis of race, color, religion, or national origin; and the Voting Rights Act of 1965 repealed local discriminatory practices against minority—primarily black—voters (it was amended in 1975 and 1982 to include linguistic minorities). The Immigration Act of 1965 removed barriers to immigration by people from primarily non-white nations and allowed a significant wave of immigration from Asian countries. The landmark decision in *Loving v. Virginia* (1967) removed all legal barriers to interracial marriage. And, finally, attempts to enact the Equal Rights Amendment (ERA) of 1972, though never yet formally ratified by two-thirds of the states, underscored the increasing demand for equal status for women in this country. Martin Luther King, Jr., lived to see all of these developments except the failure of the ERA. He observed, "Today we know with certainty that segregation is dead. The only remaining question is how costly will be the funeral?"[37]

A somewhat broader historical context is necessary for understanding why disapproving family members have license to act as though it is their duty, and evidence of their love, to oppose the marriage choices of their children and to try and prevent those marriages. Although the divisive racial issues that have plagued this country are predominantly black-white, only a quarter of interracial marriages are black-white. Intermarriage for U.S.-born Asian American women is very common. Intermarriage has been prevalent within American Indian communities since Europeans arrived, extending then to mixing with African Americans; it has even preserved tribal heritages that would otherwise have been lost.[38] Latinos, already a mixed-race group, continue to mix into the rest of the U.S. population at a high rate.

Intermarriage has occurred throughout the world since time immemorial. It may be more visible, or more divisive, in the United States than elsewhere, and it touches most American families with only a few degrees of separation at most. That is, if one's immediate family has not been touched by intermarriage, most people know of intermarriage in a friend's or acquaintance's family. A 1993 issue of *Time Magazine* acknowledged the rising rate of interracial partnerships with a cover featuring a computer-generated multiracial woman and a two-page spread of portraits of the children of interracial pairings, accompanied by several articles.[39]

The November 3, 1997, headline of *USA Today* read, "For Today's Teens, Race 'Not an Issue Anymore,'" reflecting the results of a *USA Today* Gallup Poll of 602 adolescents across the country.[40] An eye-catching chart headed "Interracial Dating" noted that 57 percent of teens who date have dated interracially. This figure rose by 40 percent in slightly less than two decades, according to a 1980 Gallup Poll. Of the dating group, 30 percent more teens in 1997 said they would consider it. More interracial dating is likely to lead to more interracial

marriage. We are headed toward an intimately interracial and multiracial country. But make no mistake: Intermarriage does not mean the
end of racial prejudice or bigotry—not necessarily even within those
marriages. Interracial marriage is not this country's solution to its long-
lived, seemingly intractable racial problems, but it is one indicator that
race relations are changing.

Since the *Loving v. Virginia* decision in 1967, hundreds of thousands
of people have unwittingly participated in a quiet revolution in which
love is a salve, a bridge, and a beacon of hope and healing. By 1995,
almost 3 million people in the United States were living the words of
commitment, *I do.*[41]

Revolution? In the last quarter of the twentieth century, the rate of
interracial marriage has climbed steadily. These marriages now affect
the contours of racial identity and politics in America. Consider Los Angeles County alone, where one out of five generation X-ers has recently
married someone of a different race.[42] According to the 1990 census,
one out of four interracial couples in the nation lived in California.[43]
And, for the first time in history, the children of these unions, many of
them now adults, will have the opportunity to recognize their biracial
or multiracial heritage in the 2000 census. As this cohort of persons
of racially mixed parentage marry, most of their marriages will, by
longstanding definitions of race, also be interracial.

The forerunners of this loving revolution were ordinary people who
committed themselves to the heroic journeys of which fables and fairy
tales are made: obstacles, tests, tragedy, persistence, and ultimately, for
many more couples these days, triumph. Love, not lust or curiosity,
guides the heart to a marital commitment despite taboos and warnings.
Several of the people I interviewed had never intended to date interracially, much less marry. They said things like, "too much trouble," "too
much grief from my family," "not worth it," "best to stick within your
own race, or "raised against it."

When I asked them what happened, they all gave the same answer,
some sheepishly shaking their heads, others looking me assertively in
the eye: *Love.* "I couldn't live without her"; "I'd met my soul mate"; "I
was a different person"; "He loved me in a way no one had loved me
my whole life"; "Our differences felt trivial"; "I felt whole"; "I'd met my
match"; "We bring out the best in each other"; "I found peace with him."

Love, as a transcendent force, compelled these couples to accept the challenges and sacrifices that had discouraged them from interracial marriage in the first place. Together, they felt more spiritually whole, better, or more powerful than they ever did alone. Love resulted in actions that have had ripple effects.

The hero or heroine's journey is cast as an opportunity to achieve clarity about reality and priorities. Carl, introduced at the beginning of this chapter, abandoned by the social service system at age ten, shared a revelation he had in the early 1940s when he was down on his luck. He had always been a fighter, winning against the odds, finishing high school, surviving. But his optimism ran out when he reached his twenties. Having hopped a freight train to cross the country, lonely and freezing, Carl thought he was ready to die. While he tried to prepare himself for this, he had an insight that stayed with him for fifty years. "If I am part of everyone and everyone is part of me, then all our fortunes and misfortunes are bound together. We have to work together to figure out how to make this world work."[44] With a decision to embrace the challenges life dealt him, Carl returned to California renewed. He attributes his ability to love Catherine, despite the hatred and fear they experienced throughout their life together, to this revelation on that lonely, freezing night.

Almost fifty years after their wedding, Carl greeted my friend and me warmly at the door of his and Catherine's home in the San Francisco Bay Area. Short and stocky, with the face of someone who has slugged it out with life, looking tired but still exuding energy in a bright tropical shirt, he invited us into their house. I couldn't help but notice that their entryway was a destination rather than a mere passageway. Photos of friends and family adorned almost every inch of wall space. So much was packed into one small area that it would have taken a long time to visit it all. He pointed out the centerpiece, a large framed photo of him and his wife renewing their wedding vows on the eve of their fiftieth anniversary, before their friends and family.

Silver-haired Catherine greeted us with a reserved warmth and invited us into the living room. She sat with perfect posture in their modest living room on a cool-toned floral couch with her hands neatly folded in her lap, dressed in a skirt and blouse suitable for a church luncheon. Carl's posture was more relaxed, but his tension was revealed in the way he held his hands together as he leaned forward to speak. Clearly this interview, one of many they had given during their lives, was part of their journey, and they knew it. Unconsciously, in the way common to couples with a long history of comforting each other, Carl leaned slightly toward Catherine. Catherine lightly caressed the back of his neck as they graciously told us of their journey, from the time when they were social outlaws in the 1940s to their fiftieth wedding anniversary just a year before. They were living embodiments of Mohandas K. Gandhi's assertion: "A non-violent revolution is not a program of seizure of power. It is a program of transformation of relationships, ending in a peaceful transfer of power."[45]

2

Love and Fear

The common prejudice against interracial relationships has a long history. People who try to legitimate that prejudice cite "natural law," Enlightenment science, and biblical scripture. In this country, state laws criminalized intermarriage well into the twentieth century. The marriage of Carl and Catherine, introduced in Chapter 1, spanned six decades and three distinct eras of changing attitudes toward interracial marriage. They married when interracial marriage was a statistical rarity and still illegal in many states. They raised three children during the civil rights era and witnessed the repeal of laws forbidding interracial marriage and the enactment of legislation designed to encourage racial integration. They lived to see a significant increase in intermarriage—and to see themselves transformed from outlaws to pioneers.

A decade after Carl and Catherine were married, in 1957, the "Little Rock Nine" were escorted by U.S. Army troops up the steps of Central High School in Little Rock, Arkansas, to enforce school desegregation. Although the Supreme Court had ruled segregation in the schools unconstitutional in *Brown v. Board of Education,* state laws were slow to change. Also in 1957, Mildred Jeter, of African American and Native American heritage, and Peter Loving, a white American, both from Virginia, declared their love for each other in a marriage ceremony in Washington, D.C. Shortly after returning to Virginia, their marriage was declared illegal, as interracial marriage had been since the seventeenth century in Virginia.[1]

Ruling against the Lovings' suit against the state of Virginia in 1959, Judge Leon Bazile sentenced the Lovings to one year in jail, commenting, "Almighty God created the races white, black, yellow, malay, and red and he placed them on separate continents. And but for the interference with his arrangement there would be no cause for such marriages. The fact that he separated the races shows that he did not intend for the races to mix."[2]

Applying the malevolent "stick with your own kind" prejudice that guided race relations in that era, the judge upheld the racial hierarchy that Europeans and white Americans had constructed when the latter began kidnapping Africans for the American slave market in the seventeenth century. The invocation of a higher moral authority, most often God, has been a common defense of racial prejudice legislation ever since.

In one of my focus groups in Seattle, for example, a white man talked about how a churchgoing member of his extended family had quoted a biblical passage about the "mixing of seeds" to show that his engagement to an Asian American woman was "unnatural." This anecdote sparked a lively discussion in which another member of the group cited another biblical passage to refute the relative's intended lesson. Another member talked about the curse of Ham, one of Noah's three sons, the biblical passage most often cited by slave owners in the American South to justify slavery, and used by bigots even today to discourage interracial relationships.

In their book on intermarriage, the Prinzings, a minister and his wife, provide a useful overview of the two biblical passages cited by the focus group.[3] The "two seed" passage warns against mixing two types of seeds on the land but does not say whether the lesson about plants applies to people. Scripture can be cited to support any number of positions, and other passages in the Bible refer to the mixing of populations without negative consequences. As for the passage in Genesis describing Noah's curse on the descendants of his son Ham after Ham saw Noah naked, the Prinzings note that scholars do not support the racist interpretation that the descendants of Ham were black. The scholarly consensus, in fact, is that the descendants of Ham and his son Canaan were probably Caucasian.

The Virginia judge's allusions to the "two seed" theory and Noah's curse misinterpret Scripture. One biblical scholar who extensively reviewed Old Testament passages regarding race mixing concluded that they do not support the prohibition of racial intermarriage. "Analysis of the laws and the practices of mixed marriage in ancient Israel leads to the conclusion that the Bible does not forbid or condemn marriages with other races or people, but only those marriages contracted with an idolater or unbeliever. It should be clear to all who come to the Word of God with an open mind that any racist interpretation of the Bible is unwarranted."[4]

Race and Pseudo-Science

Religious and moral explanations that served to justify treatment of non-white people as inferior in earlier times were not displaced by the empirical science that has flourished since the eighteenth century.[5] Although the Enlightenment spawned what we think of as modern science, its fundamental belief in hierarchy supported the idea of racial difference and the practice of racial segregation. Most scientific theorizing asserted the inferiority of non-white people and was used to justify racial oppression. A key figure in the development of racial classification systems was the naturalist Linnaeus, who classified all living things, including human beings. (The term *race* is thought to have been introduced by Georges Louis Leclerc at about the same time in the mid-eighteenth century.)[6] In Linnaeus's system, humans are divided by race and typed by physical and emotional characteristics. People native to the Americas (*homo Americanus*) were typed as choleric, reddish, tenacious, and ruled by custom; people originating in Europe (*homo Europaeus*) were typed as white, ruddy, stern, haughty, and ruled by opinion; people originating in Asia (*homo Asiaticus*) were typed as yellow, melancholic, inflexible, inventive, and ruled by rites; and people originating in Africa (*homo Afer*) were typed as black, indulgent, cunning, slow, and ruled by caprice.[7] During Linnaeus's era, European and American science classified human beings in such a way as to establish the superiority of persons of European lineage. This tradition gained ground during the period of colonial expansion in the Americas to justify the dominance of people of European heritage.

Almost a century after Linneaus, Darwin's landmark *Origin of Species,* which relied on the idea of hybridity, or the mixing of animal populations, supplanted much of this previous taxonomic work.[8] Darwin's conclusion that tremendous variety could exist within species suggested that race mixing among humans would not produce new species. Darwin's work produced great controversy and did not immediately put to rest debates about multiple human species or origins.

The scholar Robert J. C. Young recounts how the comte de Gobineau, for example, argued that monogenesis (single origin) theory was compatible with Christian theology. Using new developments in physics such as thermodynamics, Gobineau proposed that some cataclysm occurred to split the original human population into three races.[9] Subsequent work by Darwin, French anthropologist Paul Broca, English ethnologist James Cowles Prichard and others set aside the monogenesis-polygenesis debate, but were less successful in preventing the misapplication of Darwin's conclusions. "Social Darwinists" misconstrued his findings to justify the classification and ranking of human difference that originated in the previous century. "Race"—that is, phenotype and geographical origin—was taken as evidence of inherent difference. The species vs. variety debate was abandoned, allowing the work of Linneaus, Gobineau, and others to be used as a justification for colonial expansion, white superiority, the kidnapping of Africans, and the importation of slave labor.[10]

Scholars such as Young and A. Ferber note that in the United States and elsewhere, scientists returned to the idea of polygenesis. The American scientist Agassiz, for one, suggested that species developed on different continents and that little migration occurred, keeping the "species" separate.[11] Polygenesis underlies many notions of race even today, but it is not recognized by credible science. It implies that the mixing of races is unnatural and that as "superior" races mixed with "inferior" ones, the human race would be degraded.[12] Eventually this line of thought produced the conclusion that non-European populations were not fully human.

Morality, economic greed, and religion converged in a way that was disguised as science. In his treatise on colonial expansion, Young notes that in the 1860s Agassiz regarded race mixing and the production of interracial offspring as unnatural and a sin, whereas T. H. Huxley, an

[handwritten marginalia: Mixed individuals vary across time]

English scientist splitting hairs in the distinction between mongrels and hybrids, regarded mixed-race children as inferior.[13] Scientists attempted to distinguish between mongrels (mixtures of the different races) and hybrids (mixtures of distinct species),[14] and argued that racial mixing lowered fertility, despite contradictory evidence;[15] the science of the time supported the inferiority of hybrids.[16] The question posed of many mixed couples—*what about the children?*—revisits this era, in which any social difficulties exhibited by a mixed-race child were likely to be attributed to racial degeneration rather than to environmental or race-neutral factors.

The eighteenth- and nineteenth-century opposition to race mixing aimed to protect European and American interests in an era of colonial expansion; in the twentieth century, opposition to race mixing naturally extended to other groups. These groups too were socially constructed as races or species inferior to the white population, which held political and economic power.

The anti-Chinese sentiments that emerged in the nineteenth century were fueled by economic fears. Scientific rationalization for discrimination and cruelty toward Chinese allowed racism to flourish and extend to other Asian groups who immigrated to the United States. In the early twentieth century, for example, after the influx of Chinese laborers was halted by the Chinese Exclusion Acts, Japanese laborers were initially sought for manual labor on the West Coast. Within a few years, however, in 1907, negative sentiment toward the Japanese led to the Gentleman's Agreement with Japan, under which Japan agreed not to issue passports to emigrants to the United States, except to certain categories of business and professional men.[17] In return, President Theodore Roosevelt pressured the city of San Francisco to rescind an order segregating Japanese American children from white children in the schools. The order was repealed, but bias and discrimination against the Japanese continued. In 1909, a progressive California politician, Chester Powell, invoked a moral argument against intermarriage between whites and Japanese based on pseudo-scientific reasoning: "[Racial discrimination] is blind and uncontrollable prejudice . . . yet social separateness seems to be imposed by the very law of nature. . . . [An educated Japanese] would not be a welcomed suitor for the hand of any American's daughter [but] an Italian of the commonest standing

and qualities would be a more welcomed suitor than the finest gentleman of Japan. So the line is biological, and we draw it at the biological
point—at the propagation of the species."[18]

Chester Powell chose to contrast Japanese to Italians, who generally
have darker skin than northern Europeans and have been subjected to
much discrimination but are still considered Caucasian, to argue that
racially discriminatory attitudes are founded in science. Powell also
distinguishes between class and race and argues that class is a much
less important issue than race in determining appropriate marriage
partners. Powell's explicit statement that the reproduction of the white
race is a goal of marriage reveals a major objection to the intermarriage
of white people.

Legalizing Opposition to Interracial Marriage

Within two decades of the arrival in North America of the first African
slaves, Virginia developed the first law against black-white intermarriage
and sexual contact in 1661, the same year that the first American Bible
was printed.[19] Soon twelve other states had legislated severe penalties
similar to Virginia's. But love is a powerful force and such marriages
took place in spite of the laws. When the anti-miscegenation laws were
repealed in 1967, Virginia still had laws imposing severe penalties on
intermarriage.[20] The early laws forbidding black-white unions were soon
followed, in many states, by laws prohibiting intermarriage between
whites and Native Americans—with the exception of the descendants
of Englishman John Rolfe and Pocohantas![21]

As Asians immigrated to this country in the nineteenth and twentieth centuries, the states in which they settled passed laws forbidding
white marriages with them, as well. Some of these laws remained in
force through the 1940s and 1950s and discouraged American soldiers
and sailors stationed in the Pacific from marrying Asian women. The
American film Sayonara depicts the red tape used to discourage these
marriages. These laws followed the waves of immigration by various
Asian groups, first the Chinese, then the Japanese. Because of Filipinos' multiracial background, California passed additional legislation
that classified them as Malays and included them in the existing anti-
miscegenation laws. Asian Indians had much the same experience as
their presence grew in particular regions of the country.[22]

The Asian immigrants were largely men of marriageable age. Although most came as temporary sojourners, expecting to make their fortunes and return to their homelands, their dreams of wealth were generally unrealized and few men returned home. Matters of citizenship played a part in these laws, which ruled out naturalization and all but prevented the formation of families. Property restrictions were also at issue. In California, for example, women of Mexican descent could marry white men, but men of Mexican descent could not marry white women. Because Mexican women could inherit their family's land, intermarriage enabled white men to increase their wealth. With this exception, we see the intersection of gender and racism in the service of economic greed.[23]

Anti-miscegenation laws were developed not to prevent *any* interracial marriage but to protect "whiteness." Interracial marriage between people of color was rarely policed and legislated in the same way that white intermarriage was.[24] Interracial communities of significant numbers of Punjabi Indian men and Mexican-descent women arose in the Imperial Valley of California beginning in the 1920s;[25] African and American Indian communities emerged beginning in the seventeenth century;[26] Filipino men and Mexican-descent women in central California and Filipino men and American Indian women in the northwest created communities with some similarities in traditions beginning in the 1930s.[27]

Laws attempted to discourage Asian laborers from becoming permanent settlers both by forbidding them to own land and by extending anti-miscegenation laws to include them. There would have been many marriages between Chinese men and American women, but for the legal penalties. Culturally, Chinese were depicted as heathens and were sometimes lynched.[28] In 1924, the Cable Act revoked the citizenship of any American woman who married a Japanese man.[29] Structural forces thus prevented the rate of intermarriage between whites and Asians that uneven sex ratios would normally predict. These laws forced Asian men to return to their homelands to marry and then return to the United States with their brides, or, in the case of Japanese men, to send for "picture brides." Eventually, as loopholes for the immigration of Asian women closed, Asian bachelor societies arose. When the exclusion citizenship laws were eventually repealed, an influx of young Asian women married a cohort of much older Asian American men.

The laws imposing fines on white persons who crossed the racial border were applied differently to men and women. Laws were seldom enforced when violated by white men, who held the most privileged social and economic position. White women, however, were severely punished for having relations with black men, often with fines or years of indentured servitude.[30] A "double" double standard prevailed when both race and gender were factors. Black men were severely beaten or killed for crossing the racial divide—or even when they were *suspected* of having crossed that line. Black women's lives were treated as inconsequential.[31] For some black people, this reign of terror fostered the desire for racial apartheid and a mistrust of white persons.[32]

The history of interracial relationships informs the present, as black-white relationships, more than any other type, are reduced to sexual stereotypes. Black men are thought to lust after white women; white men are thought to be envious of black male sexuality; black women are supposed to be more sexually satisfying than white women; and white women are dehumanized as trophies in competition between men.[33]

The system of racial apartheid and oppression that defined the early years of this country's racial history remains in force today. Racial and sexual stereotypes are still very powerful, and double standards still abound. White men were ever vigilant about black men's sexual access to white women—and they still are.[34] Freedom to choose a partner, traditionally the prerogative of men in a patriarchal structure, made black male access to white women a barometer of race relations. But because of how whiteness evolved as a social construction and a criterion for rights and privileges, black men continue to be punished for attempts, real or imagined, to cross the color line. Eldridge Cleaver, the 1960s Black Panther, once said that you desire what you cannot have and become prisoner to that desire. "Every time I embrace a black woman I'm embracing slavery, and when I put my arms around a white woman, well I'm hugging freedom. The white man forbade me to have the white woman on pain of death . . . I will not be free until the day I can have a white woman in my bed."[35]

The dearth of positive models and images for interracial couples suggests the unfortunate, confused relationship between sex and race. I have asked people in workshops and classes to make a list of the words and phrases they have heard refer to these relationships. The slang phrases are almost all derogatory: race traitors, nigger lovers, zebras, cab chasers, and so on. The language of the gay male community, in particular, blatantly fetishizes and sexualizes interracial relationships: potato queens (seeks white men); rice queens (seeks Asian men); bean queens and taco tasters (seeks Latino men); and dinge and jungle queens (seeks black men).[36] The objects of gay male sexual desire are reduced to sexualized body parts and fetishized in both gay and heterosexual cultures.[37] Phrases such as "once you go black you never go back" connote white male fears of the stereotyped stud sexuality they have created for black men.[38] Within the African American community, the racial authenticity and solidarity of men who "talk black but sleep white" are questioned.[39] In the climate of stereotypes and prejudgments, it becomes hard for people to fathom that two people might make a commitment to one another because of shared visions and values that form the basis of long-term love.

Antimiscegenation laws were overturned as a result of *Loving v. Virginia* (1967). When the Lovings returned to Virginia after being legally married in Washington, D.C., their marriage was declared illegal and they were prosecuted. They were jailed briefly and then fought legal battles for almost ten years, until the Supreme Court finally heard the case of *Loving v. Virginia* and handed down a decision that overturned all the existing state laws against interracial marriage on the grounds that they violated the Fourteenth Amendment, guaranteeing the pursuit of happiness.

Only six years earlier, in the midst of civil rights reconstruction, fourteen-year-old Emmett Till was brutally murdered in Mississippi for allegedly whistling at a white woman.[40] Violent opposition to interracial relationships—or the suspicion of them—still occurs, and many black men feel endangered, especially in the South. As George, a black man in his late forties who participated in a Seattle focus group, put it, "We just stayed on our side of the tracks. Crossing a certain road into a white neighborhood in Chicago as a black man meant only one thing. You were eyeing the white women and that only meant trouble."

When Des, also from Chicago but born a generation after George, described how he had anxiously taken his white fiancée home to meet his family in 1995, he told a story familiar to African Americans for generations.[41] Des laughed as he talked about wanting to tell his fiancée to duck down in the car, afraid that her blonde head and white face in his neighborhood could bring bullets flying. His wife Janet observed that her relationship with Des forced her to be conscious of where it is psychologically and physically safe for them as a couple, something she had never had to think about before. Through her marriage to Des, her status as "white" has changed and become linked with her husband's racial status. But Des and Janet experience more freedom from fear than previous generations of interracial couples.

Today social taboos maintain some boundaries between the races. Tenzer's 1989 survey of white women found that a majority would consider dating black men if it were more acceptable, and a 1992 national survey, *Sex in America*, provides evidence that the taboos are eroding, and quickly, for white women and black men. Single white women were ten times more likely than single white men to report that their most recent sexual partner was black. Furthermore, all racial and ethnic groups are experiencing increases in intermarriage.[42]

A series of Gallup polls starting after the repeal of anti-miscegenation laws in 1967 through 1991 confirms these findings.[43] For both blacks and whites, attitudes in favor of interracial marriage have steadily increased, peaking for African Americans at around 70 percent. In 1968, only 17 percent of whites polled across the nation approved of interracial marriage in contrast to 48 percent of African Americans. A Gallup poll in 1991 found that 70 percent of blacks and 44 percent of whites approved of intermarriage. Higher income, more education, and living in larger communities were factors associated with increased approval of interracial marriages for both blacks and whites.

Whereas all of these variables continue to be related to more open attitudes toward interracial marriage, evidence suggests that the younger generations of America will influence race relations in significant ways. In 1997 a Gallup poll asking black and white Americans whether or not they approved of intermarriage reflected the most significant change in attitudes. For the first time, both groups professed approval by a significant majority, with blacks at 77 percent and whites at 61 percent. The most significant explanatory variable was age. Younger respondents had extremely high rates of approval, much higher than either their parents or grandparents. The trend suggests that as America ages, the negative attitudes toward interracial marriage will continue to erode and give way to a more tolerant, accepting climate for these marriages.[44]

Openness to interracial marriages also varies by region. According to the Gallup polls, the West Coast showed the greatest approval in 1991

(60 percent), followed by the East Coast (54 percent), the Midwest (50 percent); the South had the lowest approval (33 percent). In my interviews with couples and groups, I found great variability *within* region based on the individual's personality, family history, and, to a lesser extent, class and level of education. The regional differences seemed largely connected to the history of race in each region, the economic prosperity of the region, and the racial demographics. Hawaii, for example, though not included in these polls, has a long-standing history of interracial marriage, with relatively little of the violence that has plagued the mainland.[45] Many servicemen who married Asian women while stationed in Asian countries were aware that Hawaii provided a more tolerant environment in which to settle.

Dana, a black woman raised in California, provides an example of regional difference. Dana met her white husband, Doug, in college. Both sets of parents loved their child's partner from the start. Race was not a primary factor. Dana and Doug had each chosen exactly the kind of person their parents had hoped for. Dana likes people and knows how to get what she wants. She is outgoing, much like her white mother-in-law. Doug values Dana's opinion, is ambitious, treats her mother and father well, and has a good sense of humor. He fits into the family and is a good husband. Both Dana and Doug were raised to evaluate people without regard to race, and they have chosen to live in a racially integrated city for their own and their children's sake. They acknowledge that their lives are easier because of the people who paved the way before them.

Dana's level of education puts her in frequent contact with white men. Higher education seems to be associated with a more open attitude toward interracial contact and flexibility in gender roles. Given that many black women are more educated than their black male peers, and that the convention in marriage is for women to marry someone with equal or more education, it is possible that these factors, combined with the shortage of available marriageable black men for the current cohort of single women, may increase the rates of black women marrying non-black men. Tucker and Mitchell-Kernan suggest, in addition, that women still tend to consider the income-earning potential of partners and that this may further open black women to interracial marriages.[46] Dana's story was one of several to demonstrate that exposure to different people and upbringing made a difference in attitudes toward interracial marriage.

Winniya, an African American woman in her early fifties, originally from a small town in Kansas, was raised by a mother who had taught her to believe that no one was any better than anyone else. She provides an example of variation within a region and age cohort.

> My father died when I was five, so I didn't have the opposition of a father. . . . When I married my current husband, who's white, the opposition came from my daughter. I already had two children. She said, "I don't want this white man coming into my family." I think her opposition was part of a natural process thing. I don't think the opposition was because he was white, but because here was another person who was going to take some part of her mother away. But I've been married to this man for thirty years. Now my children are young adults. When my firstborn was involved in an interracial relationship with someone, I said, "Well you know, that's just part of the course because look at her mother." I hadn't initially really connected it because I had raised my young people just to be able to relate to people as people not by race or economics or whatever. I don't know, I mean I think my girls have not had a lot of positive experience in African American heterosexual relationships. When they tend to run into people who treat them well, they happen to be of another race. I would think unconsciously my experience had something to do with that because my son and daughter were five and six when I married and my other daughter who's from this interracial marriage, she's now twenty-six. She sees herself not as a black person, not as a white person. She tends to see herself as a multiracial child. That's how she says she somehow gravitates to white men, although she met this black guy that she says she's going to marry. My other daughter married a gentleman who's Russian and my son married a woman who's Mexican. I have no opposition to who they are with and where they go so long as they are happy.

Winniya is both ordinary and extraordinary, just as her mother was. Winniya's upbringing allowed her to be open to the possibility of an interracial relationship at a difficult time in our nation's history. She was a statistical rarity in the 1960s, when few black women married white men. But now she in turn has raised three children who participate in this revolution. Just as some people have feared, one interracial marriage in a family may lead to more. Many young people today, beneficiaries of the civil rights movement, are evidence that Martin Luther King's wish that his children be judged not by the color of their skin but the content of the character is coming true, one person at a time.

Class versus Caste

For at least 250 years, whites used pseudo-science to justify their representation of themselves as a class of people superior to all others. The most insidious result of the debate around hybridity and types was that boundaries became rigid. Hierarchy was really about belief in a fundamental difference in temperament, intellect, and even the ambition of persons constructed as racially different from white people. This way of thinking, enshrined in the academic discourse of science and theology, provided the basis for a caste system of racialized reasoning. African Americans were the group who suffered most initially from this system because of the potential threat they posed to the economic control of the colonizers and their descendants.[47]

Caste differs from class in the degree to which the boundaries between groups of people are permeable. Caste connotes an absolute taboo and the forbidden. The boundary is nonnegotiable and there are no exceptions. The manner in which persons of mixed heritage have been classified illustrates how race originated as a caste rather than a class category. Although for a short period of time, persons of black-white heritage were recorded as mulatto, a mulatto was considered a type of black person rather than a type of white.[48] Psychologist Wade Boykin notes that historically, when black and white persons marry, the white person experiences a shift down in status and becomes marked in many ways as a minority; he or she loses the white status.[49] But this dynamic does not work the other way around; blacks who marry whites do not gain standing as a result. The only direction for mobility in a caste system is down.

Jeanne was ten when her sister married a black man who was totally accepted by her white family in Indiana, a very liberal clan who had been involved in the socialist and communist movements of the 1930s. She remembers the family's social demotion in their overwhelmingly white Midwestern town.

> My grandparents were of high status in our small town in the 1950s. My grandfather owned a very prominent business. I had an older brother who was in the army, he became my male role model. But he also had a twenty-five-year marriage that was interracial. So my family was—this became part of my identity then because I was subject, even though I'm white. Now I, we, were no longer really held in high regard. Everybody

knew in the town that you had this part of you that you carried around. So you were socially ostracized, called names, no invitations to other people's houses. My mother was running my grandfather's business by that time in the 1970s. I just started thinking about her gutsiness. She would say, "Here we are, get used to it." So I kind of grew up with that.

The tendency to delineate who is an acceptable member of the group and who is not seems to be part of human nature, perhaps a result of our competitiveness for resources and our great capacity for psychological insecurity. White slaveholders, as every colonist in the world has done, constructed both the indigenous people and the imported laborers as different from them in essential ways that were attributed to biology. Thus began the construction of a caste system. Visible differences in skin color, eye shape, and body build, between plantation owners and slaves (or plantation workers in more modern times in Hawaii), between supervisors and railroad builders and miners, and between landowners and farmers, were invested with meaning. Like scarlet letters, these physical markers signaled status or its absence in relation to those with economic control. As sociologist Pierre van den Berghe has written on illogical definitions of race, "The human group that defines itself, and/or is defined by other groups is different by virtue of innate or immutable characteristics. These physical characteristics are in turn assumed to be intrinsically related to moral, intellectual and other non-physical attributes or abilities. A race, therefore, is a group that is socially defined on the basis of physical criteria."[50]

Physical differences are used to invent the social construct of "race," which is then used to subjugate and oppress others. Unlike a class system based on economic difference, the subjugation and control of one group by another on the basis of alleged differences in intellect and morality give rise to a caste system. The rigid integrity of a caste system is preserved by forbidding sexual relationships, not to mention marriages, across caste lines.[51] When such marriages did take place, historically, the privileged race member (and often his or her family), experienced downward movement into the caste of his or her partner. Sue, a white woman in her forties, talks about living in the grip of her father's fear and prejudice:

The thing that bothers me is that my father died in 1990 and he went to his grave being prejudiced, and I try not to hate him for it. When I was younger I hated racist white people. I almost thought I wasn't white. I had to realize, I was born white, I'll die white, and not to worry about it. But he was dying of cancer, and he didn't tell me and he wouldn't let his new wife tell me because he didn't want me to bring "those black children" with me down to the hospital. . . . I think for my father there was just this hard-core prejudice, fear of what other people would think. . . . It's like he didn't want the people in the hospital to know he had these black relatives. It would make him not white or something.

While the concept of *class* involves a social and economic hierarchy, it is not a closed system in the way *caste* is; mobility can occur in both directions. I believe that the subtle difference between caste and class explains why some interracial pairings are met with more hostility than others. For example, black-white marriages still meet with more opposition than do white-Asian marriages. Although Asians of different cultural backgrounds were initially racialized, their bodies used as caste markers, and while white-Asian intermarriage was outlawed by some states, in time Asian heritage has been transformed from a caste to a class category. In order to understand why Asian Americans have been allowed this transformation while African Americans have not, it is necessary to consider the way in which gender influences caste status. Most Asian-white marriages are of white men to Asian American women, which is more acceptable to most white Americans than the reverse, since whiteness is the normative racial assignment through male gender. Black-white marriages, by contrast, are mostly between black men and white women and present a threat to whites because black men, having gender privilege, mark white women as no longer authentically white. (Relationships between white men and black women have been relegated to virtual invisibility.) The transformation from caste to class for African Americans has been slow to occur, but it has been evident in the latter part of the twentieth century in spite of ingrained white prejudice, thanks in part to legal reforms.[52]

There is a long way to go, however, before black-white intermarriage is widely accepted. Christie, a thirty-two-year-old white woman who married a black man, describes her experience:

Well, it's when I was back in high school when I began to have close friends of another race and they began calling my house. I felt the opposition with my dad, you know, making comments to me and then when they, a person of another race came to his office where I had worked to see me, that kind of set it all off. He then had a little discussion with me. He said, "You know, in our family," you know, he was expressing family values or whatever, "I have no problem with you having associations with people of a different race or whatever at school. But when it comes to close or intimate relationships outside of that, we don't approve of that." That didn't set well with me. It really upset me and so it was from then on that I knew kind of where he stood. Then I went on to college and I began dating people outside my racial group. There was opposition, you know, with my family not liking it. Then I became very serious with my husband. We had dated for about five years. They pretty much fought it.

Etta, a forty-six-year-old divorced black woman from Illinois and the mother of three adult children, had a similar story:

> It's how we grew up, basically, and yeah, you know, my parents weren't against everyone who was white, they weren't against that. . . . My dad was against us girls, you know, marrying a white man, but he didn't mind us bringing them home. It's just like the white person don't mind them bringing the black person home, but don't want them in the family, you know. . . . And it's not like we're gonna treat them bad, or anything like that, but, you know, stay in your race to marry.

When people were asked to explain the rationale for the injunction, "marry your own kind," most of their answers were irrational and invoked racial stereotyping. Some were unable to offer a coherent explanation and simply said "you know," as if everyone understood the reasons. When pressed to explain the "you know" response, people became uncomfortable but were sometimes able to articulate their reasoning, perhaps for the first time. When Margaret, a white woman whose daughter married in the mid-1970s, was asked for the fourth time during the interview why she thought her daughter should have married within her own race, she offered the following explanation:

> My daughter is such a beautiful girl and intelligent and all that. I just thought maybe that if she married somebody that would have her economic and educational background, not that's there's anything wrong with . . . there's a lot of very wonderful black and other race people. But I just feel, I still feel people should stay within their own race when they get married. I just don't know why I feel that. I just thought he'd probably marry her and then about eight or nine years down the line he'll feel more comfortable to marry someone within his own race. I was mainly thinking of her. I can't understand why a black

man wouldn't want to marry someone within his own race. To me the guy was just out for a beautiful woman or something. That's the way I felt. He was using her or something.

Margaret, in her anxiety that she might say something offensive, shared the sentiments of many whites who came of age in the 1950s, an era in which popular culture, especially movies, struggled with race relations between white American men and Asian or Polynesian women, and with the confused and troubled history of black-white relations. She, like many of her peers, could not understand how love could overcome prejudice and cross racial boundaries. Her son-in-law came from a middle-class black family, but she nevertheless equated being black with being poor and uneducated, belying the class system that guided her thinking. She believed that her daughter was "marrying down" and that her son-in-law was using her daughter to "marry up," something he could not do by marrying a black woman.

Margaret's fear that her son-in-law was "using" her daughter suggests that her daughter was a helpless victim with no responsibility for her choice of husband;[53] this stereotype has been used for centuries to justify the mistreatment and even murder of black men, especially in the American South. She also unconsciously articulated a widely held belief among whites that black women are not as attractive as white women, when she described her daughter as "beautiful." She gave no thought to what her daughter might see in this man.

The flip side of Margaret's prejudice was expressed by Beverly, a black woman from Louisiana, whose brother married a white woman. Here she describes her mother's reaction to the marriage, a reaction that she shared in part:

> White women are not just satisfied with one black man, or white man. They have to have them all. They'll come in a poor black community and get the ugliest black man they can find. Have a baby for him, spit on him, break the marriage between the black folks, black woman and black man, and send him home broke. I'm not being prejudiced. I'm just telling you, they will, they're not satisfied with just one black man.

Both Margaret and Beverly reflect the mistrust, animosity, and distance between black and white—the result of how the races have been socially and culturally constructed. This construction of race is one subject of the Rodgers and Hamemrstein Musical *South Pacific*, in which the female Ensign Forbush breaks off her affair with her French lover, the expatriate widower Emile de Becque, after she discovers that he has mixed-race Polynesian children. Her irrational response to this discovery makes no sense unless we understand that the fact of his children's race, and de Becque's liaison with his deceased Polynesian wife, change her racial construction of him. He is no longer authentically white in her eyes and she consequently demotes him to caste status, in spite of her love for him. She cannot be contaminated by his previous wife, especially when the children provide undeniable evidence of the marriage. Ensign Forbush confesses her feelings to Lt. Cable, who is involved in a similar situation with a Tonkinese girl of Indo-Chinese parentage. Like Forbush, Cable decides that he cannot marry the woman he loves because of the racial difference and the prejudice the couple would experience back home, a prejudice that he sadly acknowledges he shares and expresses in song:

> You got to be taught to hate and fear.
> You've got to be taught from year to year.
> It's got to be drummed in your dear little ear.
> You've got to be carefully taught.
>
> You've got to be taught to be afraid
> of people whose eyes are oddly made,
> and people whose skin is a diff'rent shade,
> You've got to be carefully taught.
>
> You've got to be taught before it's too late,
> Before you are six or seven or eight,
> To hate all the people your relatives hate,
> You've got to be carefully taught!
> You've got to be carefully taught![54]

As the philosopher Bertrand Russell observed, "Fear is the main source of superstition, and one of the main sources of cruelty."[55] Fear and hatred have spawned lynching, firebombings, beatings, and all manner of atrocities against racial minorities and interracial couples.[56] Fear, insecurity, and territoriality propel the stigmatization that creates horrific consequences for unacceptable members of the group.[57] Racial construction is stigmatization in the service of caste assignment. Jews, before, during, and after the Nazi genocide, were racialized, both in

Europe and America, in ways that made them a caste. Franz Fanon observes,

> At first thought it may seem strange that the anti-Semite's outlook should be related to that of the Negrophobe. It was my philosophy professor, a native of the Antilles, who recalled the fact to me one day: "Whenever you hear anyone abuse the Jews, pay attention, because he is talking about you." And I found that he was universally right—by which I meant that I was answerable in my body and in my heart for what was done to my brother. Later I realized that he meant, quite simply, an anti-Semite is inevitably an anti-Negro.

Since the pervasive and overt anti-Semitism of the postwar era has abated, however, Jews have been transformed from a caste into a class.

The typing and classing of people on which prejudice and discrimination are based appears to be universal. Children are exposed to it early, as demonstrated by this story from Mike, a white man of sixty, originally from the Spokane area of eastern Washington:

> I had this terrible falling out with my first cousin, like, thirty-five years ago, because he continued to use the word *nigger* and was very bigoted. We actually got in a fist fight over it because I didn't want my kids around that. I didn't want them hearing that. It's like in Ireland. One of the most telling shows I've ever watched was a Channel 9 something some twenty-five years ago or so. They were talking about the troubles in Ireland and the bigotry between the Protestants and the Catholics and so on and so forth. The little kids, three years old walking down the street, saying, "Goddamn Catholics. We'll take care of 'em." A three-year-old child! Well, you know, they didn't just think that up. They're being taught that. Taught to hate. Anyway, I didn't want that for my kids, my two little boys at that time. They were about a year and a half. But I didn't want them hearing that and being around that and neither did most of our family. I don't think we spoke for fifteen years. He just stopped coming to things. But you know, I don't see us as any cutting-edge type of family, but basically, we didn't want our children raised thinking those kind of things.

The Role of Gender in Perpetuating Class and Caste Distinctions

The rigidity of the caste system also intensifies curiosity about the forbidden and the different. What is off limits easily becomes sexualized and even fetishized, as it is deemed exotic and erotic.[58] Sex and sexuality are at the core of anxiety around interracial mixing, and women become central in contentions about interracial marriage. By the rules and conventions surrounding caste systems, only white women procreating with white men can have white children. The protection of white women, particularly white women of child-bearing age, easily becomes the rationale for violence. Sociologist Abby Ferber has documented some of the extremism and illogic surrounding race mixing. She quotes an article entitled *"Sexual Contact with Negro Can Result in Black Baby by White Parents"* to show how irrational fears can lead to hysteria: "even . . . without impregnation, sexual intercourse with a black male leads to an infusion of the black sperm into the system of the White female which affects her body chemistry toward negroidal traits . . . a White woman who engaged in sex with negroes should be considered no longer to be a part of the White Race . . . negroidal influence can show up in future births . . . she has in a chemical way become part of the black race even though she still has the appearance of a White person."[59]

White supremacist thinking is based on the possession and protection of fictionalized whiteness as property. The legal scholar Cheryl Harris outlines the ways in which the invention of whiteness made whiteness property while also providing white people with certain rights. Even poor and working-class whites could assert their supposed superiority to their black coworkers.

> In a society structured on racial subordination, white privilege became an expectation and . . . whiteness became the quintessential property for personhood. The law constructed "whiteness" as an objective fact, although in reality it is an ideological proposition imposed through subordination. This move is the central feature of "reification": "Its basis is that a relation between people takes on the character of a thing and thus acquires a 'phantom objectivity,' an autonomy that seems so strictly rational and all-embracing as to conceal every trace of its fundamental nature: the relation between people." Whiteness was an "object" over which continued control was—and is—expected. The protection of these expectations is central because . . . "If an object you now control is bound up in your future plans or in your anticipation of your future self, and it is partly these plans for your own continuity that make you a person, then your personhood depends on the realization of these expectations."[60]

Sometimes people are pushed, in effect, into the arms of another racial community when they are ostracized by their own circle for straying beyond it. Patty, a Seattle woman in her late twenties, described what happened after she ended a serious three-year relationship with a black man:

> Seattle is a small place if you grow up here. So you run into the same people you've known all your life at college, movies, dance clubs, the grocery store, you know. So after the breakup, that was four years ago, friends were pushing me to date. I had gotten really hurt so it took me a while, but finally I was ready. My girlfriends set me up with [white] guys who they knew but once they [the guys] found out that I'd been engaged to a black guy, it was like . . . I thought it was strange—I'd hit it off with a guy and then he'd vanish—he wouldn't call me or return my calls. This happened a few times. Finally, after practically forcing her, a friend told me something she had heard from another friend. I couldn't believe it. She even asked, "Is it true?" I didn't know what she was talking about. She then said, "Once you go black you never go back. You know, once you've been with a black guy you wouldn't want a white guy?" I was shocked, embarrassed—I didn't know what to feel or say. How stupid can these people be? Since then, I've mostly dated black guys because they are not looking down on me like the white guys I've met.

Like many women before her, Patty's life became more complicated because her alliances with black men changed her racial status in some white people's eyes. She actively experienced the way that race is constructed not through biology but through ideology. So long as she remained single, she retained the white, middle-class identity she grew up with. When she had a black boyfriend, she was demoted and became an untouchable in the eyes of other whites. At the same time, black women who do not even know her resent her.[61]

In patriarchal societies, the male partner's identity heavily influences how his female partner is perceived.[62] Couples in which the male partner is white seem to retain status and privilege, regardless of the race of the woman, that white women married to men of color do not. A focus group member in Madison, Wisconsin, illustrates this point:

> What really strikes me more than anything else is just that gender really makes a big difference in partner identity. Like in the case of the Asian female partner married to usually a white male, in terms of interracial marriages . . . if you ask them if they are an interracial family, the

white male can say, "I don't see ourselves as an interracial family. I see ourselves as human beings," because he doesn't have to think about race or gender. He says we're a family like anybody else. On the other hand if you talk to the Asian male who is married to the white female, he says, "Oh yeah, we're an interracial family." And it's a different dynamic. One is very colorblind and the other one can't help but be color conscious.

Spickard's work on the internment of Japanese Americans during World War II makes a similar point. He documents that 1,400 inter-married Japanese Americans were interned with approximately 700 mixed-race children.[63] The Western Defense Command (WDC) allowed some internees to return to civilian life, depending on the race of the husband. Families with white husbands could relocate anywhere, whereas families with Japanese American husbands could relocate only outside of WDC jurisdiction. It was thought that the race and culture of the man would determine the loyalties of the household and that families headed by white men should not be exposed "to infectious Japanese thought" and compelled "to live in an environment from which they sought to escape."[64]

Several films of the last half of the twentieth century depict the con-tinued American struggle with interracial sexuality. *Jungle Fever* (1991) captures the way in which curiosity and lust for the forbidden are driven by multiple motives and serve multiple purposes. Flipper, a black professional married man, has an affair with his Italian American secretary, Angie. For each of them, the other is exotic and the affair is all the more exciting because the race mixing is forbidden. Caste and class issues also are at work. Working-class Angie should be attracted to Flipper as someone who offers class mobility. But to her friends and family he remains a member of a lower caste by virtue of his race. As in the film *Guess Who's Coming to Dinner,* caste supersedes economic class and educational or professional credentials. Angie's father, as the protector of his race, beats her for contaminating herself, and him, in this affair. Flipper's good standing in the black community is also threatened, and he must tell his best friend that the relationship is merely sexual in order to prove his blackness and assure his friend that he is not "selling out."

While fictional depictions of black-white relationships typically por-tray white anxiety about white women with black men, some portrayals promote a different agenda, one more consistent with white colonizing patterns. Asian women, for example, have often been the objects of white male sexual fantasy. They have even been thought to have a sexual anatomy different from that of white women. Moreover, Westerners have constructed Asia itself as feminine, making Asian men virtually invisible—or feminized in way that eliminates them as competition for American white men.[65]

White male fantasies of subservient, alluring Asian women motivated films like *Sayonara, The World of Suzie Wong, and Teahouse of the August Moon* during the postwar era, films depicting romantic involvement between Asians and white American men. The exotification of Asian women went hand in hand with U.S. legislation barring intermarriage of whites and Asians during this era, and coincided with American military presence in Japan, Korea, and the Philippines. Asian women were depicted not only as foreign but in some cases as the enemy and therefore forbidden. They were also depicted in postwar films as needing rescue or salvation by white Americans, braiding together the power matrix of gender, race, and nation. Asian women had to have re-deeming feminine virtues in order to appeal to American audiences—willingness to sacrifice, subservience, gentleness. Asian men are virtually absent from these films, which portray the white American male as hero, whereas in fact American military men were neither particularly welcome nor held in very high regard in most of Asia.[66] American military men, symbolic stand-ins for the U.S. government in these films, are redeemed in their role of rescuers of vulnerable women, despite the destruction caused by American forces in Asia, including the atomic bombing of Hiroshima and Nagasaki. These films depict a variation on the missionary theme. The Unites States, portrayed by a soldier or sailor, conquers Asia, portrayed by a woman. The gender symbolism is never critically challenged because gender, like race—particularly blackness—is a caste. Asia cannot be reconstructed as masculine; the boundary is rigid.

Asian Americans, for their part, sometimes voice the same objections to intermarriage with whites that we have seen in the African American community—that their women are exploited by these relationships and their men devalued.

The rigid hierarchy of the caste system is also apparent in the clas-sification of children born to mixed-race couples. Beginning in the seventeenth century, the "one-drop" rule declared that a child of such a union had the mother's race, which was almost always black.[67] The one-drop, or "hypodescent," rule, declared that all combinations of white and black produced black offspring. Black men and black women, black women and white men, white women and black men produce "black" babies, but "white" babies can be conceived only by two white parents. As Davis points out, blackness was a potent contaminant that stood in contrast to the purity associated with whiteness.[68] The boundaries between races became more rigid and more irrational with this law.

Black-white children and their black mothers had no legal access to their fathers' or owners' assets. The one-drop rule, which further formalized the construction of whiteness, protected the economic interests of white men and in some cases, no doubt, increased their slave holdings. Thus, the one-drop rule maintained the caste system of race.[69] Popular culture has acknowledged the power (and irrationality) of the one-drop rule. In the 1996 film *A Family Thing*, a middle-aged white Arkansan played by Robert Duvall is shocked to discover that his biological mother was black. His self-image is suddenly shattered, as he looks into the sideview mirror of his truck and calls himself a "blue-eyed nigger."

The insidious use of the one-drop rule can also be seen in how rules of classification change over time. When patterns of intermarriage showed an increase in white women marrying men of color, the rules for classification changed, and the children were to be identified by the father—or the parent of color. In 1989, the rules changed again and children were to be classified by their mother's race.

Love and Fear

Interracial marriage exposes conflicts in the American psyche around race and sex, two subjects about which even educated, articulate persons may have difficulty conversing. Where else do you see a family profess love for one another but ostracize a member for loving someone from the out-group? Only in interracial and same-sex partnerships. One of the men I interviewed recounted how he moved back home with his parents in his mid-twenties when his older brother married interracially. Jim felt he had to make up for his brother's transgression. Ten years later, his racism has left him without love. Jim still lives with his parents and he does not date. He has no contact with his brother because it would upset his elderly parents too much. And in order to reduce his conflict in choosing between his parents and his brother, Jim believes that what his brother did was wrong because "he should have known" it would upset his parents as much as it did. Jim's parents told him that his brother paid a high price for love. He becomes teary-eyed when he is told that his love for his parents seems to have cost him, too. Because Jim lives amid fear and fearful people, love is burdensome rather than enlightening and joyful. Contrary to what his parents have taught him, it is not love that extracts a high price, but fear. Fear became a mechanism for control in his family. When the fear of interracial marriage goes unspoken and unexamined in a family, the ways in which it gets expressed are always convoluted, always negative. Fear always extracts a tragic price.

Jim and his family could be of any race, but the wholesale rejection that his brother experienced was more typical of the white families I interviewed than the black families, though it also existed in Asian American families. My research confirmed what many people would predict; black families are more open than other groups to intermarriage, though less open to intermarriage with whites. All non-black groups were more resistant to intermarriage with blacks than with any other group. Whites were most resistant to intermarriage with blacks and Asians, and more open to intermarriage with American Indians and Latinos or Hispanics. These latter groups are already racially mixed groups in which European features are more evident. Perhaps this familiarity makes people from these groups more acceptable partners to whites.

In the case of first-generation immigrants, the fear of intermarriage seems to focus less on race than on preservation of culture and fear of losing their children to a foreign culture. This fear also creates much grief and misunderstanding, however. One of my subjects, Shashi, who loves his Indian parents, arrived with his family in New Jersey when he was ten years old. He appreciates how much his parents sacrificed so that he and his younger sister could have an easier life. At the time of his interview, Shashi was a professional man living at home. He was torn because he was dating an American woman who had recently given him an ultimatum: marry her or end the relationship. He wanted to marry her, and they were clearly compatible in many important ways. They communicated well and had been able to discuss the difficult issues they faced. Although hurt by some of his parents' actions, Tina understood the role they played in Shashi's thinking. Tina had been warmly welcomed by his parents when she visited as a friend of Shashi's sister, and had enjoyed the family's company on that basis for a year. Once she and Shashi began dating, however, Tina was no longer welcome. Shashi was unsure whether his parents' attitude would change if he married Tina. But he knew that in order to preserve their status as good Indian parents, he would have to marry a woman from another Indian family in good standing. If he did not, it would mean that his parents had failed in their parental duties. His individual choice could jeopardize the collective well-being of his family. Afraid of ruining their social standing and of experiencing their rejection, Shashi was in the position of having to choose between his parents and the woman he loved. Whatever his choice, he would suffer.

Common values, shared religious beliefs, and mutual love are not always enough to overcome the long-standing fears created by this country's traumatic history of race relations. The fear of intermarriage is often experienced as self-protection, even when the results are just the opposite. Beverly, the black woman from Louisiana, spoke of her aged mother's opposition to her brother's marriage to a white woman: "She doesn't want to see him after he married. He knew that. She told him she wasn't welcome in her house. Don't bring her around. If they weren't married, she still didn't like her, but he could bring her around. Her own sister married a white man, and she refused to see her after that—never saw her again, just because he was white."

For some families, overcoming the spell of irrational fear and hatred requires the transformative power that comes with the birth of grand-children. Rachelle and Norm, Jewish and Chinese American respec-tively, witnessed this transformation in Norm's parents, who boycotted their wedding, expelled their son from the clan, and refused to let him visit his father in the hospital after a heart attack. With the birth of their first child, Norm's parents acquiesced to Rachelle and Norm's pleas to "at least see the baby once." Rachelle's parents were deceased, so Norm's parents were the only living grandparents. Norm and Rachelle prepared themselves for more grief. Rachelle recalls, "I saw it in his mother's ex-pression. And then she said 'He looks like little Norm,' and scooped him up in her arms, tucking his head into the crook of her neck, her tears streaming down her cheeks onto his head. . . . His father just watched—

I think he knew he'd lost a grip on his wife. Relations are a bit strained, but we do see each other occasionally and the baby has grandparents."

What I found particularly noteworthy was certain people's ability to love despite the rejection they experienced. Beverly never met her white uncle or her aunt until she left home at age sixteen. She sees her uncle, married to her mother's sister for thirty-five years, as one of those people able to love and care in the face of rejection. Her mother refuses to have anything to do with him and always has, but fear and hatred have not spoiled his own ability to love. "He does everything for the kids. He takes care of them—even their kids. And if anything happens to my mother—he snuck and got her an insurance policy and he paid for some of her hospital bills. He won't let her know. And with her, he doesn't care, you know. He wants to take care of my mother. But he helps her. Moneywise. She doesn't know. He'll give it to us to give to her."

It was as though her uncle accepted his sister-in-law's limitations and knew not to take it personally; they had never met. He did not engage in a battle and was even able to offer love in the face of her mother's rigid antagonism toward him. Of course, he had not been traumatized directly by the history Beverly's mother had lived.

While history is full of the tragedy of racial bigotry and the scars it leaves on everyone, I was struck by how many partners who had been rejected by their in-laws left a spot open in their hearts should they, too, open their hearts again. In Martin Luther King's words, "Hatred paralyzes life; love releases it. Hatred confuses life; love harmonizes it. Hatred darkens life; love illumines it."[70] This does not mean that we can forget history, but it does suggest that there is hope.

3

Sex, Race, and Love

R acism destroys families and replaces love with hate and fear. Because of racism, families have disowned the beloved daughters and sons for whom they worked extra hours to buy a special toy, whose skinned knees they bandaged, whose band concerts, plays, baseball games, and dance performances they proudly attended. The couples we encountered in Chapter 1, Catherine and Carl and Jeff and Joy, represent many, many others who have been denounced or disinherited simply because they happened to fall in love with someone of a different race. It is nearly impossible for any marriage to compensate totally for the wounds inflicted by exile.

Rejection by one's family can haunt a marriage, creating underlying resentments and irritation. Sometimes the marriage is asked to bear the burden of compensation for the loss of family, or it can become the arena for displaced anger at family members. Karen, a white woman from Arkansas, attributes her brother-in-law's failed marriage to the lack of family support from both sides of the family.

> My husband is a twin, and his twin brother also married a white woman. And her parents had the same initial reaction as mine, but they kept it up. They kept it up. They cut her off, from paying for her college—they didn't. They completely would give her nothing. And I think after a while, that starts to wear on somebody. They ended up, after six years, getting divorced. And her parents' comments at

that point, "Well, now we have our daughter back," and "At least you didn't give us any mixed kids." You know, all this kind of stuff. Then after they got divorced, they could relate to her ex-husband, because it was no longer a threat. It was like he was okay as person. To them, it wasn't that he was a bad person, but they didn't want their family that way. . . . Marriage is hard enough. To be put in that situation. I could see it in their relationship. Every time they had a disagreement about something, it's like, "Well, is this because we kinda feel we have to stay together, because your parents pushed you out, or is it because we really want to be, and you're always questioning that?"

The reaction of these white parents suggests that they saw their daughter's marriage as a significant breach of their identity and possibly also their status as "white people." By cutting off their daughter or treating her as a marginal member, the family was able to maintain its racial authenticity. This kind of coercion is more common in white families, and in some Asian families, than in families of other races. June, a white woman in her fifties raised in New York City but now living in Wisconsin, recalls the family drama over her announcement in 1965 that she intended to marry a black man:

When I called and told my mother, she screamed and dropped the phone. She had met my husband and thought he was a nice person, though she claims to have told me, "Don't marry him." I was living in New York City, and was involved with the civil rights movement. My husband, now my ex-husband, was involved with the Black Nationalist movement and a lot of political activity. To me this was a positive thing. . . . My parents are quite old. My dad was born at the turn of the century; my mother is about ten years younger. I was more or less disowned. I was told not to come home, not to try to have any contact with my parents or with my family or other family members. So I called my grandmother, who had always been my ally and had been very understanding. She sounded fine on the phone and said she would talk with my mother. Later, I got a call from my brother. Evidently, she had a stroke right immediately after this telephone conversation. I could see the letter from her several years later saying she had heard this terrible news, dropped the phone and fell to the floor. Her son came rushing from his business because he heard her fall to the floor saying, "Mama, Mama, who did this terrible thing to you?" and all she could say was, "June." So at any rate, I carried a lot of guilt for a long time. But she sounded very understanding. She even said "Goodbye." I had no idea that this had occurred. So then my mother ended up having a hysterical amnesia attack which lasted for months. She didn't know who she was or where she was, and this was all on my shoulders. Up until that point, I thought my intended marriage was a very progressive move. I had thought how much better—to be—to make this commitment and marry someone rather than just live with someone. . . . I also really think that if I had, if it had been the other way around, if I had been a male marrying a person of color, that this would have been more acceptable because there had been various wars. There was an acceptance of war brides from other cultures.

Karen's and June's stories resonate with the generation of white women who married interracially in the 1960s and 1970s in the mainland United States. Even Katherine Hepburn and Spencer Tracy, the progressive white parents in *Guess Who's Coming to Dinner,* had difficulty with their daughter's intentions. The wife reminds her shocked husband, "We told her it was wrong to think that whites were superior and when we said it, we never said, 'But don't fall in love with a colored man.'" The split in American consciousness between political ideals of integration and personal preferences for segregation shows how difficult it is to surmount racist notions of class and caste. This split comes to the surface when families are faced with the prospect of an interracial marriage.

The terms *endogamy* and *exogamy* have been used in the literature on intermarriage to distinguish socially acceptable from socially unacceptable marriages. Socially acceptable, or *endogamous,* marriages conform to social convention and take place within an in-group (also called homogamous marriages).[1] Certain behaviors (culture and class markers) and symbols (race, skin color, accent) become markers of in-groups and out-groups. In endogamous marriages these markers maintain social distance between groups and preserve resources, authority, and power. Essentially, for dominant groups, endogamy serves as an exclusionary device.[2] *Exogamous* marriages are marriages with someone from an out-group, as defined on the basis of race, gender, religion, nationality, or class (or some combination thereof). I interviewed a young woman from Ghana who was then living in Ithaca, New York, with her white husband, whom she had met and married in Ghana, and their three children. She said that if she had known back then what she knew now about American race relations, she would never have consented to move to this country. She did not regret marrying her husband, only that their marriage was considered unacceptable in the United States and that they had paid the price for that in terms of social ostracism and discrimination.

Intermarriage on the basis of class is sometimes classified as either *hypergamy* or *hypogamy*. *Hypergamy* refers to marrying into a higher class, "marrying up," while *hypogamy* means marrying someone of a lower class, or "marrying down" or "beneath one."[3] Class, in this scheme, is determined not only by wealth but also by race, gender, religion, color, type of accent, school attended, physical attractiveness, and other factors. From a white person's point of view, the marriage of a person of color to a white person is often seen as hypergamy for the person of color and as hypogamy for the white person. Ironically, not all of the people of color I interviewed saw intermarriage as hypergamous, but they sometimes attributed hypergamous motives to other people of color.

People who oppose interracial marriage typically cite higher divorce rates as their rationale. But data showing higher divorce rates for mixed marriages derives from older studies of Jewish intermarriage[4] and black-white marriage.[5] In a study of intermarriage in Hawaii—where the usual views of hypergamy and hypogamy do not prevail—Johnson found that when only resident marriages were considered, twenty-nine out of forty possible exogamous marriage combinations based on race sustained lower rates of divorce than endogamous marriages based on ethnicity.[6] Specifically he found that white men, white women, and Filipino women had significantly lower rates of divorce when they married people of different races than when they married within their own race. In contrast, Hawaiian men sustained higher rates of divorce in exogamous marriages. Johnson notes that in Hawaii, where white persons are a minority and are openly perceived as outsiders, acceptance or insider status for whites may derive from intermarriage and an assimilation of local values.[7] The principles of hypergamy and hypogamy may also operate in the areas of income and education. For women from families with significantly higher income and more education than their husbands had, the rate of divorce was higher.[8] Johnson found a strong trend for endogamy on the basis of income similarity. Educated, affluent women may strain traditional gender roles in these marriages. In most societies, the social and cultural mandate is that women should either marry "up" or marry within their own class, as in fairy tales about maidens and princes.

White men's choices of partner are not as socially constricted as women's are. Why not? The simplest explanation is gender privilege. A woman's identity is associated much more closely with the status of her partner than is the case with a man. In a patriarchal society the woman essentially becomes a member of her partner's clan. A white man derives his privilege both from his gender and his race. A man of color derives his privilege from gender. The woman of color has neither privilege. Relationships between white men and women of color—initially American Indian and African American women, then Asian women—have never been scrutinized as closely or as critically as those of white women married to men of color.[9]

Sherrie, a young woman who grew up in a Midwestern farming community, was raised to value openness, particularly openness to class difference. Although her brother had made a cross-cultural marriage and been accepted, she was initially disowned for her marriage to a man from a lower-middle-class black family. Her experience illustrates the subtle ways in which class and caste intersect with race and gender.

> At first they disowned me and then accepted me. Except they disowned me based on this other person, and then accepted it. So obviously it was something else because he and I were still the same people. And that's how I can tell. During the time that I was living with this person, my brother became engaged to a woman who was clearly of a different class than he was. But in this particular case, he was moving up. He was marrying into an extraordinarily wealthy Greek orthodox family, very old family. I think it sort of impacted my parents' self awareness of . . . their situation in the family. They saw themselves as classless people who could go anywhere and move into any sort of society. And they always tried to make us, they tried to fight against this self-coded hick farmer's thing by taking us everywhere and making sure that we could move into any society. And I think it dawned on them that we were. It's just that he happened to move in one direction and I happened to move in a different direction. And it was like it finally occurred to them that they had succeeded.

As women have gained more rights through civil rights legislation and cultural transformations, more attention has been paid to marriages of women of color and white men, an encouraging development that suggests the rules of hypergamy and hypogamy are flexible and the concepts open to interpretation. In his foreword to Adams's study of interracial relationships in Hawaii, sociologist Robert Park observes:

> Race relations, like many if not most other relations among human beings, must be conceived as existing in three dimensions rather than, as we ordinarily conceive it, in two . . . between individuals and between groups of individuals. . . .
>
> Changes may be, or seem to be, merely fortuitous. At other times they assume a cyclical or secular form. All three types of change are involved in the processes of growth and all three are more or less involved in what we may described as the "race relation cycle." [Change in race relations] at any time and place . . . once initiated, inevitably continues until it terminates in some predestined racial configuration, and one consistent with an established social order of which it is a part.[10]

More than fifty years ago, the sociologist Robert Merton suggested that two processes enable interracial marriages to survive despite the stigma and taboo against them. One is love, which persists and can thrive even in hostile conditions; the other is the democratic ideals of the United States, which allow some fluidity across socioeconomic and racial lines.[11] In combination, these two factors, love and democratic ideals, have enabled an increase in interclass and interracial marriages. Plenty of movies, fairy tales, epic dramas, and popular songs suggest that many working- and middle-class girls dream of interclass marriage, which today may include interracial marriage.

Race, Caste, and Class

So why has there not been more intermarriage? Until recently in America, race as caste rather than as class has made racial lines difficult to cross.[12] Many persons of color have achieved middle-, upper-middle-, and upper-class status, yet discrimination on the basis of skin color persists. It is not at all uncommon for professional (and professionally attired) blacks—judges, businessmen, lawyers, doctors—to be bypassed by a taxicab in favor of a white passenger, or accused of shoplifting, or pulled over by the police for no other reason than that they are driving in a white neighborhood.[13] Recent years have seen an upsurge in lawsuits brought by minorities against corporations for discriminatory practices in the workplace.

Acrimony has also arisen in communities of color surrounding persons of mixed-race European heritage. Spike Lee's film *Jungle Fever* depicts a circle of black women who complain about black men's preference for lighter-skinned women, a sign that these men have internalized some of the attitudes of white men. Asian American women have been castigated for diluting Japanese, Filipino, Korean, Vietnamese, and Chinese bloodlines through their marriage to white men. Although Diane Fujino's research on interracial dating suggests that a prototypical Asian American man is rated positively on variables associated with hypergamy for women—for example, earning potential—he is rated as less physically attractive than a prototypical white man.[14] One explanation may be that height is highly correlated with attractiveness in men. On average, Asian American men are shorter than men of European or African descent. Height is associated with power, and power is equated simplistically with masculinity.

A caste system influences how we evaluate an attractive partner. As Merton observes, "in a racial caste structure, the criteria of pulchritude are commonly derived from the physical traits characteristic of the dominant caste, so that even in these terms, lower-caste members will usually be deemed unattractive."[15]

Researchers have used "exchange theory" to explain exogamous marriages and how the concepts of hypergamy or hypogamy work in them. Exchange theory is based on a traditional, post–Industrial Revolution model of gender roles in which men hold structural power through financial provision for women. Exchange theory assumes a marital contract in which the structural (political and economic) power of men and women is implicitly unequal. Women exchange some resource (for example, economic) or value (for example, beauty) for the status that comes with marriage to a man. But exchange theory does not account for gender or race as caste, which diminishes its power to explain intermarriage.

Robert Merton's classic work on black-white pairings was based on exchanging race for economic and or educational status. Fujino argues that there is mixed and marginal evidence through the twentieth century to support these variables as a basis for exchange. Of course, different patterns existed for different racial and ethnic groups based on region and era.[16] Given all of the possible heterosexual pairings of black and white women and men, Merton predicted that the most common pairing for white women and black men should be a lower-class white woman with an upper-class black man; the least common pairing should be an upper-class white woman with a lower-class black man.[17] In fact, however, these predictions were not borne out by the numbers. It becomes apparent that although he used the term *caste*, Merton based his hypothesis about race on class and neglected the rigidity of the caste system that prevailed in American society during the 1930s and 1940s, when he did his work. His model works better today for other forms of racial intermarriage in certain regions of the country, as Sung's research on intermarriage patterns for Chinese Americans in New York in 1982 suggests.[18] But Merton's predictions for black-white mixing do not hold even today, largely because of the way in which caste remnants are attached to blackness and because gender also has characteristics of caste. When gender and race are understood as master statuses with caste connotations, marriage between black women and white men should be much less frequent than marriage between white men and women of any other color.

At the beginning the twenty-first century, however, financial independence for women, changing mores, extended periods of fertility, and the ease and prevalence of divorce require us to reconsider what exactly is being traded. We may need to rely on notions of complementarity to explain interracial attraction.[19] Psychologist Celia Falicov observes that notions of endogamy may be too simple to explain contemporary cross-cultural marriage (which is not always the same as interracial marriage).[20] Fujino has concluded from her research that exchange theory is unlikely to work if single attributes are used to explain the exchange.[21] Exchange theories based in psychological theory are at a basic disadvantage when the structural power differences of gender and race are not weighed, when regional histories of race relations affecting the climate for interracial marriage are not considered, and when the meaning of love has not been captured in the explanations for interracial marriage.

Sex, Race, Love

Without being able to fathom the normal trend toward intermarriage when people have contact, intermarriage has been studied from an assumption of abnormality and pathology, much as same-sex relationships have been studied. In this way, the social sciences have sanctioned opposition to interracial love in the same way that they have opposed same-sex unions. Theories of black male sexual prowess, black female sexual appetites, unusual female anatomy of Asian women, and other myths abound in social science research.[22] Franz Fanon suggests that white male genital envy and insecurity are at the root of white men's anger toward black males who marry white women.[23] An indirect corroboration of this theory, at least at the level of folklore, came from a random survey of white women, in which Tenzer found that a significant number of white women surveyed believed that white men saw black male sexuality as different from theirs in a way that promoted white male insecurity.[24] Fanon suggests that lynching, torture, and cruelty are a form of sadistic sexual revenge. Fanon, among others, suggests that the black male has been castrated, whereas the Asian male has been emasculated or feminized in a way that has reduced white male envy. White male sexual interest in women of color, particularly black women, is seldom discussed. When it is, the white man absolves himself of responsibility or assertiveness by constructing the black woman as sexually aggressive and rationalizing his assaults on her.[25] He also absolves himself of responsibility for his liaisons with Asian women by constructing them as geisha or prostitutes meant to serve him.[26]

Franz Fanon has written about the dependency complex of colonized people, whereby they internalize the image of the colonizer as superior.[27] One strives to achieve that for oneself. "It is the racist who creates his inferior," he writes, adding that the colonist essentially projects onto the colonized a neuroticism about race in which race is confounded with class and access and freedom.[28]

> Out of the blackest part of my soul, across the zebra striping of my mind, surges this desire to be suddenly *white*.
>
> I wish to be acknowledged not as *black* but as *white*.
>
> Now—and this is a form of recognition that Hegel had not envisaged—who but a white woman can do this for me? By loving me she proves that I am worthy of white love. I am loved like a white man. I am a white man.
>
> Her love takes me onto the noble road that leads to total realization. . . .
>
> I marry white culture, white beauty, white whiteness.

When my restless hands caress those white breasts, they grasp white civilization and dignity and make them mine.[29]

But Fanon's words suggest that even he has internalized stereotypical attitudes toward interracial relationships. He forgets that the lower caste status by gender of white women prevents them from conferring status on black men. Although we cannot ignore the politicization of interracial relationships and intermarriage, to see them only in this light makes them two-dimensional, devoid of the power of love to instill hope, to heal, and to connect people. At the same time, however, through the politicization of intermarriage, white and black women's bodies become commodities, essential vehicles through which race is defined.

Psychologist Ernest Porterfield summarized three psychoanalytical explanations for intermarriage that prevailed for generations, all based on a pathologically motivated pairing, particularly of white women and black men, but not substantiated by any significant data.[30] First, a person may be hostile and may marry to act out a revenge fantasy or to control what he or she has been denied. This theory is usually used to explain why black men marry white women. Implicit in this theory is that white women will have control through whiteness, and black men through gender. The second explanation suggests that an individual may be rebelling against a parent, usually a father, and most often a white daughter against her father. This dynamic is supposed to explain why a white woman marries someone considered "beneath" her, whether by class or by race; by ignoring the filial obligation to her father she also "betrays" her race. By the third explanation for intermarriage, a person marries outside his or her group out of self-loathing and a wish for self-punishment.

These folk theories have been around for a long time, acted out in film, song, play, and everyday conversations. They suggest that people who intermarry are different from or marry for different reasons from those of the general population, whether this difference is viewed as positive, negative, or neutral. Few of these theories allow for the possibility that people who marry outside their racial or socioeconomic or gender group do so for the same reasons that people marry within their group.[31]

A second group of "normative" theories focuses on the idea that intermarriage reflects a group's acceptability. Intermarriage has long been used as an indication of the social distance between groups, social distance being a measure of how fully (or how little) a given group is accepted by other groups.[32] A high rate of intermarriage suggests that a group has been accepted or assimilated into the dominant Euro-American culture.

Throughout the twentieth century, black writers have articulated the structural forces that have maintained a distance between black and white populations and psyches. As the barriers between the races began to crumble with the civil rights movement, Milton Gordon, a prominent sociologist of the era, interpreted racial intermarriage as a sign of assimilation, a sign that a minority group's difference from the dominant society had diminished.[33]

Several studies, however, suggest that assimilation operates differently for different groups of people. Using 1980 census data, Lee and Yamanaka found that the rate of intermarriage with the non-Hispanic white population was highest for Asian Americans.[34] They attributed this higher rate to the smaller social distance between Asian Americans and whites, compared with the social distance between whites and either blacks or Latinos, and concluded that this was the result of Asian assimilation, specifically Chinese, Japanese, Filipino, Korean, Vietnamese, and Indian, into American society.

Fujino challenges this conclusion and cites four factors that throw it into doubt. First, U.S. servicemen married Asian "war brides" who were neither acculturated nor assimilated at the time of marriage. Second, there are high rates of intermarriage between white and Asians despite "glass ceilings" in the workplace that limit Asian American assimilation. Third, many Asian Americans have a strong bicultural identity, with strong ties to their native Asian culture. And fourth, many Asian immigrants still struggle against barriers in housing, employment, and other areas of civil rights.[35]

Hwang, Saenz, and Aguirre offer an analysis that combines these two differing conclusions using a 5 percent sample of the Public Use Microdata Sample of 1980 census data to derive a sample of in-married, interracially married, and interethnically married Asian Americans. They suggest that the effect of two forms of assimilation, cultural and structural, should be differentiated. Cultural assimilation, or acculturation, was measured by the combination of two variables, immigration status and English language fluency. Immigration status was divided into

American born, pre-1965 immigrant, and post-1965 immigrant. Structural assimilation was a combined index of educational achievement, occupational status, and income. They found that high acculturation (American born, fluent in English), rather than structural assimilation led to higher rates of intermarriage for Asian Americans. These findings strongly suggest that other factors such as attitudinal prejudices may place constraints on the impact of structural assimilation for Asian Americans in a way that is different from the experience of white immigrants.[36] Although signs of both structural and cultural assimilation are evident, assimilation is predicated on immigrant groups' relinquishing values and practices deemed inferior or inappropriate by the host culture. Assimilation thus carries with it an attitudinal bias that may prevail in private between individuals and groups of people in the form of prejudices against intermarriage.

Using patterns of Anglo-Chicano intermarriage in Arizona, California, Texas, and New Mexico, Fernandez and Holscher also concluded that simple assimilation is not the sole explanation for intermarriage.[37] With few exceptions, theorists have concluded that Chicano intermarriage occurs because of increasing assimilation into the Anglo or white dominant culture. But Fernandez and Holscher underscored the conclusion of psychologists Salgado de Snyder and Padilla that interethnic marriage must be understood in context.[38] In regions with large numbers of structural minorities, such as Chicanos and Mexican Americans in California and the Southwest, it is possible that the dominant group is assimilated into the Chicano culture or that there is a significant mutual influence between groups that reduces social distance.

Typically, assimilation is thought of as a unidirectional process in which one group assumes the characteristics of the dominant or host culture. But it may be also a two-way process, as Johnson and colleagues suggested in a study of interracial marriage in Hawaii, where many cultures have blended into a local culture and white, European-based culture is only part of the blend.[39] The operative distinction in Hawaii seems to be "local" versus "not local." Whites are considered not local unless they have successfully assimilated local values and behaviors. In contrast to the privileges associated with whiteness in the continental United States at some level, white phenotypes in Hawaii are considered "not local" regardless of the number of generations one's family has resided in the islands.

For yet another view of assimilation, I interviewed several white persons trying to assimilate into minority communities, mostly women, but also a few men: an indigenous American Indian community, a South Asian community, a Mexican American community, and an African American community. Sometimes the apparent reversal of the desired direction of assimilation reflected the unique aspects of a micro-region of the country or metropolitan area. Common markers of these attempts at assimilation were the adoption by white persons of the accents of the ethnic group of their partner. Involvement in community activities and efforts to learn about the culture, food, music of the partner's native culture were common on the part of those persons attempting to blend in. One woman living in a Northwest reservation area of coastal Washington told me that there were several women her age, fifty to fifty-five, who had married blond-haired, blue-eyed men who had learned to fit beautifully into the community over the years. She noted that they had made this transition so well that they felt odd when they went into the metropolitan areas. A white woman married to an South Asian Indian man had adopted her husband's accent, as she talked about how hard it was to be accepted within the Indian community in spite of being married for thirteen years. She made efforts to learn the dialect, cooked Indian food, and shared child care with the other women, but she ultimately remained an outsider. The motivations for trying to assimilate varied; some wanted to reduce the distance and potential conflicts caused by cultural differences; others, to make things less confusing for the children; some felt a real affinity for the culture; and many sought acceptance by the partner's family or culture, which they felt was warmer and more accepting than the culture in which they themselves had been raised. One woman said of her thirty-four-year-old white brother, who had married a black woman, "He just seems to feel more at home in her family. I don't think it really has to do with our family. He's just happier."

Sociologist Peter Blau, like others before him such as Alba and Golden, introduces structural factors such as nativity, generation, segregation, sex ratios, and group size to explain patterns of intermarriage. He has suggested that the smaller a group is relative to another group with whom it has frequent contact, the more intermarriage will take place.[40] Using 1970 Census data, Blau, Blum, and Schwartz found that this thesis worked for almost all forms of diversity they explored in their sample of 125 metropolitan areas in the country.[41] For example, the demographic characteristics of national origin, native language, and occupation showed this pattern—but race did not. In a subsequent study using the same data, Blum refined these findings and concluded that more intermarriage occurred when there was more equality between persons of different races in the community.[42] Blau, Beeker, and Fitzpatrick, still working with the same data, found that the more opportunities there are for groups to affiliate, the greater the likelihood of intermarriage.[43] With increased integration of communities, neighborhoods, schools, workplaces, and places of worship, intermarriage should increase.

Ironically, the civil right movements and its repercussions in the 1970s and 1980s have heightened racial consciousness and the awareness of internalized racism to the point that affiliation with white people has been interpreted as a sign of disloyalty. A backlash against intermarriage may thus be an unintended consequence of the civil rights movement and its aftermath. Chicanos, for example, a political category of persons of Mexican descent in the United States, are of mixed heritage. But, as Garcia observes, as a racialized group that has been disenfranchised in this country, "What seems to be of principal concern to Chicanos is that intermarriage often results in a weakening of ties and a declining sense of responsibility and commitment to La Raza."[44] Ernest Porterfield has noted the effects of black pride on decreased familial acceptance of white partners.[45] In his study of black-white intermarriage, several white wives who had initially been accepted were ostacized, ignored, or otherwise ill treated as black family members became involved with the Black Pride movement of the 1960s and 1970s. In the racial and ethnic pride movements of this era, many persons found that healing the wounds inflicted by racism meant total immersion in the movement and rejection of symbols of the dominant culture, including human "symbols." This process has been well documented by many researchers of the process of developing a black[46] and Chicano identity.[47] A few of the white participants in my study described experiences similar to those that Porterfield documented in the 1970s. Suzanne, a white, middle-class woman married to a middle-class black man for more than twenty years, described her experience with her husband's family:

On my husband's side of the family, he was this big, like, national at one point, very militant. So my brother-in-laws were like, you know, "How could you turn against us," you know. And then I would come to the house where they would tell me he wasn't there. Or I would come into the house, if I got that far, and everybody would sit on the couch so I wouldn't have a place to sit. And I had to sit on the edge or something. And they would tell me that their mother doesn't allow you to sit on the edge of the couch. So my husband had to set them straight, set them all straight.

Cynthia, a twenty-three-year-old white woman in a relatively new marriage, spoke of how her black sisters-in-law still tested her and treated her rudely:

They treat me as though I'm stupid or don't even exist. They refer to me as "she" even when I'm right there. Now, I know that some black women think white women are out to steal black men, but I didn't go out looking for a black man to marry or even date. We worked together, shared some friends in common. We like the same music and I enjoyed his sense of humor. I married him because we are good for each other and love each other. I try to ignore them sometimes. Recently, I've started telling them they are being rude. My husband's confronted them, and they say something like, "She's your wife, not ours."

Historical factors may drive these dynamics, including a process in which black identity formation may denigrate anything associated with the dominant culture. Perhaps not coincidentally, Gallup polls suggest that although blacks have always had a high rate of approval of interracial marriage relative to whites, the rate not only stopped increasing in the 1970s but decreased in each poll through the early 1990s.[48] Cynthia's sisters-in-law may interpret their brother's choice of a white wife as a negation of their value as black women. They may see themselves as self-appointed representatives of one of the most oppressed groups in this country's history, past and present, and may feel the need to act in solidarity to make their point as part of a broader protest of black women. And while this point may not be lost on their white sister-in-law, she may focus on the rudeness because of the structural privilege whiteness has provided her: She can afford to limit her analysis to the personal relationship she has with these women. Her awareness buffers her so that this rudeness, as bad as it is, is not felt as deeply as it might be if she were black and they were white.

Sex Ratio Theory

The one factor that is overlooked in many discussions of intermarriage is that of the balance or imbalance of sex ratios. Sex ratios allows us to examine structural factors that account for differential patterns between gender across race, and similar patterns for gender that prevail across race for intermarriage.

During the course of this country's history, sex ratios between men and women have varied. When sex ratios are balanced, there is less racial out-group marriage. According to economic laws of supply and demand, sex ratio theory suggests that when one gender is in oversupply, it becomes a "buyer's market" for the gender in shorter supply. For example, Vietnamese American women of the marriageable cohort age are in short supply for the marriageable cohort of Vietnamese American men, which would lead us to expect significant rates of intermarriage. When figures from the 1980s suggested an significant oversupply of Vietnamese American men in San Diego, as well as in general patterns of those who immigrated in the 1980s,[49] unmarried Vietnamese American women did experience the predicted increased relational power with Vietnamese American men.[50]

African American women's rates of intermarriage have increased, as African American men of marriageable age have been in short supply due to incarceration, lower levels of education than black women, death, and unemployment—all symptoms of chronic institutional racism.[51] A decade ago, Staples estimated that there were 150,000 more black women than black men enrolled in college.[52] Imbalanced sex ratios can lead to the redefinition of sex roles, sexual freedom outside a relationship, and increased regard for partners in short supply.

There is, however, a double standard for men and women. Guttentag and Secord, who have explored this theory in depth, suggest that the laws of supply and demand are heavily influenced by structural power, which is not usually factored into psychological theories.[53] Structural power derives from and is embedded within social institutions and conventions; it is not equitably shared by men and women. Men hold more structural power than women, regardless of race, even though this is gradually changing in most Western societies. The interaction between the laws of supply and demand, which these researchers call *dyadic power* and *structural power*, yields some predictions that are verified by current patterns.

When there is an oversupply of one gender, people of that gender will partner with people from the group that is most plentiful. The classic example of this phenomenon can be found in the colonization of countries by Europeans who then married or partnered with native women, a strategy often critical to colonial expansion. In more recent times, military men abroad for any length of time have an increased likelihood of finding a partner from the indigenous culture.[54]

Structural power is not just male-dominated; it is also white-dominated. When Asian labor was imported into this country in the nineteenth century, at a time when sex ratios were the most imbalanced this nation has ever seen, Asian men, first Chinese, then Japanese, then Filipino, were forbidden to touch white women, let alone marry them.[55]

The philosopher Lewis Gordon provides an analysis of the structural power enacted through race and gender that links the dialogue between them. Gordon points out that from a white point of view, the assumed race of the human race is white. To be non-white is to be racialized in an anti-black world. To be raceless is to be "pushed up" toward whiteness. Gordon also notes that for centuries the Western tradition has configured the gender of the human race as male. So although power may be defined as genderless and raceless, the default values for power are male and white.[56]

Gordon contends that a hierarchy of sexual desirability naturally follows from this view of gender and race. Given the traditional Western view of power as white and male, white women can be constructed as black by their gender. This might help to explain why pairings of white women with black men are more common than pairings of black women with white men, a phenomenon that flies in the face of early exchange theories. White women and black men are not so distant from each other in social location.

I was struck by the personal information given by men of Asian-black, Asian-white, and black-white heritage in a study I conducted of mixed race siblings. These men illustrated the social construction of masculinity within a racialized context. In contrast to biracial men of black heritage, the men of mixed Asian-white heritage confessed to insecurity about the stereotype of Asian men and small penis size, and the degree to which penis size might affect their sexual attractiveness to partners. Some of these men engaged in body building to increase their bulk in an effort to offset the slightly smaller bulk and height they attributed to their Asian heritage. The men of either black-white or black-Asian heritage said that they sometimes attempted to "act black," which they defined as intimidating or aggressive posturing, in order to enhance the social perception of their masculinity. Even when these men had small builds, they felt that their construction of self as black compensated for small size or other less masculine characteristics stereotypically associated with Asianness. I suggest that these observations and the forgoing arguments offer some explanation for some of the inequities that sex ratio and conventional structural theories cannot predict or explain.

With the structural power of men in general and white men in particular, certain double standards prevail.[57] Thus despite Guttentag and Secord's observation that "the individual member whose sex is in short supply has a stronger position and is less dependent on the partner because of the larger number of alternative relationships available to him or her," that position is still influenced by gender and its attendant structural inequities.[58] When there are significantly fewer women than men, the men become very protective of women's sexual freedom and women's freedom of movement becomes more restricted. However, when there are significantly fewer men than women, sexual freedom abounds for men; they have less commitment to monogamous or sustained relationships that prevail when gender ratios are equal. Under these conditions women are likely to be, and feel, exploited—although such conditions can also lead to greater independence for women if they make an effort to reduce their dependency on men.[59]

Researchers found that both black and white women's behavior for the 1970s through 1980s simply follows from the laws of supply and demand they call dyadic power. When women were in oversupply they married at a later age, more women remained single, there was a larger group of divorced women at any point in time, and more divorced and widowed women did not remarry.[60] However, when men were in short supply, male privilege changed the formula. Men actually marry later when there is no shortage of partners; more men remain single because they can have multiple partners that way; there is a larger pool of divorced men because there is no pressure to compete for scarce women to remarry; and divorced and widowed men disproportionately remain single. In addition, free from the cultural and social repercussions that single mothers experience, single fathers do not face the same stigma or constraints.

Whereas both men and women may go outside their in-group for a partner where they are oversupplied, women experience more constraints than men do: barriers of race, expectations of hypergamy on a status variable, and the perceived declining attractiveness of women as they age. Guttentag and Secord reviewed rate and age of divorce, marriage, and sex ratios and found that the theory holds for both black and white men and women. But whereas white women who have gone outside the in-group for partners and subsequently lost their authentic white racial status can still be seen as physically attractive, black, Asian, Latina, and Native American women are typically seen as less attractive. Collins notes that these constraints may explain why divorced black professional women are less likely to remarry than their white counterparts.[61] Many white men who have married Filipina women through correspondence relationships do not necessarily consider these women as physically attractive as they do white women. What they find attractive are the imagined or real qualities these women provide that white women are now thought to lack due to feminism. Essentially, white women, and American women in general, have made a claim for adult status and treatment. There is a perceived oversupply of assertive women and an undersupply of traditional women. Obedience, willingness to cook, clean, and cater to a man's whims, whether these qualities are fact or fantasy, makes Asian women more attractive than American women to these men. Their unfamiliarity with the culture increases their dependence on men psychologically, physically, and emotionally. There is thus no question about who is dominant in the relationship and the gender roles are clearly defined and unchallenged—at least initially.[62]

When there are significantly fewer men than women (10 percent fewer or more), women may necessarily need to seek men outside their designated in-group.[63] This has long been the case for white women, and in the past decade black women have begun to join their ranks in this respect; marriages between black woman and non-black men have doubled in less than a decade.

In an unpublished survey of 350 black women, Chapman found that almost two-thirds (205 women) had dated interracially and others who had not said they might.[64] This figure is lower than the one Staples obtained with a different sample of participants more than a decade before. This figure and recent changes still stand in contrast to 85 percent of black single men in Staples's study who said that they had had at least one interracial dating experience.[65] Many of the women in Chapman's sample thought that interracial dating gave them the possibility of increased economic opportunity. Chapman speculates that as more black women attain advanced degrees, the likelihood of interracial marriage may increase. Her speculation is further supported by Heiss's analysis of racial differences in attitudes toward family matters. He found that black and white women of the same class background were more similar than different.[66]

The children and grandchildren of the civil rights generation live a different racial reality from that of persons born before the 1950s. Intermarriage has increased because it is no longer illegal and there are now opportunities to develop meaningful relationships across color lines. And despite double standards, double entendres, and mixed messages, many young people do not experience race as a caste or even as a class barrier as frequently or as formidably as their parents, grandparents, and great-grandparents did. Structural factors are changing—not only along racial lines, but in terms of gender roles and economic positions associated with these statuses. There is a greater chance to make friends at school and in the workplace, where people spend a significant number of their waking hours. Women have more opportunities for independence from their families and husbands. They also have opportunities to delay marriage as fertility has been extended through technology. Birth control reduces the need for early marriages or forced marriage as a result of pregnancy. As structural barriers to equality between race and gender continue to be challenged, the matrix of gender and race changes. The result will be more interracial marriage.

4

The Business of Families

Racial intermarriage touches millions of Americans. With almost three million people in the United States part of an interracial marriage as of 1995, it is no longer a rarity.[1] And with one degree of separation—that is, all of the family members of these couples—it easily touches many millions more people. If we allow a second degree of separation—friends, coworkers, acquaintances—it is already likely that intermarriage affects most people in this country. Based on the intermarriage rates of the late 1980s, anthropologist Roger Sanjek observes:

> If we were to grant each intermarried white spouse sixteen relatives and assume these kin do not reject the intermarried couple, potentially one-sixth of white Americans now have a nonwhite affinal relative and are likely to have a racially mixed kinsperson, the offspring of the interracial marriage. Looking at things from the other side, many more than this proportion of Hispanic and Asian Americans have white and half-white relatives, since one-sixth themselves are interracially married. The logic of the numbers suggests that most Asians and Hispanics now have white relatives. Such existing, potential, and growing kinship links are far fewer between black and white Americans, or between blacks and Hispanics or Asians, for that matter.[2]

The reception of interracial marriage is certainly one barometer of American race relations. Many factors have brought Americans to a point where they are more open to intermarriage than ever before. A 1997 Gallup poll found the highest approval rating of interracial marriage ever by black (77 percent) and white (61 percent) Americans.[3] Like the Gallup polls, the National Opinion Research Center (NORC) has followed white and black Americans' attitudes toward racial intermarriage and has found increased acceptance and decreased objection. By 1994, when people were asked, "Would you favor a law against racial intermarriage?" 84.9 percent of 1,626 white Americans answered in the negative. As predicted, even more black Americans—96.8 percent of the 258 polled—also answered no.[4]

Nevertheless, interracial marriage still can create conflict within families, as we have seen. A NORC poll in 1990 asked Jews, blacks, Asians, and Hispanics how they would feel about a close relative marrying someone from outside their racial or ethnic group.[5] Blacks were most strongly opposed, with 57.5 percent of 1,362 respondents against it; next came Asian Americans at 42.4 percent, then Hispanic Americans at 40.4 percent. Jews were the least opposed, at 16.3 percent of 1,362 respondents, but also had the largest response neither favoring nor opposing intermarriage of a close relative (63.1 percent). Just over 46 percent of Asian Americans and Hispanic Americans were neutral on the question, neither favoring nor opposing such a marriage. These data still show that despite the increasing acceptance of intermarriage in this country, families are not necessarily pleased when it becomes personal.

My attempt to understand why some families felt so much conflict around intermarriage led me to ask focus groups and individuals, "What differentiates those families who extend themselves to a new family member who is perceived as racially different from those families who cannot do this—ever?" The answers I received repeatedly implicated family dynamics: communication, rules of family membership, respect for individuality, status consciousness, and the degree to which people or family environments controlled individual members. When combined, the family dynamics suggest that if race is part of the "cultural capital" of the family, then racial reproduction is an intended product of the family whether it is white, black, or Asian.

Sometimes the cultural capital was ethnicity; in that case, opposition to intermarriage varied depending on the gender of the family member getting married. In matrilineal cultures, the lineage resides with the women, regardless of whom they marry. Jerry, a Navajo man who in the past decade has dated several women racially different from himself, has two grown children, a son and a daughter. When he was asked, "Which would make more difference to you—if your son married a non-Navajo person or if your daughter did?" he answered without hesitation, "My son." Because Navajo lineage is matrilineal, his daughter's children would be Navajo regardless of whom she married. His son's children, by contrast, would not necessarily be able to claim this heritage if he married outside the Navajo clan. In patrilineal cultures, the reverse appears to be true. A white Catholic woman named Rose noted that when she and her brother, two of four siblings, had both married interracially, her family had shown more concern about her marriage than about her brother's. Ironically, in patrilineal cultures women are often responsible for the transmission of certain cultural values, which complicates interethnic and interracial marriage for white women.

Thus the question *What about the children?* addresses not only concern about social reactions but also the race or ethnicity of the parent, through which lineage is passed or marked. Gender and race interact to determine what race will mean for the children of interracial marriages. If the family is a site for reproduction of race, then it may be viewed as a business, complete with a leader or management team, public relations department, workers, and a product—future generations of same-race relatives. Marriage as a business transaction can be conceptualized as a franchise, a merger, or an acquisition in which the definition of family, its mission statement, and its style of leadership influence whether or not family members see themselves as an interracial family—or the degree to which being seen this way is acceptable or threatening to them.

The Business of Families

Family Product. The most significant product of families is future genera-tions. Rosenblatt, Karis, and Powell, in their study of interracial couples, suggest that disowning interracially married family members may be a way of disowning racially different in-laws.[6] Rosenblatt and Karis note that divorce and death may end this relationship and that the disowned family member may then be received back into the fold.[7] Denounce-ment attempts to avoid possible contamination by a status or stigma the family wishes to avoid. The NORC data and my own interviews suggest that white people are not the only ones who fear contamination; blacks, Asians, and Hispanics share this fear, though for some different reasons. For people of color for whom racial designation may overlap significantly with cultural identity (for example, black with African, Asian with Chinese or Japanese), the opposition to intermarriage may be related to fear of the loss of culture.

Definition of Family. What is a family? Who are kin? Some people do not consider the partner's family to be family. A new marriage may constitute a totally separate family. Some families do not even consider the partner family. Understanding the difference between core and extended family may also shed light on why families react to interracial marriage the way they do. If racial reproduction is a critical product of a family, and family also includes the partner's kin, then intermarriage will pose a significant problem for families. And if the couple has children, as most couples do, the children have a blood tie to both clans, which strengthens the links immeasurably. Late marriages, those that occur past child-bearing age, may receive less opposition for this reason.

That children are indisputable evidence of an interracial liaison, evidence that cannot be hidden from the world, has significant bearing on the reception of such relationships. Rudy, a fifty-year-old white man living in Seattle, married a Filipina of similar age. He suggested that if they had been able to have children, his family would have reacted much more strongly against the marriage, for mixed-children would have challenged his family's racial identity in a way that a Filipina daughter-in-law did not.

> One other issue made a big difference in how my wife was received into the family. She was beyond the childbearing years so everyone knew that there would never be any children as an issue of this relationship. I think she thought it was a very positive kind of thing. I think it was extremely positive because they knew that there would be no offspring in particular in among my sons. . . . I think that my family, all the men, are very big. I have one son 6'4" and the other is 6'6". Big strong guys. I think the thought of them having a 5'2" flat-nose Filipino dark-color kid running around with my German surname would have unsettled them a bit. Why? Because it's entirely different than the images the family has had of itself of always being big strapping guys six feet or taller. It would be just a different concept of family identity. You've seen the

families where you have brothers. One is a big guy and the other, you know, looks entirely different and everybody goes, "You're brothers?" You know sometimes families get certain images of themselves.

Rudy's frank reflections on his family also suggest that white, mainstream images of masculinity are incompatible with Asian features. The value his family places on maintaining its self-image is clearly associated with male power, defined as big, tall, and white. One of the truths uncovered by my six-year study is that people can hold internalized prejudices that originate in fear and still love the object of their fear very much.

Family Mission Statements. Through marriage and the production of children, families grow. In this sense families are like small corporations that aim to grow larger. Metaphorically, marriages can be viewed as franchises, mergers, or acquisitions. The family mission statement, as well as its self-definition, determine which of these metaphors applies to a marriage. Ten questions help to clarify the role played in the family by race, and its incorporation into the mission statement:

1. How does the family assess its worth?
2. What are the products associated with the family?
3. For what type of growth does the family strive?
4. What image is important to the family?
5. What role do family members play?
6. How are rewards, compensation, benefits, and security allocated or secured?
7. What is the policy toward gender equity?
8. What is the model of leadership?
9. Are there opportunities for increased responsibility or leadership?
10. How much structure and independence can family members expect?

Answering these questions may help us understand why endogamous marriages are typically viewed as more desirable than exogamous, interracial marriages.

The Merger. Applying the business model of a merger, intermarriage connects two different clans to each other integrally and intimately. Leadership is negotiated and includes people from both clans.

A merger in itself does not guarantee what type of leadership model will prevail, nor does it mean that family members will have no independence. Some sense of similarity and shared values is part of each family's self-image. How the two families benefit from the affiliation with each other is usually made explicit.

If racial reproduction is an important product, families of color are less threatened than white families by mergers with other-race families because racial construction assigns children a non-white status. Since the 1970s, however, there seems to be more pressure on people of color to keep marriage racially endogamous. If the family is concerned with cultural reproduction, more responsibility is typically placed on women to marry endogamously. If a white family is invested in racial reproduction as a main product, a racial intermarriage will be vehemently opposed. The marriage may be perceived as putting the family, or the race, at risk for takeover. Just as business may sell off unprofitable divisions, the family may use threats of rejection or disinheritance to try and discourage intermarriage. (See Figure 1.)

The Franchise. This model of family recognizes a degree of separateness, and separate leadership, but also connection to the original corporation. It is concerned more with the new leadership, the newly married couple, and the degree to which they represent the image of the original corporation and can replicate and promote the products associated with the family. The clan of the racially different spouse is not integral to the acceptance of the couple. This model assesses the couple as a unit and their potential to enhance the original corporation. If race is not a meaningful product for the family, individual skills, talents, and values become the significant factors in evaluating the new individual.

If race and racial reproduction are critical to image, status, or product, an interracial marriage will not be granted a franchise. The couple will have to start their own business and it will have a very different image from that of the original corporation; there can be no mistaking the original family business with the new business venture. This type of disenfranchisement may still allow some personal interaction between families but without a stake or investment in the fledgling business. In effect, the family neither abandons nor rejects the individuals but distances itself emotionally or geographically. (See Figure 2.)

The Acquisition. This model of business keeps strict control of resources and public image. The new spouse becomes one of the family—

Racial Reproduction

Unimportant   **Important**

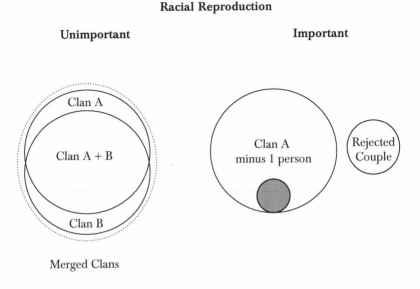

Merged Clans

Figure 1 Family Business Model of Merger

in effect, the family's property. Because of the competitive nature of business, hypergamous relationships, in which the acquisition in some way enhances the family's image, are naturally preferred. The inclusion of the newcomer's extended family in the acquisition is negotiable but not automatic; they usually remain peripheral. In part, it depends on whether the extended family has "capital" that enhances the corporation's image. If the family runs on a strictly patriarchal model, men's wives always become an acquisition of the family and are expected to comply with the family's way of doing business. More latitude is given to women's husbands, but they too are expected to fit a certain image. If not, the family may not accept the acquisition.

If race and racial reproduction are important, the marriage and its offspring may not be recognized. This is the only model that will not recognize a marriage. Or the couple may receive crumbs of attention and small gifts as token symbols of connection. In this case, the family member can usually return to the corporation through divorce; but if children have been produced, other family dynamics may prevent this return. The family member will be disowned and the family unit may be recognized. The new family unit may be abandoned, leaving them

Racial Reproduction

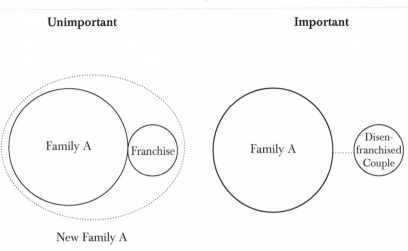

Figure 2 Family Business Model of Franchise

open to be acquired or taken in by the partner's family. The culture of some families, regardless of color or culture, uses an acquisition model. Such families assume that whomever one of them marries automatically becomes one of them. (See Figure 3.)

It becomes apparent that in any of these business models, when race or racial reproduction becomes a critical product, the expectations of loyalty take on increased importance. In essence, the collective's integrity takes precedent over the individual's need. This dynamic, often salient in immigrant and religious families, makes exogamous marriage very difficult, whether it is interethnic, international, interracial, or interfaith. Among the people I interviewed was a young Ethiopian man studying for an advanced engineering degree in the United States. He fell in love with a white Jewish woman, and at the time of the interview they were planning to get married. But he had made a unilateral decision about the religion in which their children would be raised; furthermore, he let his fiancée know that he would never be able to bring her home to meet his family. For this couple, what might be an ordinary merger or acquisition model is going to be an unrecognized marriage. Their marriage will have to withstand much stress and they

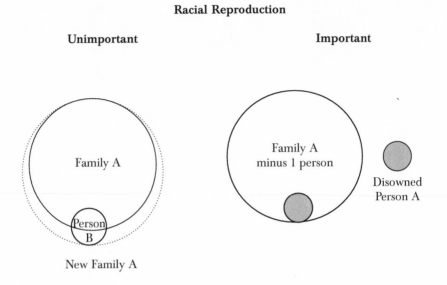

Figure 3   Family Business Model of Acquisition

will have to hope that the woman's family will love and support them. Otherwise they will have to fall back on friends and acquaintances in lieu of the family or families that have abandoned them. Love is not always enough to keep a marriage intact.

Gender always plays a role in business models. If race, and therefore racial reproduction, is a critical product of the family business, women are central. In such families, women become important assets or property; through them, culture and race are secured. The result, regardless of the business model, is that competition for and ownership of women become important. This is the basic premise of white supremacism.

Within each business model, I focused only on the response from one partner's family. The response from the other family is important, particularly if the couple has been rejected, disenfranchised, or disowned. In exogamous marriages, couples may play out situations in order to comprehend how, whether, and when racial reproduction and sameness are important and how this will affect them. For example, one side of the family may reject them, while the other side may accept them with love, providing the couple with a source of emotional security and support.

Models of Leadership

The leadership of a family determines how business is transacted; strong leadership can even transform one business model into another. Sometimes leadership is shared, but in most families one person has the last word. In some families a patriarch or matriarch who may not be involved in daily operations nevertheless sets the tone of acceptable behavior, particularly in times of crisis. Several models of leadership are possible: the *chief executive officer* or president; the *monarch;* and the *council* or *board*. The style of leadership in a family may change as the younger generation comes of age and older members die. Sometimes different leaders oversee different departments or branches of family business.

Chief executive officer (CEO). The CEO functions as president of the family. Sometimes this position is shared by two parents, but usually one or the other fills the role. While the CEO has the ultimate authority within the extended family, his or her decisions are informed by advisors who make recommendations and in many cases are free to make decisions without consulting the CEO. Communication takes place in both directions between the CEO and family members. CEOs differ as to how much advice they want and the degree to which they delegate decision making or share leadership. The more they delegate and abide by the decisions of the persons to whom they have delegated authority, the more room there is for individual expression and direction. This style of leadership occurs infrequently in immigrant families. As the youngest generation reaches adulthood, the CEO attempts to step down and transfer power to a designated successor.

A CEO who will not delegate responsibility and wants direct control over all decisions functions as a micromanager. This kind of CEO discourages the development of future leadership and encourages the dependence of other family members, a dependence that is usually tied to money or privileges controlled by the CEO and borders on a monarchical style of leadership. Whether delegating or micromanaging, if the CEO does not attempt to understand ideas, or is inflexible or incompetent, he or she is likely to turn into a dictator or inflexible monarch. This was the case in some families I studied and it took sons and daughters by surprise. Parents who had been excellent communicators and who had delegated authority gracefully sometimes turned into dictators when they strongly opposed a marriage on ideological grounds. The business of family usually dissolved or was weakened significantly, and the marriage—rather than the CEO's inflexibility—was blamed for wrecking the family.

Monarch. Another style of leadership I observed in my research was that of a *monarchy*. The monarch is often the oldest member of the family, a grandparent or even great-grandparent. Even families that function on the CEO model in normal times may have recourse to the monarchy model in times of crisis, particularly if the image of the dynasty is threatened.

This style of leadership may come into play only when there is a very significant decision to be made; otherwise the family may function more or less democratically. Though this person may have advisors, as the CEO does, the family follows his or her direction unquestioningly. Critical thinking and discussion are discouraged. Because the monarch holds so much power, people may censor their real views in order to remain in the favor of the leader. Monarchy thus encourages secrecy and duplicity. The family usually has to have substantial wealth or resources to bind members through potential disinheritance, which is associated with a significant change of lifestyle. Such disinheritance effectively provides barriers to thes family member's moving in the same social circles and thus amounts to abandonment rather than merely disinheritance or distancing.

Council or Board. The council model bases family policy on the opinion of the majority. This style of leadership is found in two very different circumstances. In the first, a community council of elders, such as that found in some Indian communities and tightly knit ethnic communities, pressures parents to put pressure on their children. The council is not always formally organized and may informally be composed of influential leaders of the community.

More commonly this style of leadership is found in single-parent families or in families in which the oldest generation is still young (under sixty) and is the second generation of immigrants. The families that operate under this form of leadership typically have fewer conflicts over generational issues. The council discusses issues and considers deviations and exceptions to family protocol by person and context. Membership may vary depending on the issue and whom it affects. Communication is freer and takes place in all directions; no single person can make a decision without the knowledge of the council.

Although this style of leadership appears very inclusive, if one person deviates from agreed-upon practice, the pressure to conform can be very extreme indeed. In a council model, a dissenting individual thwarts the expectations and demands not of one person but of the whole group. Some families that have historically followed a CEO or monarch model may be flexible enough to adopt a council style of leadership in the event that an interracial marriage threatens. In this way family members who are closer, or closer in age, to the errant individual may be used to exert pressure.

The experience of Eric, a Filipino in his late thirties, provides an opportunity to analyze the model of business and leadership that determined his family's response to his sister's black husband.

> We don't take the material wealth of the person as something of the most significance. We look more on his . . . how he deals with the other family members. How he relates himself to our friends, and especially to the elder members of the family. That is how we size up the man or the woman. It's not on the material achievement, or whatever. He grew up in the country and was brought up strictly to be respectful, like we were. The blacks are very close, they have a great respect for their elders. And that's what I like most, because that is very similar. It strikes a similar tone with the background of Filipinos. I would also say work ethics, the value of, I don't know how you call it, being close in the family. He sees to it that he attends to the needs of the family, the children especially. Education and the material needs. Oh, he's good-looking, too. He's got to be accepted because he's trying his best to blend with the whole family. You know, we also talked about it. And I said, look, the guy's honest enough that he wants to be part of the family, so we accepted him.

Eric's narrative clarifies his family's mission statement. The family clearly values the collective over the individual good, yet with room for some freedom. His description rules out a franchise business model; he is explaining the ways in which his brother-in-law's acts led to his being accepted by the family. Many of the ten questions that help to draw out the family mission statement are clearly answered. Relationships and respect are important assets here. The business of family is hierarchically organized, and respect for elders is a significant part of its organization. Race is not a central piece of the business transaction of this marriage.

Whereas white families have traditionally seen intermarriage as an irreversible contamination of social status (when race is construed as caste), and as resignation (if race is construed as class), families of color and devoutly religious families have reacted against intermarriage for a greater variety of reasons. Rather than racial contamination, fear of the loss of ethnic solidarity or the erosion of faith may motivate their opposition.[8] Many cultural or ethnic groups put the family unit before the individual. There are areas in which individual prerogatives are not tolerated, intermarriage being one of them if it threatens the integrity of the family culture in the next generation. Eric described his mother's concerns about the cultural compatibility of her daughter and her daughter's intended husband.

> He's got a sister in Iowa that he visits once in a while and we have met two other family members, the girl and his mother. His mother is very kind, good. The sister's just like my brother-in-law. But food was a concern. My family asked, "Can you eat the food?" Yeah, you know, the food is number one because how will your wife cook? She will cook one for herself and one for her eldest daughter and she will cook something else for you and that will be very expensive, my mother said. So the food is number one. The friends that you go along with—she asked, "Will you allow your children to grow up with Filipinos?" They will be adopting the culture of the Philippines. And he said, "I don't see anything wrong with that." And that's the only two concerns of my mom.

Eric's narrative suggests that his family saw his sister's marriage as a merger of clans. The CEO was probably his mother, and she had obviously delegated some responsibility to her adult children to assess the situation and, possibly, offer their advice. There was probably also some vestige of council leadership in Eric's family, perhaps the result of the adult children serving as culture brokers between Filipino and American culture. It was important to the mother that her family continue to be viewed as Filipino, though it was not clear that doing so would rule out the family's also being an African American family. The third generation of this family—the offspring of Eric's sister and her husband—is not likely to adopt the culture of the Philippines. The culture of her grandchildren will be foreign in many ways to Eric's mother regardless of whom her daughter marries.

Other families have strict rules of exclusion, and they are typically more status-conscious and use a more constricted range of assessment of the marriage. Most of the white partners I interviewed came from middle- or working-class backgrounds. Psychological insecurity about class standing may have contributed to the rigidity and fear their families expressed about the inclusion of a racially different family member. In such cases, white families almost always stereotyped families of color as coming from a less privileged background. These marriages were then considered a step down by the white families—though they were not necessarily seen as a step up by the families of color.

The confounding of race and class was also witnessed in families of color who sometimes incorrectly assumed that white partners were from middle- or upper-middle-class backgrounds. Rosanne, a twenty-six-year-old white woman from the Midwest, said of her mother, "I believe that some of my parents' reactions to my marriage were based on a negative stereotype about socioeconomic class. When in fact my husband's [black] family were much better educated and really had what I would call a higher educational economic status than my own parents. But yet because he was 'colored,' as my mother said, they perceived him as lower-class." All families esteem certain values that indicate what they consider to be desirable markers of in-group members. Responses such as Rosanne's mother's suggest that class discrimination is a thin disguise for racial prejudice. The business model of her family is likely to be a franchise in which Rosanne will be released to start her own family enterprise so that she will not become a liability to her family. The style of leadership here is likely to be a CEO model, because, while her mother indicated disapproval of the marriage, she did not express complete rejection such as would come from a monarchical leadership style.

The influence of grandparents was significant for many of the participants in my study. Generation tends to have a significant impact on views of race and intermarriage, which complicates the family's deliberations on these issues. People now in their late middle age or old age were influenced by decades of racist doctrine and usually had parents who believed in racial segregation. Younger participants in my study often faced grandparents who came from a different world and were ignorant and uncomprehending of their grandchildren's more enlightened attitudes.

In general, families that expect and value individuality operate more democratically and feel less threatened by the exceptional paths or

journeys a family member may take. They may also have a greater capacity to evaluate potential new family members as individuals, despite
their prejudices. Families that felt threatened by difference interpreted
a son's or daughter's choice of an out-group partner as a deliberate rejection of the family values (which it sometimes was), or even madness.

Family dynamics can combine to promote growth, individuality, and
critical thinking, but this is not what all families strive for or desire.
Conformity and agreement may be valued if instability is experienced
as threatening. When families abandon, reject, or distance themselves
from sons' and daughters' marriages, these sons and daughters are
more likely to move away geographically in order to avoid the pain of
being "so close, yet so far away." These new family enterprises often
formed new families from friends, as many gay and lesbian couples
do. Some of these couples formed or joined multiracial family support groups.[9]

Redefining Family

The first phase of my research allowed me a wonderful glimpse into
the way in which families deal structurally and psychologically with race
when it becomes a very personal issue. In the second phase of research,
I posed the question, "Does your family see itself as a multiracial family?
What would this mean?" People often responded that the immediate
nuclear family of parents and siblings was now considered interracial.
These answers also shed light on how they defined family. Whether
these definitions were consistent or not across marriages provided
another glimpse into the meaning the family placed on race and how
they negotiated it. Some people defined family in the most restrictive,
traditional, nuclear terms, while others defined it as a larger, extended
system of aunts, uncles, grandparents, and cousins.

Two of the Los Angeles focus groups were composed of persons who
saw their families as interracial and celebrated the diversity within them.
I asked them why they thought other families had so much trouble doing
this. Their responses fell into four general categories.

The first category takes us back to the business models of family.
If you believe that you marry an individual rather than a family, then
for you marriage represents a spin-off type of business, a franchise,
rather than an acquisition or merger. Your new branch of the family can

be viewed separately. Sons-in-law and daughters-in-law never become full-fledged members of the family, though they may be welcome at family gatherings. Respondents thought that this model held more for white families who were no longer ethnically identified than for families of color.

Children were central to the definition of family in this category of responses. Mike's sister married a black man whom he and his family liked. When I asked him, "Do you now see your family as an interracial or mixed-race family?" he answered:

> No. I really never thought about it. Um, I think probably if they had children together I would have more of a tendency to think that way, but they're both older. And I just think about it as a family, not necessarily a mixed race-family or a non-mixed race family. . . . I think having children, yes, they would have mixed-race children. And then I probably would have responded yes. Because there would be mixed-race children and they would all be definitely part of our family. But I don't somehow think of him and her as interracial. I just think they're a couple.

A second category of responses was slightly different. In this group, families might decide that the member who engaged in the interracial marriage had been different all along—not quite like the rest of the family. In this way families compartmentalized the marriage as an aberrant transgression and not a reflection on the family. This strategy seemed to protect and maintain the family's racial identity.

A third set of responses identified geographical distance and mobility as reasons why families might not think of themselves as interracial. When the interracial couple lives far away, by choice or by chance, their families do not have to face the possibility of viewing themselves as an interracial family in the community. One woman in her thirties said that she remained geographically distant from her family as a way of maintaining the best family relations possible. She and her husband and children visit, but they do not challenge the daily reality of her parents and siblings. She does not have to endure what she anticipates could be hurtful, subtle rejections of her children or herself or husband.

Distance allows people to avoid resolving the question, "Do you see yourself as an interracial family?" Margaret, whose daughter married a black man in the 1970s, gave a glimpse of her thought process in answering this question: "Well, they have an interracial family, my daughter and her husband. My three sons are all married to white people. Well,

I guess you could call us an interracial family since she's certainly part of the family. Well, I guess it is. See, they live way down there and she hardly ever comes up here so we don't see them all that much."

Margaret thought aloud the logic but had clearly never contemplated the question before. Geographical distance allows her not to think of *her* family as interracial, but rather as someone with a daughter who has an interracial family. In a way, Margaret sees her daughter as having started her own business of family—a disenfranchised member of the corporation but still with some emotional ties.

The fourth type of responses arises from changing the rules which guide racial classification. Roberta, the white grandmother in her fifties whom we encountered earlier, has an Asian-white grandchild. When she was asked, "Do you now see your family as an interracial or mixed family?" she responded, "If I see my family as an interracial family? Oh, yes . . . black, white, we're all white." Roberta defined race here as a matter of black and white, although her Japanese son-in-law and biracial grandson are not white according to centuries of U.S. racial classification. Her construction of race, and of her grandson as white like her, made this relationship less objectionable to her. She also demonstrated the subtle change that is taking place in the one-drop rules. In a previous era, she could not have considered this child white; he would even have been considered foreign.

The difficulties that white families have with viewing themselves as interracial seems to move beyond definitions of family. The meaning of the word *interracial* is part of the struggle. President Clinton's Race Advisory Board Chairman John Hope Franklin wrote, "Stereotypes remain because Americans cling to the idea that it is best to try to ignore race. That, in turn, forces people to bury—and therefore harbor—beliefs they form from stereotypes heard at school, in the media and from family members."[10]

Some people are more open to racial difference when it is viewed in the arena of international or cultural difference—that is, when it is couched in international rather than interracial terms. I interviewed several white men and women who had married African spouses. They felt that their parents were more accepting of these black African partners than they would have been of American blacks. This is further evidence of how deeply blackness is perceived as caste in some people's psyches.

Families struggle with viewing themselves as interracial but do not always resolve the question of whether they are interracial or not and what that means to them. Subtle boundaries almost always remain. The introduction of children, however, does seem to make a difference because of perceived blood ties. How the parents and extended family racially construct these children, and the conflicts over the appropriate racial designation for them, reveal that race is a social construction. The literal fact of children blur what are often artificial boundaries, and this blurring helps to explain why children are so often a focus of family concerns when an interracial relationship becomes serious. Interracial couples are usually asked their intentions about having children much earlier in a relationship than are other couples. People also feel freer about offering unsolicited opinions on this question and can even suddenly become self-appointed experts on the developmental issues facing multiracial children.

Ideals of individualism, independence, and romantic love do allow people to cross lines of faith, race, ethnicity, and class. As one of my subjects in Seattle put it, "Independence is encouraged for different reasons. And sometimes independence leads to independent decisions, such as who you marry." Personal independence does change the definition of who can become family and ultimately forces us to reexamine our definition and transaction of the business of family. Increasingly, racial reproduction will be less predictable, and maybe eventually less important. Time will tell.

5

Open and Closed Families

My attempts to answer the question, "What differentiates those families who can welcome someone racially different from those families who cannot?" led me to a simple way of thinking about families as either open or closed systems of relationships. The results of my analysis are not an attempt to catalogue families but to provide a framework for thinking about complex family dynamics. Not all families will fit neatly into open- or closed-system descriptions. Open families most resembled an individualistic society in which interdependence is maintained; intermarriage is acceptable. Those that appear somewhat open I term "pseudo-open." They may encourage interracial or interethnic friendships and be fine with interracial dating, but they oppose interracial marriage. In contrast, "pseudo-closed" systems were sometimes able to grow over time to greater acceptance of an interracial marriage—but this often took years, and sometimes the birth or death of a family member. Closed systems typically corresponded with monarchical family models, showed less tolerance of individual deviation, and saw race as a critical piece of the image or product and property of the family. Let us look more closely at these family models.

Open Families. Open families responded to tensions in such a way as to encourage, rather than limit, growth. They were not without conflict, but communication was a two-way process, and respect for individual choice ultimately prevailed. Even when they became a source of conflict,

94

individual differences were respected. Open families had a clear sense of the boundaries between individuals and did not see an individual's actions or opinions as necessarily representative of the whole family. Family identity was derived not from a single individual but from the character, relational efforts, integrity, achievements, and recreational interests of the whole. Leadership was held usually by a CEO, rarely by a council, and never by a monarch.

Mike, whom we met earlier, reflects on the process by which his sister's black husband was welcomed into his white family, who had little contact with African Americans.

> I didn't have any trouble liking him. He's a pretty good guy. He treats her good. Pretty much lets her do what she wants to, and she travels a lot. Her business takes her on tours around the world and that stuff. None of that seems to bother him, and that's good. She's the type that needs quite a bit of freedom. She likes being with him. That suits the hell outta me. We have a very close family and everybody works pretty damn hard at accepting everybody else and their decisions and so on. I wouldn't have anticipated a lot of problems and there hasn't been. Though we are strictly, you know, a white middle-class family. But we're basically a family of working people. He's a working-class guy.

The family mission statement is revealed here through Mike's description of the criteria for fitting into the family. He acknowledges the value of individuality and the match between his sister and brother-in-law and their working-class origins. He expresses respect for his sister's judgment in choosing a mate.

> There isn't much that is more important than being happy, I don't think. And if you can help the other person be happy by going along with whatever it is they're doing, until you can make some kind of a rational decision, yeah, he doesn't beat her, you know, he works, gets along good with her kids, and gets along with the rest of the family. Why should I or we object? Why would I even voice my objection? If he's beating on her or something, that's a whole different thing, but that wouldn't matter who it was. Race wouldn't make a difference at all. . . . If a person's rude, and so forth, doesn't matter what the hell color rude they are; they're just rude. You know if you ask somebody, "Would you rather have a nice, polite, decent, ambitious, happy black guy around, or a no-good-son-of-a-bitch white guy that was always causing trouble, fighting with everybody?" they should pick my brother-in-law.

The open family recognizes that as children grow up they become independent, with ideas and beliefs that may differ from those of their parents. Mike's words suggest that his family operates on the franchise model with a democratic form of leadership, allowing considerable autonomy for the franchise but still having certain criteria for inclusion in the family. Mike stressed character and hard work as important attributes of a desirable in-law, and on these grounds his brother-in-law filled the bill. Race was not an important issue for Mike's family.

Ann, a white woman of Scandinavian heritage from Seattle, provides another description of an open family. Her daughter married young, a white man, and then divorced. Several years later, she married a black man from her family's church.

> I remember in high school, saying to her when she asked me, "What if I ever married? It could be someone like Watanabe, a Japanese or Oriental, what would you all think?" I used to say, I do remember saying, "No problem, people are people. We accept them and love them if they are who you pick." But I do remember saying the words of caution, "You have to think about the children." I mean, I can remember saying that to her, think about the children you bring into the world and what you would be dealing with in this society. And she was probably sixteen or seventeen back then, raising that question.

Ann's feelings about the importance of child-rearing and the value of acting with and giving love reveal her sense of her family's mission.

> It makes you cry . . . the old thing even in the Old Testament, [that] the sins of the generations are passed on. So however they were raised with those kind of comments, in their atmosphere and their world, then their attitude and their mind is the same way, and maybe they just don't have big enough hearts. . . . You got to have an open door, a big heart if you are going to have the ability to reach out in any sort of way from taking in children to interracial marriage. You have to have, like, unconditional love.

Faye, a thirty-year-old white woman from Colorado, also described an open family in talking about her family's response to her choice of a Chinese American husband.

> My family just thinks my husband is the greatest thing since apple pie. My brothers don't call to talk to me. They ask me how I'm doing, then quickly ask me to put my husband on the phone. I don't know if there is

a certain way my parents raised me that made me this open specifically. I didn't grow up religious at all. I think the only thing I can think of, is my family treated people like people. We didn't talk about race or religion. They just talked about people. If they were a person, I didn't care what they were. My parents are a little older. My mom is already in her sixties. My dad died when I was seventeen and he was already in his seventies. My dad never met my husband so I don't know how he would react. But I'm pretty sure he wouldn't care. My brother has dated ABCs, as my husband calls himself, American-Born Chinese. My brother is engaged to an Asian woman and he's dated Asian women a lot and my father met some of them and he never had a problem. He thought his girlfriends were fabulous, just like anybody else.

Basically, this family's "mission statement" emphasized character and quality of interpersonal interaction. Race was not part of the mission statement, at least not when it came to Asians. So she was free to choose someone who really did fit into the family in spite of possible cultural differences. It is likely that the family business model was an acquisition or franchise model. Her family's approach was not necessarily color-blind, however. That they did not talk about race is not necessarily a positive thing. Like many white families, they may not have been particularly motivated or well equipped to talk about it—although it is possible that race was not mentioned simply because it was not considered a factor in assessing character.

Open families sometimes reversed, or at least complicated, conventional ideas of acculturation. It is usually thought that the minority person has to adapt to the dominant society, but several people from open families were able to open themselves up to the culture of the partner's family, and discussed how much they appreciated this opportunity. These experiences sometimes had positive ripple effects in their extended families. Sometimes the minority culture and worldview were more consonant with their own experience of the world. For example, Garrett from Florida explains why he married a black woman.

[From the age of about thirteen to twenty-five] most everything I did was in a predominantly black environment. The church I went to, or if I went to listen to music. If they had a festival, at least the area where I lived, the culture there was jazz. . . . I would probably say that the fact that I do have a black wife is that she seems more of the role or more who I was exposed to. As a matter of fact, I've only dated one white girl in all my life, not that I really had this tremendous preference; it's just that where I grew up, [black] was positive. I had a lot of black friends that lived around me so I had a great peek into a lot of black culture. Of course, I can't fully understand what it is like to be black, but being around black culture has given me some great insight.

The experiences that they accumulated over the years, including that of being the "outsider" in certain settings, enhanced some interviewees' ability to be even more open. Faye provides an illustration of this.

My husband grew up in a predominantly white area with very few Chinese people and I grew up mostly in a white area with few minorities. I learned a lot about Chinese culture. He hasn't had to go out of his way to learn about white culture because he's been surrounded by it all his life, so there's not that much for him to learn. But I learned a lot about Chinese and it's very interesting. I really, really enjoy it. . . . I think a lot of white people, when they go out in public and they hear people speaking in different languages, they worry, "What are they talking about? I have to know." Somehow, now when I hear people speaking especially Asian languages, I hardly notice, and in fact it reminds me of home. It makes me comfortable when I hear people speaking Asian languages out in public. I hear it all the time being around his family.

Pseudo-Open Families. The pseudo-open family is not distinguishable from an open family until a relationship moves to a level of serious commitment. When this happens, a pseudo-open family may fall back on internalized stereotypes that pose a significant challenge to the marriage. Because pseudo-open families consider themselves liberal, enlightened, and free of racial prejudice, they will typically couch their objections in cultural or class rather than racial terms. Some pseudo-open white families were open to any choice of partner except black; some pseudo-open black families were open to any choice but white. These reflections were in line with the National Opinion Research Center's poll, summarized in Chapter 4, on opposition to intermarriage.[1]

Rich, a white man from Florida in his early thirties, describes his pseudo-open family.

Early in my upbringing, I was told by my parents that race wouldn't be an issue unless, I emphasize, unless she was black. So I'm sure that had some influence on me. You have to understand that this was the attitude in the part of the country where I was from, Florida and the South. It's not like they said, "I don't like black people." My parents' attitude was they have no prejudice against black people as long as they don't try to marry their son. Otherwise everything is fine. In fact, I had a lot of black friends growing up in Florida and at school. One time I played a joke on my parents. I had a lot of friends who were foreign exchange students. I'd help some students out at the university, of course, during the holidays when they had no place to go. Most of them stayed on campus. So I'd invite them home. I brought students from Venezuela, Japan. I invited one student from Africa home for Thanksgiving as a favor to a school acquaintance. I didn't know anyone from Africa. It was an educational experience to make her acquaintance and learn a little bit about that place. Well, my parents were surprised because I didn't specify that I was bringing home someone from Africa and someone female. They were very nice to her. As soon as she got on the plane, they were stammering over themselves to check out whether or not she was a girlfriend. When I told them she wasn't, they had a big sigh of relief 'cause I remember my mother told me a long time ago, they didn't have anything against a race, they just didn't want me to marry a black woman.

Rich's parents' racial prejudice was overt, though they had enough control of their anxiety not to visit it upon their son's guest. They would probably not object to black-white intermarriage if polled, but they obviously would if it became personal and affected their own lives.

Another way in which the pseudo-open family operates is that while the most recent generations are truly open, the oldest generation (the grandparent generation) still holds much executive power in a monarchical style of leadership. Tensions increase and family harmony is threatened. If the parental generation cannot negotiate between their parents and their children, the ability for growth and welcoming of a new family member is significantly impaired. In the pseudo-open family, race may be neutralized when the individual has outstanding features that override race, such as star status, in which another aspect of his or her identity outweighs the family's prejudices.

Closed Families. The hallmark of closed families is the rigidity of rules maintaining distance between "us" and "them," the in-group versus the out-group. These families, while seemingly democratic in times of peace and harmony, tend to become monarchical in the disowning process, directing other family members' behavior toward the banished member.

In closed families communication moves in a single direction from the decision makers to the lower-ranking members, that is, from parents to children. The flow of communication may not change even when children are grown and well into their adult years. Cultural, ethnic, or religious traditions are often key parts of identity and help determine the boundaries that mark in-group and out-group status. One of the recent immigrant groups having great difficulty breaking closed ranks are adult children of South Asian families. Many of these adult children were either born or raised from an early age in the United States and are very Americanized. Intermarriage naturally emerges as a possibility for this generation, but their parents often insist that they marry someone culturally similar with similar class standing. Parents have even hired private investigators to find out whether their children are having secret relationships with people who do meet with their approval. Some of these parents also try to arrange marriages and sometimes place ads in newspapers for suitable spouses for their children. They are openly rude to girlfriends and boyfriends who are not of the "correct" racial, cultural, and class background.

Much of this rigidity stems from unchallenged prejudices or unrealistic expectations. In a culturally and racially diverse nation with tremendous geographic mobility, educational opportunities away from home, and integrated workplaces, it is unrealistic not to consider the possibility that a son, daughter, grandson, granddaughter, niece, or nephew will fall in love with a member of an out-group.

Closed families are not necessarily dysfunctional families (until it comes to crossing the color line), which are unstable, chaotic, lack the capacity to nurture, and can be abusive. But they do tend to have certain rigidities, fears, and prejudices that are not easily changed by facts or experience. Their ability to act lovingly in the face of these feelings is limited or non-existent. Interracial dating is explicitly forbidden. Closed families do not always engage in overt forms of racial discrimination, but they usually do their best to pass on a way of thinking that perpetuates the borders between the races, a way of thinking that forecloses critical thinking about race. They teach their children from an early age "to hate and fear . . . all the people [their] relatives hate," as we hear in *South Pacific*. Often the prospect of an interracial marriage takes on mythical proportions and the partnership is seen as an act of blatant disloyalty, even as an act of war.[2] In these families filial piety is assumed; sons and daughters are indebted to their parents and must repay them for their sacrifices. Marrying the right partner is a filial obligation. The children of these families are caught in a horrible bind: sacrifice their own needs and desires or alienate their parents, perhaps permanently.

Closed families have narrow criteria for whom they will accept as one of the clan, and will open their ranks only to persons who guarantee betterment of the family position. Regardless of how a family becomes closed, the opportunities for growth and change are limited. In an extreme example of a closed family, Randall, a forty-six-year-old African American, talks about his ex-mother-in-law's inability to see him as a person.

> My daughter and my son are black and white. To make it brief, my wife called her mother in California one Christmas day and put our daughter on to talk to grandmother. She didn't say a word to our daughter and my wife gets back on the phone and her mother says, "What the hell is the matter with you? I don't want a nigger in my family!" And this is her grandchild! She wouldn't even speak to us. My wife just hung up and never spoke to her again. But when we separated, that was the first thing that she [my wife] fell back on—trying to degrade me for my skin color and call me nigger, called me SOB and all kinds of stuff. I thought it was because she was angry at me, but a few years down the road, she still holds that kind of attitude.

Randall describes a puzzling and sometimes problematic dynamic for persons who marry persons from closed families. To what degree have the adult children of these families internalized some of the deep-seated fears that fuel racial prejudice? That a person marries someone of another race does not necessarily mean that he or she has fewer racial prejudices than someone who does not. Randall's ex-wife betrayed her prejudices when she racialized her anger during their divorce. This anger allowed her to separate from Randall psychologically and emotionally, and in the heat of the moment she exposed deeply held prejudices that had been buried during her marriage but now realigned her with her family. Even so, her mixed-race children might present an impediment to complete reunification with her family of origin, in which race matters greatly. The business model for Randall's wife's family was a corporate sell-off in which their daughter was sold off as a liability and abandoned, not even recognized. The only way she could return to the corporation was without her husband and children. She did take the children and went to live in another town, where the visible presence of her children could not contaminate her parents' racial identity.

Divorce can bring disowned children back into the fold of a closed family, and certain behaviors can facilitate this process. Displays of prejudice and disgust can cement membership in the group. To speak well of one's ex-spouse or maintain a friendly relationship threatens closed families because it leaves the door open to reconciliation or even to another interracial marriage.

The rejection and disowning that are hallmarks of the closed family are not limited to parents and grandparents. Sometimes adult children disown their parents, as in the case of Linda, who married a white man years after being widowed by her Filipino husband. "My [Filipina] daughter really disowned me for several years," she said. "It is only this Christmas that we got a card. But in the card she didn't mention anything about having feelings against us or for us. She just sent the card to me." In closed white families, whiteness is valuable property, to be closely guarded.

Closed families and Family Cutoffs. If the threat of an interracial marriage exceeds the family's capacity for flexibility and constructive response, it may respond with "solutions" that set the stage for family dysfunction. Emotional or physical cutoffs are one such "solution," similar to being fired from a job with no warning. When a family cuts off one of its members abruptly, that person is stunned and suddenly isolated, possibly robbed of his or her identity as a family member. The family has given a corporate message—you are on your own; we make no further investment in you. There are degrees of detachment, based on the family model, ranging from distancing (franchise model) to rejection (merger model) to abandonment (acquisition model).

With abandonment, the most extreme form of cutoff, women suddenly lose the possibility of refuge from violent relationships, a common problem in relationships regardless of race. This dynamic was illustrated in an unusual focus group in Seattle, in which several women had been cut off from their families for marrying someone of another race. All were white; two had married Mexican men, one had married a black man, and one a Pacific Islander. Unfortunately, all four husbands were batterers. Women who are repeatedly battered experience not only physical abuse but psychological trauma that diminishes their ability to feel lovable or capable in intimate relationships. Like most battered women, these women felt trapped in their relationships. Although they were miserable, they felt responsible for the success or failure of the relationship, another characteristic typical of battered women. Some had been held hostage by their husbands, who threatened that if they tried to leave they would lose their children. Becky, a twenty-seven-year-old white woman, described the psychological transformation she experienced and how the abandonment by her family left her without a safety net. She was not able to resume relations with her family until she divorced her husband.

> I felt worthless, you know. He kept telling me that I was no good and he was the best thing that had ever happened to me—after he had punched me in the face, kicked me in the stomach, whatever. After a while, I just wasn't the same person I was when we dated. I had always been a real people person, but friends said I'd changed. . . . I saw them less and less because I felt like, why would they want to be with me—and I didn't want them to think badly of him. I wanted to leave, but where would I go? I felt that if my relationship failed, my parents, you know, would feel like they were right in their racist convictions. So I felt like a lot was at stake here. I had ended up in a family in which the men did this to their wives. So it wasn't like I could go to my in-laws. You know, I knew this really didn't have to do with race 'cause the other women, like I was the only Anglo in the family, the other ones were Mexican women married to Mexican men. They were being beaten, some worse than me and it wasn't all of them. . . . But I'm embarrassed to say that I just have this gut reaction whenever I see a Mexican man. I literally feel it in my gut, sometimes in my jaw. The first thing that comes to mind is, "I wonder if he beats his wife or girlfriend, too." My neighbor is the one who helped me to get out. I'm back on speaking terms with my family, but I still, maybe never, can tell them what happened.[3]

These women were in a double bind: They could come home only if they "failed" in their marriages. Emotional and physical cutoffs are manipulative, emotionally abusive control measures intended to insure conformity and the upholding of group norms.

Among the participants in my research who were cut off by their families, the experience of being disowned was most common for older participants whose parents were in their sixties or older. Sometimes the banishment was conditional—one Chinese American subject's father maintained an implicit no-contact rule, but after some years he capitulated to his wife's need to see and claim her grandchild. Most often these cutoffs suggested an irrational and fragile sense of racial identity that naturally followed from attaching family identity to something as socially constructed as race. Beverly's family's experience reveals this irrationality. Her black mother told Beverly's brother that he could not come home once he married his white girlfriend, but if he did not marry her, he could still come around—even with the same girlfriend.

In their classic study of ethnocentrism, including anti-Semitism and racism, psychologists T. W. Adorno, Else Frenkel-Brunswik, Daniel J. Levinson, and R. Nevitt Sanford observed the dynamics that led to the closing of ranks in closed families:

> Certain common trends seem to exist, and these are generally the same as those found in anti-Semitic ideology. Most essentially, outgroups are seen as threatening and power-seeking. Accusations against them tend to be moralistic and, often, mutually contradictory. One of the main characteristics of most outgroups is that they are objectively weaker than the groups whom they supposedly threaten. Sometimes this weakness is perceived by the ethnocentrist, but this does not seem to lessen his sense of being threatened. The conflict as he sees it is between an ingroup trying to maintain or recapture its justly superior position, and an outgroup, resentful of past hurts, trying to do to others what they have done to it. But the conflict is seen as permanent and unresolvable; the only alternatives are dominance and submission; justice requires dominance by the superior ingroup, and the subordinate group will always remain resentful and rebellious. Because he considers hierarchy and power conflict "natural" he has difficulty in grasping a conception of group relations in which power considerations are largely eliminated and in which no group can control the lives of other groups.[4]

Pseudo-Closed Families. These families look very much like the closed families described above. Three conditions seem to be associated with their transformation from a closed to an open position: the potential loss of a family member when they realize their son or daughter might marry anyway; the birth of a grandchild; the death of a family member, particularly of a family member who led the opposition to the intermarriage. In addition, the family must be more comfortable with individual autonomy than a truly closed family is.

A pseudo-closed family may also open up if the prospective in-law appears to be an exception to prevailing stereotypes, or if the new relationship outlives the dire predictions of the family. Robert, a black man in his early thirties, described the reactions of his and his wife's families. His father was open, his mother pseudo-open, and his in-laws pseudo-closed in their responses to his marriage. His description captures some of the ways in which race and gender operate differently for men and women because of the structural power of male privilege and white privilege.

> The way I was raised, my parents grew up mostly in Chicago, and Chicago was very racist in the sixties. And so I thought my dad would really be against my wife and I. My wife is white. But he wasn't at all. My mom had a problem with the concept, but not with my wife. Just more being an African American woman, she's the only one who has a problem with this and this is weird. But she kind of got over with it pretty quickly because my wife is just a dynamic person. So my family didn't really have a major problem. But with my wife's family, we had major problems.
>
> Before my wife and I got married, we were really best friends and so her family got to know me that way and really liked me that way. But then when we started dating, it was more "This is wrong, this isn't gonna work." And they gave us all these reasons why we should not have a dating relationship and why we shouldn't get married. They said like the number one thing was they are Christian and the Bible was against it. I said, "Show me where in the Bible that is against it." Then her dad said that society is gonna be against it. And I said, "Show me where society is gonna be against it." They gave us all these arguments that really made no sense. It was so bad that her family had nothing to do with our wedding. My wife and I put on our wedding with the help of my parents. But her family had nothing to do with it. She just said, "Well, if you guys don't want anything to do with it, that's fine." Her father went so far as to say, "Just cut her off." More or less like that. And it's still hurtful for my wife because now it's funny how I go from this person who used to be, at least this is the way I look at it, nonexistent, but now the number one son-in-law because everything changed.
>
> Now we go to their house for vacation. We take our son over there and they're very accepting. Everything changed for the best now. I think now they don't look through the color. They see that we worked at being married for about ten years. But it's kind of interesting to know that it was that way once before. My wife has a lot of problems with it 'cause she brought it up with her mom the last time were in Colorado on vacation how it still bugs her because her mom's wedding dress, the only one that could fit into it would have been my wife and she couldn't wear it because they didn't want anything to do with us. The day of the wedding

her mom was here and left to go wherever they were living at that time and she didn't come to the wedding. She was mostly controlled by her husband, I think, in that aspect of being involved with us and being involved with the wedding. The way I looked at it, if they are not going to be with us, then they are against us. Then they can do their things, and we will do our things. I didn't want their negative baggage because we had enough going on trying to get married and putting it on ourselves. I figured they'd come around eventually if this is gonna happen—and they did.

I asked Robert what he thought brought about the change in his wife's family.

I think a lot of it had occurred with her dad, my wife's father. A lot of it has changed because they've seen how everybody said that our marriage wasn't gonna last; then they saw that it has lasted and we have less problems than the rest of them. My wife and I do a lot of things together and that's how we met. We have a lot more interests in common than the rest of them have with their husbands and wives, so we get along so much better because we have so many interests. Like we're both great baseball fans; we go to baseball games together. I think that some of it too, has to do with seeing that my wife and I have gotten along really well.

Pseudo-Closed versus Pseudo-Open Families. It may appear to be splitting hairs to separate pseudo-open from pseudo-closed families, but significant conceptual differences exist. Pseudo-open families consider themselves open, but when their ideology is tested on a personal level, it collides with their emotions. Because pseudo-open families are open until a relationship becomes serious, they have had time to become acquainted with their potential relative. Pseudo-closed families, by contrast, refuse to do this, often until years after a marriage has taken place.

For example, a young white Seattle woman described how her family was open to her black boyfriend so long as the relationship did not appear serious. Once the couple announced their intention to marry, the family did everything in its power to get her to give him up. They used expensive and otherwise manipulative ploys, such as the offer of a trip abroad. When she declined, her father stopped speaking to her. She agonized for six months during this period of manipulation, which she interpreted as a test of the seriousness of her feelings—a generous interpretation that speaks both her resilience and her respect for her parents' intentions in spite of her deep disagreement with them. When she and her fiancé refused to budge, the family finally accepted the engagement and now treats them well.

Unlike pseudo-open families, pseudo-closed families initially experience no conflict between ideology and emotion. Only when they recognize the autonomy of an individual member and his ability to leave the family business, never to return, does this potential loss open the possibility of a conflict between ideology and emotion. When they realize, too, that they no longer have control over this family member, some families capitulate conditionally—allowing visitation under certain conditions, for example. Both types of family, and the strategies they employ, are coercive and manipulative.

Pseudo-closed families still see their social standing as fragile. They implicitly derive their status from the authenticity of their racial or cultural identity as perceived by the community in which they live and work. Pseudo-closed families may pretend to be open by avoiding the subject, taking care not to put themselves in situations where the issue will arise—or, when in the presence of the objectionable partner, treating him or her as invisible, referring to him or her in the third person, and so on. A relative might ask "How is Cedric's work going?" when Cedric is at the table. She might avoid using the person's name but engage in superficial conversation: "Is your wife doing well?"

Lori's white family is an example of the type of pseudo-closed family that derives its identity and social standing from its reference group, where change in that group can allow for change within the family.

> So my husband and I are hanging out at his family's, a small town in Indiana. Two weekends later my mom calls me. It's so funny. "Guess what, guess what?!" Two of the neighbors now, they're letting their daughters bring their black husbands around. She was so thrilled. She didn't know that the neighbors had black son-in-laws. They didn't know that she did—that my parents had one. Everybody was keeping it quiet, but once [she brought] John out of the closet, the rest of the neighborhood could come out too. And my mom thought she was just a trailblazer; she was so proud.

Julie, a white woman married to a black man with two grown children, feels bitter that she lost years of openness with her family because of their need to "maintain appearances." She and her husband lived far away, so her family could visit them outside the scrutiny of their white neighbors, thus preserving their standing in the community and still having contact with their daughter. This case was so extreme that Julie's parents had even kept the race of their son-in-law a secret from their extended family. On the occasion of a cousin's wedding, the family was suddenly faced with the problem of how to reveal the secret they had kept for years.

> I said, "Mom, how are we going to tell people? I just don't want to go to the wedding and say, 'Here I am. Here's my black husband and my two college-age kids.'" And then she was, like, "Well, I told my brother," and she's talking about how she is going to tell my father's one brother. So I go upstairs and take a nap. All of a sudden I hear this noise downstairs. My uncle has done a surprise visit. He lives not too far. So my son's downstairs. I think my daughter was away. So my mother goes over to the hot tub and says to my niece and nephew, "This is Julie's son, Malcolm, and this is Laurie. Do you want a drink, Ron?" And they went and had a drink and he was like, "Why didn't you tell me?" you know? "Well, you know how [Julie's father is], like Archie Bunker." But he was still, like, "Why didn't you . . ." and "you could have . . ." And my uncle . . . I could just tell right away—he just touched my back and how he acted and stuff—that everything was cool with him. And my father, I mean this [how his brother would react] was his biggest worry all these years. My cousin's wedding was an opportunity. Later my dad asked if my husband was coming to the wedding and I said he'd be there. And then I get to the wedding, and my dad was like, "Well how are things going?" "How is he treating you?" And I said, "Well, things are fine." . . . It just wasted all those years.

My research suggests that fathers have more influence than mothers on family reactions, as was the case in Julie's family, though of course there were exceptions to this rule.

Influences on Openness

Mobility, whether across social, cultural, or geographic lines, provides people with new points of view. It can widen our perspective on class, culture, religion, family dynamics, personality, and generation—all those variables that people sometimes think of simply as "race." Many of the non-white spouses in my study had stories of how their race had exposed their white spouses to prejudice and bigotry—regardless of whether the family had been open or closed. Such experiences make a previously abstract, intellectual understanding of racial bigotry an immediate, emotional experience. Partners often anticipated and recognized the shock their white spouses experienced, especially if they had grown up in predominantly white communities.[5] Robert, a black male married to a white woman, saw this happen to his wife.

> I think that African Americans, because we grew up in a white society, it does affect us in different kinds of ways. But I think it affects whites in different ways. At least I know, like, my wife, it affects her. She gets to see another side she never saw on TV and did not read about in books. And she has been able to embrace African American culture and people. I went to a predominantly white high school in Boston. Then I went to a predominantly white college. Even now where I work, I'm only one of two African American men professionals there. So everything I'm gonna do, it's gonna affect me in some kind of way.

With the exception of first- and second-generation Asian American families, families of color tend to be more open to intermarriage than whites.[6] Why is this? Perhaps because people of color in America already feel more pressure to be at least bicultural. Many or most of them have been acquainted with white people all their lives, whether they wanted it or not. They are more likely than many white Americans to have encountered a variety of people and attitudes; and they have learned how to cope with negative attitudes and how to anticipate shabby treatment from subtle cues. Their race does not confer on them the same advantages that whiteness does.

In contrast, many white people have led racially and ethnically sheltered and isolated lives. Anxiety about other races and ethnicities may stem more from folklore, unfamiliarity, and ignorance than from actual experience. In this country and in this culture, many white persons have been able to move through life with no sense of their race, unaware of the privileges they have merely by virtue of the color of their skin.[7] Peter, a white man in his early forties who lived for years in Japan, where he met his wife, explained how his experiences opened his eyes to the reality of racial discrimination.

> I think it is a tremendous advantage to live in the other person's culture for a while and really find out what's going on. Because my wife comes home sometimes and she says, "Jeez, this place is all racist. There's so much racial prejudice, I can't believe it. Every time I start to speak to somebody, they speak to you and they don't address me at all." The

same thing happens to me in reverse situations in Japan. Soon as they hear my accent, they would speak to my wife, rather than speak to me, so I knew where she was coming from. She was experiencing life here in America. A black baseball player over in Japan once said, "I think every white American should come over and live in Japan for a while and then they can realize what the minorities in America really go through." Simple things like sitting on a train, a crowded train where there are all these people standing and they can see an empty seat next to you and nobody will sit next to you because of the color of your skin.

In settings like these, where they were the minority, white participants experienced their whiteness for the first time.[8] Not all of them found the experience as positive and enlightening as Peter did, however. Some became defensive when they realized that their whiteness no longer conferred automatic privileges. In some cases this defensiveness was translated into overt racial prejudice.[9]

Daily exposure to white society affected James's ability to be open to white people; and his blackness also affected his wife.

You can't teach me anything I haven't been through. My school from the seventh to twelfth grade in western Pennsylvania had 1,700 students. Four of us were black and one of those was a girl. I think I got to know white people close up and personal, okay? I don't judge the whole race by the action of someone. Some of them were actually my friends and we saw each other through a lot growing up. But I do believe that taking my wife to Montana and having her see the reaction to me first of all, being black, and her next of all, being with me, helped her to really understand what I as a black man have been able to deal with. It gives her more strength to know what I can handle. I believe that it has also reinforced my abilities to be independent

Social mobility and individualistic thinking may ironically open up more closed families, particularly as people have the option of marrying later (which is associated with more psychological independence from family), marrying a second or third time,[10] living at a geographical distance, or increasing the pool of marriageable partners when sex ratios are unbalanced.[11] If interracial marriage does not open up a family, it at least opens a different path for the new family that is created. While the marriage may result in a split from the original family business, it is then left to create a new business venture, with the potential to create its own mission statement—and to prosper.

6

The Life Cycle and Interracial Marriage

As couples and family members told me their stories, it became clear that the characteristics that enable a family to operate smoothly in general also determined how easily the family would be able to accept an interracial marriage. Sensitivity, tolerance of individual differences, respect for each other's decisions, and constructive means of resolving disappointment and anger all helped to facilitate the introduction of a new member. In closed families, these qualities were missing, and the interracial couple suffered as a result.

A family's life cycle involves several phases, though not everyone moves through all of them. Marriages and the birth of children bring a sense of new beginnings and expansion. Launching children into adulthood, encountering divorce, and dealing with the death of loved ones are life phases marked by separation and loss. Midlife crises and the transition from parent to grandparent can also be difficult phases. The emotional trauma and irrationality with which some family members react to interracial or interfaith marriage prevented some couples from going through these stages.[1] Disinheritance prevents a son or daughter from integrating a partner into the family and closes them out of the celebration of births of nieces and nephews. They may even be banned from family funerals.

111

Four initial phases of integrating a new family member emerged from my research: meeting, love and commitment, introduction to the family, and blending with the family.

Meeting

Up until the last quarter of the twentieth century, it was an uncommon experience, for most Americans, to know people from different racial backgrounds in a meaningful way; interracial love relationships were rare. Beginning in the seventeenth century, anti-miscegenation legislation protected colonists' business interests and economic advantages by legislating the boundaries between whites and non-whites. As we saw in Chapters 2 and 3, constructions of race and gender were intertwined. Race was not merely a statement of difference but was intended to create clear and impenetrable boundaries. In this way, whiteness was constructed as maleness and the two combined to define personhood from a legal perspective.[2] White superiority was originally asserted over persons of African and American Indian descent but was later extended to each group subsequently constructed as non-white. With the use of pseudo-science, questionable theology, and racist legislation, race became a caste designation rather than merely a class of differences. Until quite recently—and even today, in many areas of this country— these forms of dehumanization generated fear and insecurity among millions of people and have made the color line very difficult to cross. The civil rights reforms, starting with *Brown v. Board of Education* in 1954, made it possible for race mixing to occur with fewer obstacles and in a context of legal legitimacy.

These changes, instead of causing widespread hope for racial equality, heightened anxiety, particularly among white persons who could no longer rely on the law to prevent race mixing. As many white people feared, desegregation in the common arenas of daily life did lead to desegregation in more intimate spheres. Even before the repeal of anti-miscegenation laws, research data demonstrated that intermarriage occurred more frequently where there was less racial segregation.[3] Most people interviewed in this study met at work or at college, places where they had close daily contact. These people in turn made it possible for others in their families, brothers and sisters, nieces and nephews, to venture across the color line.

Sociologist George Simmel has described how greater independence from a reference group is gained when people live and work in places where different networks operate. Socioeconomic status and educational differences may comprise part of the diversity of the setting.[4] This was the case for Thomas and his wife. Thomas, a black man from a working-class family in New York, married a Jewish woman from a well-to-do family.

> I have a cousin who had married a white female, a southern woman, years ago. And nobody talks about him, 'cause he was ostracized. So I kind of knew what their [my family's] reactions would be. So I kind of entered marriage anyway with, well, I'm pretty much on my own anyway. I always felt like an orphan to begin with. So I kind of entered the marriage with really not much of a family to really bring into the marriage. My father-in-law died long before I married my wife. My mother-in-law initially had a lot of difficulties. She knew who I was and when my wife and I first met. We met on a job interview. . . . I already had a job, but went as a favor for somebody. Met my wife. She was nice-looking. Yeah, she's kind of cute . . . just kind of talked to her during the interview and we wound up working together. Became friends for about a year and then we started the relationship afterwards. . . . When my wife had relocated down to where this job was, I had helped out in moving. So my mother-in-law knew we were friends. . . . Her fear was, my wife told me, that we were going to wind up dating. She was also very perceptive because she was right.

While daily proximity increases the likelihood of interracial relationships, geographic location also has an impact on that likelihood. Regional differences, including the region's racial history, the proportion of racial populations relative to one another, and the sex ratios of marriageable partners, all affect the number of interracial marriages. For example, although nationally black men have almost always intermarried much more frequently than black women, in Washington, D.C., black women and white men made up the majority of black-white marriages between 1879 and 1943.[5] In more recent times regional differences in the gender composition of black-white marriages are consistent, but rates vary. The rates of black-white intermarriage are lowest in the South and highest in the western states. According to the 1980 Census, 1.6 percent of black men in the South were intermarried with white women compared to 12.3 percent of black men in the west.[6]

Angela, a black woman originally from Detroit, commented on the regional variations she observed: "The first thing I noticed when I moved to Seattle was the interracial couples. . . . I thought, oh gosh, what's happening with the black women around here? I was [also dating a white man]. But that would be a dangerous thing to do in Detroit."

Nationwide, there has been a huge increase in interracial dating in the past thirty years. A 1997 *USA Today*-Gallup poll of teenagers found that the majority of those surveyed had dated interracially. Of those who had not, approximately one-third of blacks and one-third of whites would consider it, compared with 9% of Hispanic/Latinos.[7] A separate poll by the same team found that 62% of parents said they would not object if their children dated interracially, although some parents said they would discourage a more serious relationship.

Love and Commitment

Ironically, theories that attempt to explain interracial marriage rarely address the subject of love. In his study of black-white marriages in the 1970s, Porterfield concluded that interracial couples married for the same reasons that motivated other couples—first and foremost love. A compelling, all-encompassing feeling of expansion and selflessness, love is a powerful force at the heart of this quiet revolution of interracial marriage.

Falling in love seems to dissolve awareness of differences, minimizes the serious faults of the other person, and infuses one's life with a sense of specialness. Psychotherapist Nathaniel Branden suggests that romantic love is one of the most intense emotions because it is "a passionate spiritual-emotional-sexual attachment between two people that reflects a high regard for the value of each other's person."[8] From a position of loving, one can reevaluate and suspend learned judgments and evaluations—even unconsciously. Some of my interviewees had "never in a million years" dreamed they would marry someone of another race, yet all of them had. Loving someone in a way that sustains a relationship for a lifetime requires a commitment to work through the thick and thin of familial, cultural, spiritual, and class differences, from attitudes about money to child rearing. Loving interracially seems to be one of the products of a partnership of romantic love and individualism that strives for freedom of choice.

Historian E. K. Rothman has studied changes in courtship related to the social changes that have made interracial marriage more acceptable in recent years. She notes that "where the state of one's body and . . . one's soul dominated [the] eighteenth century . . . the state of one's heart became a central theme in the nineteenth."[9] In the twentieth century, with increased mobility and the growth of cities, unchaperoned dating became common and moved beyond the protection of family, friends, and even community. The promptings of the heart had fewer restrictions and obstacles to overcome than previously.

Parents are naturally anxious that their children be loved rather than used or hurt, although this concern can sometimes mask racial prejudice. Rich, the young man who routinely brought foreign students home with him from college, recalls his parents' initial reaction to his Chinese fiancée's motives: "They did express some initial hesitation because she was from China and this is different from marrying someone who's Chinese American. . . . They were worried that perhaps I couldn't tell if she was really in love with me or looking to get a green card."

It may be more difficult to distinguish mere lust or other motives from love when cultural differences are involved. This difficulty surfaced repeatedly in my interviews with women who had married foreign men. Many of them described the courtship phase of the relationship as "overpowering," "exceedingly romantic," and even "hypnotic." Several white American women married to foreign men recalled how they initially had been swept off their feet by the intensity of attention, gifts, sacrifice, and sensitivity, things that made them feel special and chosen in a way no American man had ever made them feel. Few had the experience to know that such courtship was considered routine in the cultures of their suitors. Without this knowledge, and lacking the experience of having dated other men from the same culture, it was easy to confuse these attentions with a promise of everlasting love and devotion. Several women said that the intensity of the courtship made it difficult to resist the man's proposal. Some expressed great disappointment once they were married and the lavish attention disappeared almost immediately. They felt they had been deceived, tricked, even though the husbands had not necessarily intended any deception.

Our visions of love reflect the stories of love that resonate with us. Interracial love is acceptable in the United States today in a way that it was not even a generation ago. We may still grow up assuming that we will find love among our "own kind," but when our experience is broad enough, our "own kind" becomes the whole human race. The affections of the heart are not limited to a particular skin color. The mind, conditioned by prejudices and fears, may protest, but the heart may rule. How does this happen?

The psychological needs that love satisfies are many and varied and not easily explained. The expression "we all bleed the same color" acknowledges that ultimately we have more things in common than things that divide us, that our psychological needs as people are similar. What we need from love may change over time, as we mature and change.[10] However, Nathaniel Branden believes that at least nine needs define a love relationship:

1) the need for human companionship;
2) the need to love;
3) the need to be loved;
4) the need to be psychologically visible or mirrored;
5) the need for sexual fulfillment;
6) the need for a reliable emotional support system;
7) the need for self-awareness and self-discovery;
8) the need to experience the self as fully man or woman; and
9) the need to feel alive in the presence of another.[11]

Most successful relationships will satisfy most if not all of these needs. Some families discourage interracial marriage because they expect that, with all of the stress and difficulty involved, such marriages will not satisfy these needs. Their own fear blocks their ability to understand and support their child's ability to extend their love to another person who may not be "of their own kind." Parents take the few available statistics on interracial marriage and conclude that these relationships have little chance of working.

The people I interviewed who had married interracially since the late 1980s reported little prejudice or violence against them and found people much more open than they had been in earlier generations. But some less recent data suggest that parental fears of marital dissolution were not totally unfounded. Thirty years ago, black-white couples had higher divorce rates than same-race black or white couples. Census data from 1970 show that in first marriages that took place during the 1950s,

90 percent of white couples and 78 percent of black couples were intact ten to twenty years later. Black-white couples had a significantly higher rate of breakup; 63 percent of black husband-white wife marriages were intact, and 47 percent of white husband-black wife couples.[12] Census data from 1980 for first marriages that took place during the 1960s reveal a similar pattern, though divorce in all categories had risen in absolute terms. Seventy-nine percent of white couples and 68 percent of black couples were intact. Although black-white marriages continued to have even higher rates of dissolution than same-race marriages, the increase in divorce rate was less steep, with 44 percent of these marriages still intact.[13] The analysis of 1990 Census figures on marriages that took place in the 1970s is not yet published, but it is likely that same-race divorce rates have increased and that the gap between same-race and mixed-race divorces is closing. Analysis of other interracial marriages of a duration of twenty years was not available.

Introductions to the Family

For most people, bringing someone home to meet the family signals a serious intention. My interviewees who had come from open families and were used to bringing casual friends and dates home did not feel they had to choose the occasion as cautiously as did people from closed families. All business metaphors for family integration of a new member are available to open families. If significant damage is done in the process of testing or wrestling with conflict before a family reopens itself to someone racially or ethnically different, the franchise model is still available, but the merger and acquisition models are dependent on the partner's resilience.

Regardless of the model, daughters and sons want their families to like their new partners. They also want their partners to think well of their families, though this may not be quite as crucial. Still, while the family might be constructed as the buyer, so is the potential spouse. If the partner does not seek merger with or acquisition from the family, then he or she requires less approval from potential in-laws. In closed or pseudo-open families, where resistance is expected, carefully laying the groundwork can make a difference in how the new partner is received. Introductions are generally smoother when family members are prepared; and willingness to prepare them also communicates respect for their difficulties.

Adequate preparation prevents or minimizes the shock that can provoke unpleasant responses that everyone later regrets. Angela, born in Detroit and living in Seattle, was shocked by the insensitive way she felt her brother introduced his fiancée. Rather than prepare his family, he simply showed up with her one day, unannounced. "It doesn't bother me now, but at the time . . . I met her, like, 'How you doing?' getting-to-know you type of thing. I didn't know it was serious. I wasn't even sure she was his girlfriend. And she just, like, moved in one day."

How a person fits into a family is a concern for all involved, particularly for close-knit families that enjoy each other's company. Sons and daughters hope that their new partners will fit in and that they won't have to keep their married life and their family life separate because of incompatibility. The family, likewise, wants to like the partner so that they will continue to see their son, daughter, brother, or sister at family gatherings. In open families, there is excitement and suspended judgment about meeting a serious partner. In closed or hostile families, sons or daughters may simply hope that nobody says anything too rude, but they prepare their partner for this possibility. The implicit or explicit family mission statement determines which criteria are used for assessing fit. Gail, a thirty-five-year-old black woman from California married for twelve years to a white southerner, describes her first meeting with her prospective mother-in-law. She and her fiancé had laid the groundwork even though he was certain his mother would like her.

> We'd already said hello to each other and done chit chat on the phone a few times. I had a good feeling from her . . . but [I was] a bit nervous when I went to meet his family. And I wasn't sure how they would take to me being black even though he'd reassured me they'd love me. Not that they didn't know—but, you know, in person. Them being from the South, I was expecting them to be a lot more formal and quiet. That would have been fine, too. My husband's quiet. In person, wow. We hit it right off, his mom and I. She's just a talker; she loves life; she loves people. His dad was away on a trip or something. She told me she knew he would like me. We were off to lunch in a couple of hours—without my husband—and I felt totally at ease. It's been like that ever since. She and I spend more time together than she and her son. . . . Like she says, I'm the daughter she never had. Same way with my family. We're all

women 'cept my dad. I was the first to get married. Joe was the first white person introduced into the family seriously—people had dated but not married. We're a close family, so they knew I wouldn't pick someone they wouldn't like. He fits in real well. My mom likes him a lot. He and my dad would get into these debates or arguments like a competition. They both have—had—these competitive personalities, both in sales, but had total respect for each other, even when they disagreed. My dad's gone now. They both enjoyed this sparring.

Rosa and her sister were born and raised in Mexico. Her sister went to college in North Carolina and there met her husband-to-be, a white American man. She prepared the family for the introduction by talking about him for so long that the family liked him before they ever laid eyes on him—though she never mentioned that he was white. But since she was attending an American college, the family probably assumed this.

He could speak Spanish, so in general he was very accepted when he was met. He had lived in Central America and lived around Hispanic people for a long time so he was very accepting. His dad was very accepting. His mother had died years before. I think he was even happy that he had someone to speak Spanish to. As soon as my parents met him they fell in love with each other, so they were pretty warm from the beginning. . . . My parents always said that people were people, no matter what color they were. That you had to know them before you could actually judge them. I mean you end up judging people almost no matter what you do. But you shouldn't judge them just from the outside. You should know who they are first.

If the family identity is fragile or closed, people will worry or even agonize about what Aunt Jean, or the bridge club, or Sam down the street will think. The success of the initial introduction may be one key to enlisting family support for "selling" the newcomer to extended family networks, particularly to members of the older generation.

First introductions in closed families are often mere "courtesies," as adult children know better than to expect approval or even acceptance. As difficult as these introductions are, however, there is always hope that they might lead to further interactions down the road, if the family becomes more open.

Pseudo-closed families require that people have especially good timing and patience in preparing family members for the meeting. They basically make a sales pitch, which begins negotiations for adding a franchise to the family, the only possible business model for pseudo-closed families. Closed families are unable to complete mergers, but if they open up, a franchise is possible.

Several of my participants commented that they got through difficult family introductions by remembering that the family's reaction was not an accurate reflection of themselves. Other people described first introductions as tests—tests that sometimes went on for years in closed and pseudo-closed families, where the newcomer was repeatedly reminded that he was an outsider or still on probation. In these cases, some people felt that it was important to maintain some emotional distance and not feel the need to become part of the family.

Sometimes initial preparation was done by phone, out of respect for all involved. James, a fifty-something black man from Pennsylvania, twice divorced, introduced the topic of his marriage to his father by phone. He was already aware of where his father stood on interracial relationships.

> My father came from Ethiopia when he was twenty years old. I was raised on a farm in western Pennsylvania. When my dad was alive, he was really, I can say, prejudiced. He wasn't really prejudiced, it was more segregation towards white people. My question in my mind which I never had the guts to say to him was, "Why the hell did you move to an all white area?" It just didn't make sense, though I know we got better schooling. In the eighth grade I had a white gal that I liked a lot. She asked me to be her boyfriend. Well that lasted a complete total of eight hours, I think it was. We got along quite famously, actually. Then when both of us got home, our minds and attitudes were changed. As soon as I walked in the door, I got knocked across the room. From my understanding later on in the year, she had gotten spanked from both her parents for even associating with me. So I learned to negotiate around the color lines until I left home and got into the service in the mid-sixties.

Given this background, James had realistic expectations that his father would not be pleased to learn that he intended to marry a white woman. His second wife had also been white. He knew his mother would not be thrilled, either, but he felt that he owed it to them to let them know about this serious decision. That he was middle-aged also gave him more independence; he knew they could not talk him out of it. Geographic distance also helped. There was no merger possibility here, nor did he want one. There was no franchise or acquisition possibility, either. All three of his marriages were businesses quite separate from his original family, which itself had splintered. Still, by informing his parents of his intent to marry again, another white woman, he kept the door open for a future meeting.

> So I called him from California back to the farm in Pennsylvania. He asked what kind of gal she is and I said, "A woman." He said, "I am aware of that," 'cause he knew I was becoming defensive already because of the way he brought me up. I said, "She's Spanish and Italian." Well, good luck to my mother who lived in San Francisco and has remarried. Her attitude was "You better get somebody of your own race and sit your ass down somewhere." Well, I didn't listen to her either. I was gonna be where I felt comfortable and who I felt comfortable with. People just take people for themselves and don't try to change them. I'm better off since I've learned that. Otherwise, I was like a person banging his head up against the wall. I couldn't make her change 'cause she's an old woman and set in her ways and she's just gonna have to understand that she's my mom and some of her trait and some of my father's trait rubbed off on me. I see something that I like and works for me, and I stick with it. And if they don't like it, too bad.

Ann and her husband also used the phone to let family members know what to expect at their daughter's wedding, and to convey their support for their daughter's choice and their expectations of extended family members. "Sometimes I made the call, sometimes he did. . . . I remember my husband telling his brother on the phone. I don't know what his brother did. He was probably surprised. So each of us, whomever we were talking to, we did it, we didn't do it to shock. We did it gently on their [daughter and son-in-law's] behalf. And I would say we did it with some fear and trembling of what we possibly might get in return. We didn't really know."

Some individuals were not able to sort out how the difficulty of an introduction might have been due to factors other than race. Attributing people's reactions to racism may have been a way of absolving themselves of blame for poor timing, immature judgment, or poor choice of partner on grounds of character or compatibility. For example, despite all of Margaret's confusion about her daughter's thirty-year interracial marriage to a black man, she still resents the way her daughter broke the news of her marital intentions.

She was home from college on Christmas or spring break or something. We went to a movie with Katherine Hepburn, "A man who came to dinner" or something like that. . . . After we got out of the movie, she and I were driving home and she said to me, "I'm getting serious about a fella I met at college." So I said, "Why don't you bring him over or home or something." She then told me that he was black and I almost fell through the floor. You better go ahead and tell your father. And so she went and told the family and her father. I was really upset. Her father didn't seem to be that upset. Then she went back to school. The next thing I know she called and said they were in Honolulu, Hawaii, to get married. How could she do that? She got back to school, she was in her third year and I said, "Oh, can't you finish school and so on and so forth?" So they didn't because he was in the Air Force. So they went and got married. Then he was stationed abroad so, of course, she left school to be with him. Anyways, they came to our house and we gave her and him a party and invited all the neighbors. But it was the way she did this marriage. It was so sneaky. If she'd brought him home and let us talk to him [that] would have been more intelligent instead of coming home to say "We're getting married"—and we've never met him and they're on the other side of the state.

This mother's story illustrates how in the drama that followed from their inability to understand each other, daughter and parents missed out on a critical stage of family development, the introduction of a new family member. It is likely that her daughter thought they were closed to her love for a black man and would try to talk her out of it. Johnson and Nagoshi found that pressure for in-group marriage in Hawaii, particularly with first marriages of persons of younger age, did work to keep marital choices endogamous for race or ethnicity. However, they also found that when there was great pressure exerted on first marriages, second marriages showed a greater movement toward outmarriage.[14]

Margaret's daughter might not have felt capable of withstanding the conflict and tension of a meeting between her parents and fiancé. Although the marriage proved to be stable and long-lasting, it is possible that at the time she had some doubts of her own and was afraid that her parents might exploit them and break her down. The mother, however, was deprived of helping plan her daughter's wedding. She may not have been aware of how deeply her and her husband's reservations might affect her daughter.

Beverly provides another example of how mismatched personalities and inappropriate behavior compromised an introduction that would have been difficult enough, given the mother's opposition to interracial marriage. Distinguishing racist objections from valid ones is difficult when the first introduction is done in an offensive or insensitive way. Here is her account of her brother's introduction of his white fiancée. They later divorced.

> It's like [my mother] knew in herself, in her heart, that this girl was not gonna be true. . . . She was phony from the start. You could tell, you could tell when a white person is really trying too hard to be black. Put it that way. They come off with this—they slur the words more. They cut their hair and curl it and try to be as black as possible. Cause you know they're here with this black dude and they messing with a lot of black guys and they have to be overly, overly black. And so it was phony. I mean she tried to put it on me and I say, I just laughed. I didn't want no part of it. That's probably what my mother saw, too. And then to hurt my mother, the first time meeting her and then calling her Mama, too. She made a big mistake. Really. She didn't ease her way in. Just full force, full speed ahead.

In a different kind of example of poor timing born of overexcitement and lack of sensitivity, Emma, a Filipina in her late forties who met her white American husband through a correspondence relationship, announced that she was getting married to her four children, who ranged in age from nine to seventeen. Emma had been widowed and was lonely and concerned about how she was going to be able to give her children the education they needed to get ahead in life in the Philippines. Her husband had died less than a year earlier, but she viewed marriage as the answer to her prayers.

> I wrote to several men, but I wrote to [the man who would become] my husband most often. Then after seven months of writing, he called and said he would like to see the Philippines. So I said "You are most welcome to stay in our house," I said to him, "because we have two houses. We can accommodate you at home." Then he said on the phone, "If I go there, are you going to marry me?" I said "Yes!" with excitement, without thinking of any other consequences. Then I looked for my kids when I got home and told them that he was coming to marry me. My oldest just said, "Mommy, we just lost our father. We are not ready for a new father. Even if we have nothing, please stay with us. Maybe we will survive

without you marrying another." But the two youngest liked the idea because they wanted to come to America, also. My intention in marrying my husband was to explore another world and to support my children. I told that to my husband—that my intentions were to find someone who would help to finance my kids. I did not lie to my husband.

The degree to which the family respects a son's, daughter's, or other relative's choice may also be related to their track record and maturity. Mike spoke of his respect for a sister who was in her third marriage. I asked him how much the fact that this was her third marriage influenced his family's reaction to her choice of partner.

Well, the fact that he's black didn't have that much effect on the family, really. We just wanted her to be happy. I think she's happy; she wasn't happy in her previous marriages. She's about fifty years old, so I think maybe the fact that she's older. I think that you give a person more credit as they get older. What the hell? It's her life. It's not like she's a twenty-year-old and still maybe very immature. If she's nearly fifty and she's still immature, what the hell, let her do it anyway. But the fact is that she's mature and she knows what she wants to do with her life pretty much. Like anybody else, she's looking for happiness. I think most families when they're young people, you kind of look out for them more. Because you don't know if they make good decisions. You kind of watch them. Once you get past thirty or so, you're on track—if not, you might not ever be on track. By the time you're fifty, if you don't have the judgment, you're not going to have it. But she always has had, you know, pretty good lifetime judgment.

Racial prejudice is not always the reason, or the only reason, why some families oppose the interracial marriage of a young family member. Society does discriminate against interracial couples, particularly black-white couples, though this was a worse problem in the past than it is in many areas of the country today. James, the black man from Pennsylvania, suffered for his choice of partner at the hands of black men.

I left home and got into the service in the mid-sixties. I did the whole patriotic thing, tour of Vietnam. The guys I was with, most liked me and so skin color never meant anything—at least in terms of what I thought of people. What I thought about a person is what I went by and that how I engage myself based upon whether I like this person or I didn't like this person. After I got out of the service, I went back to San Francisco and my second wife happened to be white. I got beat up by three black guys because they called me an oreo and Uncle Tom and stuff like that because I wouldn't stay in my race. I tried to get it through their thick heads, "Hey, it doesn't make any difference about race; it's what you feel." I'm strong enough, I guess, by my upbringing, to stand my ground even though I did get beaten up. It didn't change our attitudes towards each other. I guess I don't just have a color block. That sets me apart from a lot of people, especially black people. They don't understand how I can just be as comfortable with another race as I could with my own.

Blending with the Family

Several factors appeared central to success in blending into family: shared definitions of family, expectations of closeness, similarity of values, overlap in interests, and personality matches. How family was defined was a critical factor. If the newlyweds bring different definitions of family to the marriage, the blending may be less than smooth. One of them might desire only to join in family celebrations a few times a year—minimal contact appropriate for a franchise model of business. The other might prefer a merger model—a joining of clans. Couples also have to contend with the possibility that their respective families may differ in their definition of family. While Eric's Filipino American family expects a merger, his brother-in-law's family might operate more on a franchise model. When families have similar models of merger or acquisition, negotiating holidays becomes difficult because of logistical difficulties.

Other scenarios include the possibility that one partner really leaves his or her family to join the other clan. This was a common fear among many of the closed families in my study, particularly white families. Of course, such families may actually drive their offspring away with their anger, opposition, or conditional acceptance of the new partner. When conflicts arise over how the blending will take place, the parties involved need to consider individual expectations, which often reflect inherited definitions of family.

Ironically, a family that is not very close may pose less of an obstacle to interracial partners, since the goal of blending is acceptance, not closeness. Wendy, a thirty-something woman from Nebraska, came from a family that was not very close but respected each other's independence. All four white siblings married interracially—to a Filipino American, a

Japanese, an Alaskan Native, and an African American. In their isolation from one another, they each became a member of their partner's clan. When white persons do this, particularly several siblings in a family, it seems that they have little investment in or expectation of white privilege, particularly when they become integrated into their new communities. "One of the reasons we're not closer is because there are some issues that we haven't learned to deal with each other," Wendy explained. "So our choice has been to distance ourselves from one another. . . . For closeness to happen, we've got to communicate. So we just sort of respect each other's decisions to do what he or she wants for their life. It's cool. And it is more like respecting but in respecting your choice also respecting sort of the boundaries around it."

Again, the family mission statement is a guide to determining how open a family is to accepting and incorporating a new family member into the system. The success of blending depends on how well the new individual understands and respects the family's membership rules. The fewer the criteria, the greater the chance for blending. If the criteria include race, this member can never become a bona fide member. It is possible, however, that the introduction of a new family member who is well liked may reflexively change the family rules about race.

Personality is another factor that affects how well a new person may be blended into an existing family. Friendly, charming personalities are naturally more easily welcomed into a family. Robert, the black man from Chicago who married a white woman from Colorado, described how he was received into his wife's pseudo-open family, who had liked him before they were engaged, and how his open family received his friendly, outgoing wife.

> I think a lot of what changed family members' outlook was personality. Like my wife is really nice. She's just a great person. She made everybody come along in my family when we were just dating or friends just by the way she is and by the way she acts. She's not so judgmental in everything else. This is funny because my one brother-in-law says she so cool she's an honorary sister, meaning she just mixes right in with the family. Our family is loud and boisterous and she jumps right in. So I think a lot of that has to do with her personality. I think the reasons her dad changed about a lot of it is the way I dealt with him, too. A little crack in the armor. We didn't become judgmental of them the way they treated us. Once they saw that, everything got a little bit better and better. They

started to see that they were wrong about their initial assessment of our marriage. We were not judging them, and once he got to know me a lot better, then he started changing. He's a very analytical man because he's an engineer and I think a lot of what was in his mind he had assumed, because he and I have never talked about some of the things that worried him.

Ann, a white woman from Seattle in her mid-fifties, shed tears of thankfulness and joy as she reflected on her black son-in-law.

Were there personality characteristics that facilitated his acceptance in the family? Just his warmth. He has a great smile. And maybe even his sighs. When he comes into a room, you know he is there. I don't know, his personality is very pleasant. He was a manager in a restaurant . . . and when you are a manager—I've worked at a local restaurant as hostess for six and a half years—you have got to greet all kinds of people. If there is a problem with the food, you go talk to the customer, and if need be, you get the manager or the server. I was the hostess, but I mean, managing the restaurant, he just had all the staff under him.

She also noted that her son-in-law had been a professional athlete, and I asked her how that made a difference to the extended family. Sometimes star status neutralizes some of the objections based on race, but then the "star" may be seen as an "exception to the rule" for his or her race. Even when that is the case, any opening, however superficial, may lead to more meaningful dialogue and mutual understanding and respect later on.

When they learned that he was a professional ball player, then that took away the sting, you know, it changed it. Wrong or right, it changed it. It gave him identity and an image with which they shared values, they assumed he had earned a fair amount of money, that they might be secure financially, and that she hadn't picked a stereotype ghetto person. It was like a class issue. It just gave them an identity for him they could accept like, "Oh, this guy has probably been to college, so he's okay." They also could start up conversation with him, asking him what team he had played for. It also made a difference that he was a member of the Christian professional athletes fellowship. He was raised with the gospel and when he has been to our home, he'll say, "Oh, I remember that hymn, one of those old classic hymns." So that gave us all common ground and that made a big difference because I have a Baptist background and so do all my relatives. Having the

Lord in his heart, changed all that stereotyping business. There was a common ground. . . . Same for his family, though it certainly was the first interracial marriage for his side, too.

Meeting cultural expectations for behavior that might otherwise be misinterpreted by many Americans as submissive or unnecessary can nevertheless facilitate blending and illustrates a willingness not to exercise certain possible privileges. Eric, who is Filipino, talks about his brother-in-law, who is black. Although the two families involved are both families of color, Eric perceives his brother-in-law as more American, more privileged, and possibly therefore in a position to regard their Filipino family as inferior.

It took him a hard time, you know, to blend. Sometimes he would say, "Hey guys, what can I do for you this week? You want me to bring you to the grocery? And, uh, let's help you out or maybe you want to go to the park?" He tried his best to integrate with the family. And for that we liked him. It was maybe that he also talked to some Filipinos and said, "How would I win these guys over?" He kind of did. He's also alone, relatively, and we were so many, and he loves his wife, so much. Says "I cannot live without her. I love her so much," things like that. I know he loves his wife very much. He went out of his way. We recognized it and appreciated it. He understood he was marrying the whole family. But you know, the family, to Filipinos, when we take you in, we're part of your family. All the problems you have, even financial, go to the family. They'll help you. That's how we help. Somebody who blends himself with the family. We take you in, everything.

Unlike Eric's brother-in-law, Roberta did not seem to have a subtle understanding of cultural or personality differences, and this affected her relationship with her son-in-law. A white woman in her late fifties from a small Wisconsin town, Roberta explained how her daughter's marriage to a Japanese man affected her sense of family. Her son-in-law's parents died before he was ten years old and he was raised by relatives, separated from his younger brother.

Well, he's just not a warm person. He has never hugged me. I have never hugged him, not even close. And I want to give you a background on me. We have four children, my husband and me. Our oldest was killed in an accident twenty years ago. And so, here is my life, instead of the family circle getting larger, the family circle is getting smaller. So I had these expectations that when my children got married, we would once again become one big family. And so it hasn't happened. . . . The strangest thing, I think, is that he has never called me by name. He has never said my first name. He has never called me mom, mother, whatever . . . he just doesn't. I feel like it's a disrespect that he doesn't acknowledge that I am his mother-in-law. In retrospect, I wish I would have said to him that I really would just like it if you would call me something. I don't care what, but just acknowledge me, that I am, you know, your wife's mother. But I just never, never did that. And so, I'm always trying to be open, you know, with this relationship, and I'm always cordial and kind, and I try to make him feel welcome in my house.

Roberta clearly had needs from the person her daughter would marry that revolved around her own losses. She could not understand that he had reacted to his losses in a different way, she was apparently unable to sort out the influences of his personality, culture, and religious background on his difficulty in blending into the family. Her dream of an acquisition model, intensified by the death of her son twenty years earlier, was thwarted when her daughter and son-in-law started a separate business, not even a franchise.

He converted to Jehovah's Witnesses when he was first in America. They do not celebrate any holidays, pagan holidays. They don't celebrate the wedding anniversary, birthdays, Mother's Day, Fourth of July, those things they don't. So that cuts out any family gatherings, because that's when we get together. So they were living in the house, and I had cooked Thanksgiving dinner, and they had come in from some Jehovah's Witness meeting, and they had come into the kitchen, and we had sat at the table, and they had said that they weren't going to be there [for Thanksgiving]. They've been sitting at the table for almost a year, and they made no indication that they weren't going to be sitting at the table on Thanksgiving day. And so the night before Thanksgiving, I started my turkey, and my daughter announced that they weren't going to be at the house for dinner. And I was so shocked. And I know she waited to tell me so long because she knew it would upset me. And I was. Here, I had this anticipation, and she's watching and listening to me get all these groceries in . . . When I found out later that she had joined the Jehovah's Witnesses, I sought out an ex-Jehovah's Witness support group, because I wanted to learn as much as I could about this group. But when I found out that he had been in it for twelve years, then I thought, "Well, my chances of being able to do anything to get her out of that are really slim." And so, since about that time, at the beginning, I didn't have big expectations of a close-knit relationship with him because of the religious difference. . . . It is their religion, not race, not class . . . that keeps the distance. . . . I'm not going to let the relationship with my daughter end. When we're together, you know, we have a good time. But still there's that little space between us. And sure it's the religion, and him, an oppressive husband, that's just the way he is. It just keeps that space between us from closing.

The couple distanced themselves from Roberta; they essentially left the corporation and attached themselves to a religious corporation of which she had little understanding and in which she found little room for the fulfillment of her needs. There were probably more variables at work here than Roberta described. It is possible that her son-in-law's loss of his parents in childhood and her lack of awareness of cultural difference played a larger part than either of them recognized. Sometimes parents and their children have such different personalities that they have difficulty being sensitive to each other. It is possible that Roberta's daughter felt pressure to be all things to her mother to assuage the grief over the loss of her brother. Perhaps her marriage released her from this obligation; perhaps she needed the psychological separation provided by conversion to her husband's religion.

When the family's response to a marriage is disappointing, the individual's needs may be displaced onto his or her spouse. The spouse will then be expected to compensate for the family's failure and may carry the burden of having to "prove" that he or she really was the right choice of partner. Consider the story of thirty-five-year-old Christine, from Michigan.

One of the complicating factors sometimes is, like, you can't talk very much about problems with your parents because you're trying to make it sound like this is a good marriage and you don't want to say, well, you don't want to give them another reason not to like them [one's partner], like stuff like something you may be arguing about. So you don't get that support, you know, that you could get from your family. Plus, on the other side, I think it's almost like your husband has to become a superman, sometimes, because you might say to yourself, "Well, look at everything I gave up to marry you." So sometimes I found myself in a spot where he has to be even better, maybe, than a lot of other people, because look at everything I have given up. So I think that puts an edge on the marriage, too.

Although I did not set out to study how religious differences influenced the integration of family members, it became clear that these differences also made blending more difficult. When the interfaith nature of the marriage had been a major reason for opposition from family, the couple kept their religious life very private. Jewish partners whose families would not set foot in homes containing Christian symbols kept secret the fact that they had a Christmas tree at home. The birth of children often intensified conflicts the couples thought they had resolved. For example, some couples selected a day of the year, often a non-religious holiday such as Thanksgiving or New Year's, around which to create family rituals. With the birth of children, however, differences often resurfaced and conflicts could be intense. Other researchers have discussed interfaith marriages at greater length and more astutely than I attempted to do in this study.[15]

The phases of the family life cycle and the processes that emerged in my study as critical in negotiating different visions of family are no different from those of any relationship. But the aspect of race heightened the anxieties and fears of closed families and made the terrain more treacherous for interracial couples, requiring them to exercise greater maturity, sensitivity, and tact in order to avoid a rift or family crisis. The likelihood that an interracial marriage would succeed increased with the degree of acceptance and support received by at least one partner's family. If both persons were isolated, the relationship was more difficult and had a greater chance of failure.

Falling in love is natural when people share similar visions of love. Emphasis on romantic love, individual freedom to choose one's own partner, and women's freedom from some economic dependence on fathers are important factors in interethnic, interracial, and even international marriages. Less dependent economically on their fathers, women today are not as restricted in their choice of mate as their mothers and grandmothers were. Love and all that it means is probably the most important cement in any married relationship, but family closeness and support can be crucial supports as well.

Blending into the spouse's family can be a lifelong process that evolves over time, but how one defines family has a great impact on the degree of blending desired and achieved. I have discussed some of the obstacles to blending as well as some of the factors that can facilitate it. The death of a family member affords yet another opportunity for families to face down their irrational fears and prejudices, and, with any luck, to transcend them.

A Death in the Family

When I was an intern, a fellow intern who was a Jesuit priest told me that his favorite pastoral duty was being with dying people in their last days and hours. I could not comprehend this and asked him why. He explained that in those final days and hours many people are at their purest, as pure as they have been, perhaps since birth. They are ready to drop their masks and relinquish their games, lies, and resentments. He told me that in this brief window of time, some people allow what is best in them to rise to the surface. I did not really understand his explanation at the time, but I remembered it.

In their stories of family, the people I interviewed raised the subject of death as a part of the process of becoming an interracial family. James, the black man from western Pennsylvania, explained how death affected him, his wife, and their relationship.

> My present wife, we've been married eight years and her family just can't stand me. She tried every avenue to try to make them understand why she fell in love with me and they didn't want to understand. So she finally said goodbye, and if they want to come visit us they know where we are. They can find us. I welcome them into our home but I won't take any of their shit. Her mother seemed to rule to roost; she was the worst. But before she died, she loved me. You want to know what happened? Her mother saw that everything that she tried to put a wedge in between us failed. She saw her daughter happier than she was with her previous husband, who happened to be white. And she couldn't understand it because she is a little older and she just couldn't quite grasp it. But before she died she gave me her blessing. The rest of the family was just shocked. Here is this woman so dead set against me that now accepted me and loved me. That made my wife feel better.

Some family monarchs hold so much power that although others might not agree with them deep down, they dare not stand up to them. One twenty-three-year-old white man, Trevor, held off on making a decision to marry because he tended to date black women. His white grandmother, whom he loved very much, was strongly opposed to interracial marriage. He confessed that he had a track record of sabotaging his relationships with fine women, and he had come to the conclusion that this was an unconscious but deliberate way of avoiding his grandmother's disapproval. He now realized that he was waiting for her to die before he could propose marriage to his African American girlfriend—either that, he said, or else he hoped that he would become strong enough to endure the loss of her love and his status as her favorite grandson. I asked him where his parents stood and he said that they were very supportive of him. They had told him that they would accept any woman to whom he committed himself and that they trusted his judgment.

Candace, a young white mother of two children in Madison, Wisconsin, told a similar story. She described the anguish she went through in timing her announcement of her engagement to her black boyfriend of five years. The death of the matriarch, her paternal grandmother, and the last member wedded to a monarchical style of family leadership, allowed the family to redefine its mission and make race less central to its image. Candace's story was echoed by others.

> I was so clear that my husband was the right man for me. But my father had been all against it and so everyone else in the family followed his lead. I had always been treated with respect by my parents so this was a major blow to our relationship. I really tried to see if I was rushing into something that was a mistake. But after years, I knew my mistake was going to be letting the love of my life walk away. It took some time to grow up so that I felt I could survive and go on if my family disowned me. When I was twenty-six, I decided I was ready to get married; it made no more sense to wait. But my husband had been terribly concerned that I was feeling like I had to choose between him and my family, and he knew how much I loved my family. He said he would understand my decision not to marry him. But we knew our lives would feel empty without each other. My decision came a couple months after my grandmother, my dad's mom, died, so I knew my timing might be kind of rough on the family. I waited up to have a conversation with my father one night, alone, because I thought it would be so painful I wouldn't or couldn't deal with everyone else's reactions. But I was so shocked. I told him I had decided to marry Tony and he congratulated me with a smile and a sigh of relief. A genuine sigh of relief! I was confused, because here I'd been waiting for this terrible scene and possible disowning. He said he knew I loved my husband and he made me happy and treated me well. He thought he was an upstanding, outstanding person. He trusted that

if he was the person I'd chosen, he respected my decision. I just sat there in shock. Shocked. And then we hugged each other and cried. Then, in tears, he told me that he hoped I knew that he planned to walk me down the aisle. I was so happy and shocked. I just cried and cried with relief and joy. I asked him what was his change of heart. He explained that he had never objected to my boyfriend, but that my grandmother did and his going along with me would have made life so difficult for him and for us. I know this sounds weak, but my grandmother kind of ruled the family, and now, basically, my father was free. My family was free. I couldn't believe it. We ended up with a beautiful wedding with all the people I love there.

For other families, some closure was achieved when a monarch who had opposed interracial marriage repented on the deathbed and gave the interracial couple his or her blessing. In this process, meaningful admissions were made, clarity was obtained, and families moved on. Linda, a Filipina ex-nun, and her white American husband, Rudy, both in their fifties and married for seven years, talked about some of the clarity and freedom from fear that Rudy's father achieved in his last days. Linda attended her father-in-law's sick bed constantly for the two weeks before he died. No one else was as attentive. Ironically, he had seldom even acknowledged Linda's presence in his home prior to his dying.

I knew he had fear, but it was of himself, not really me—he didn't know me. . . . But I was there all the time before he died, bringing him cool cloths, covering him with blankets, feeding him, making him as comfortable as I could. He did not have much time left. I couldn't understand why his children were not spending time with him. He had so little left. I saw his fear melt gradually, and then I saw him open up. I just prayed for him. I didn't say much, but I could tell in his eyes when he finally saw me as just the person I was all along—but it was only the day before he died. . . . That day he asked that we have our picture taken together, which I did. I hoped that helped him die with peace. I loved him despite his fear, because he was my husband's father.

Elaine and Curtiss talked about the long process of family unification, a process that required an impending death. Both Midwestern children of ministers, this black-white couple explained how Elaine's mother's death allowed a closeness that was out of reach as long as she was alive.

On my husband's side of the family, there was a lot more of, "Well it's really too bad you couldn't find somebody who was black to marry, this is really too bad." And they'd say this to me, too. But probably because both our fathers were ministers of the same denomination [this] made it okay in this respect. The families were always very polite to each other, when they would get together. But once my mom got seriously ill and ended up dying of cancer, both sides of the family started to communicate more with each other. My husband's mother moved into Madison, and my parents [father and step-mother] moved into Madison, and now all of our holidays are both sides of the family coming together at our house. After my mom died, which is, I mean, it's sad that it had to be in that respect, but I think it kind of made people look at the perspective of what really matters. And it took quite a while.

Novelist Louise Erdrich says it well in *Love Medicine*: "Your life feels different on you, once you greet death and understand your heart's position."[16] The African American poet and writer Maya Angelou has written, "I answer the heroic question, 'Death, where is thy sting?' with 'It is here in my heart and mind and memories.'"[17] Death completes the circle of life and allows for a transformation that may bring new visions of family and purpose.

1

Parents, Children, and Race

Parents and strangers alike have used the issue of interracial children to discourage interracial marriage in the first place. People who married anyway were discouraged from having children. The *What about the children?* question is a key to understanding the American racial climate and landscape. For most of America's history, mixed-race children were shunned, but over time their situation has improved.

In her novel *Caucasia,* Danzy Senna addresses many of the issues mixed-heritage children experience through the voices of two sisters, Birdie and Cole. Without warning, their parents decide to separate the two loving siblings because of underground political activities in which their white mother is engaged. The elder daughter, Cole, who has more recognizable African features, goes to live with her black father; Birdie, who "passes" for white even among black people, goes to live with her white mother. The girls have no say about being separated or with which parent they will live. Birdie, forced to live as a white girl for four years, is reunited with her father, a college professor, when she is in her mid-teens.

> He explained to me his theory—that the mulatto in America functions as a canary in the coal mine. The canaries, he said, were used by coal miners to gauge how poisonous the air underground was. They would bring a canary in with them, and if it grew sick and died, they knew the air was bad and that eventually everyone else would be poisoned by the fumes. My father said that likewise, mulattos had historically

been the gauge of how poisonous American race relations were. The fate of the mulatto in history and in literature, he said, will manifest the symptoms that will eventually infect the rest of the nation.

He pointed to the chart, "See, my guess is that you're the first generation of canaries to survive, a little injured, perhaps, but alive."[1]

Nowhere is the active construction, negotiation, and enforcement of the fiction of race more clear than in the racial assignments of mixed-heritage children. Race is made central to their lives and, as a result, these children become central to discussions of race. Participants in my study repeatedly shared five of the ways in which children were central to the construction of family racial identity and the general social construction of race. Two questions from a related study of multiracial individuals were particularly relevant to further understanding the family processes affecting multiracial families: "Do you think your parents were prepared to raise mixed children?" and "Is there anything that you wish could have been different growing up that would have made your life easier, happier, or better?"[2] Not only did persons of mixed heritage have to understand race in a way that did not oppress them as children of color, they also had to make room for themselves in a world that did not include them in public dialogues on race; they were invisible and, simultaneously, feared.

Birth of Children

The birth of interracial children not only marks a new phase of the family life cycle, it introduces five significant issues that are usually irrelevant in same-race families:

1. It permanently records the interracial relationship;
2. It creates different-race blood kin;
3. It can change some people's perception of a parent's race;
4. It potentially changes the race proportions and cultural mores within a family; and
5. It provokes reflection on racial socialization.

A permanent record. For families who regard racial reproduction as an important product, a son, daughter, or other relative who marries outside the race will be marginalized. Pseudo-closed families may take them back into the fold if the marriage ends without children; partner gone, the family can pretend to forget the relationship or discount it. The thirty-seven-year-old daughter of a Japanese woman who had married an African American soldier told me that her mother had been removed from the family books that recorded births and deaths. When they went to Japan to visit, when she was in her early twenties, her Japanese grandparents refused to see her mother if she brought her children to the house. She recalled ducking down in the car and hiding as they took in curious glimpses of their grandparents and the house in which their mother was raised.

Another white woman states it succinctly: "My parents never met my children. They didn't want to acknowledge them. . . . It does change after you have kids, because once you have kids, then you are not going back. I mean, even if you would divorce your husband, you still have your children. And they're still biracial. So there's no going back."

Creation of Blood Kin. The birth of children creates undeniable proof of the interracial relationship. In desperation, parents sometimes suggest abortion ("No one will ever know"), or adoption ("It's the best thing to do" or "It's in the best interest of the family"), regardless of their adult child's wishes or circumstances. Among the people I interviewed, men and women of color were least likely to report that their parents counseled them in this way. The parents of white women were much more prone to this kind of desperation, which suggests that white women are central to the construction of whiteness. Interracial children highlight other gender differences in the culture as well. Women with children, especially biracial children, have fewer chances for remarriage than childless women. And because the children of divorce tend to remain with mothers, becoming incorporated into new families when their mothers remarry, interracial children are more threatening markers of race and racial authenticity for families in which race matters.

Families threaten to withdraw love, approval, and assistance more often with white daughters than with any other group, although Asian American parents can also be very unmoving in their opposition to interracial marriage. As we have seen, however, the birth of children sometimes breaks down a family's resistance and can help to legitimize a marriage in the family's eyes. Children bring a new focus to a marriage, and the process of rearing children can draw family members together.

Childless marriages, whether childless by choice or by circumstance, are usually viewed as less meaningful, less good, and can even be seen as based only on sex, and often as only temporary.

The birth of children presents a paradox. Although it makes the interracial nature of the marriage undeniable, which is upsetting to closed families, it may also generate hope that the marriage will be meaningful and lasting, with a stable environment for the children. The common belief that children are better off with two parents than with one, and with married rather than divorced parents, can outweigh family anxieties over the interracial nature of the relationship. As Diane, a forty-year-old Japanese American, said, "One thing that made a difference was once we had children. We were married for six years before we had kids. Once we had kids, although my mom's side of the family, still, like I said, never had anything to do with us, other people think, 'Okay, maybe they are serious about staying together. It isn't kind of a fling.' My husband's family, which is black, accepted this was their grandchild, so they were a little more connected that way."

For families who seemed to have no difficulty embracing a new family member, the birth of children was met with wonder and joy. Celebration, love, and hope marked these births. The birth of children may transform closed families into pseudo-closed ones, as was the case for Thomas and his Jewish in-laws.

> In terms of children, my wife's family has been very, very accepting of our son. In fact, I was actually moved when they had his first birthday party. I mean all these people showed up. There were people who showed up for my son's birthday who didn't come to our wedding. And it's almost like he's in, you know. It doesn't matter; he's blood. That's how they treat him. I know in some families that it's, no matter what the issues, if you are an in-law, it's always different when there's a child. But I've just been very pleased with the fact that my child has prepared the family for the coming of a second interracial child to another interracial marriage in the family.

Blood ties are psychologically powerful for most people, and in pseudo-closed families, the birth of children may encourage people to revisit their definition of family. And once they are open to redefinition, they may find it possible to love the children as family, at least conditionally. That is, they may accept and love the children as family while still regarding them as part of an "inferior" branch of the family. Some relatives will try to avoid the subject of race, which is uncomfortable for them, and focus on other things. But this is not always easy when faced with a new baby who looks black or Asian or mixed (to a closed white family) or who looks white or Asian or mixed (to a closed black family). Charlene, a white woman from Wisconsin married to black man, saw this dynamic at work in her parents. "I think they like to look at other things that make the kids like them. Like they are accomplishing things in school, and things like that. They don't like to talk about color or make any kind of deal out of that side. I don't think they feel comfortable talking about that. I think it will take another twenty years."

Perceptions of Parent's Race. In general, white women seemed to be most affected by how their biracial children changed them in the eyes of strangers. No longer quite white enough in the white world, and under suspicion in the non-white world, life gave these women a crash course in racial self-defense. For many of these mothers, awareness of white privilege was heightened by witnessing racial discrimination, however subtle, toward their children.[3]

Women of color did not have to deal with issues of their own racial authenticity as much as white women did. The issues facing them concerned whether their children, not they themselves, would be accepted by the racial or ethnic group in question. Particularly in immigrant communities, race and nationality were co-constructed. Some parents saw the mixture of their children as primarily an issue of nationality and only secondarily of race: Were they "American"? Their fathers' whiteness was often a confirmation of their "Americanness." In this way, the gender and race of the parent were symbolically equivalent to the nation. But, by this logic, many mothers and minority community members questioned the legitimacy of these mixed-heritage children; if they were only half Asian, or only half black, could they claim a legitimate place in the Asian or black community? This was an issue for Asian and Latino communities in particular.

Sociologist Rebecca King provides an interesting example of how blood quantum, or the percentage of heritage you can claim through your ethnic lineage, is used to settle questions of legitimacy in the Japanese American community. She studied the process by which the Cherry Blossom Queen was chosen in different Japanese American communities around the nation. It became evident that the Japanese

American community was struggling with blood quantum as out-marriage is so frequent. The co-construction of race and ethnicity becomes apparent in the struggles around the ethnic legitimacy of mixed race Japanese American contenders for Cherry Blossom Queen.[4] Questions abound. How much heritage must you be able to claim? Where do you draw the line at claiming to be Japanese—at one-half, one-quarter, one-eighth? What does it mean to have a young woman with a very European appearance represent the Japanese American community?

African American women faced difficulties when their children looked white—blond-haired, blue-eyed, and fair-skinned—and they themselves did not. One black mother of a white-looking daughter told me that it took three attempts to get her daughter's teacher to acknowledge that she was the mother. After this conversation, which took place at a parent-teacher conference, the twelve-year-old daughter was convinced that the teacher's behavior toward her changed, and not for the better. Some black mothers said that other African Americans accused them of thinking that their light-skinned children were superior to other blacks. "Passing" as white, particularly in previous generations, was another strategy for subverting and renegotiating race and the privileges and access that go with whiteness.[5]

Janis, a white woman married to an African American man living in a suburb of Wisconsin, described how the birth of her children made her more aware of racial constructions.

> I think my nuclear family came to view itself as multiracial as a result of a trip . . . to Nashville, where my husband's family had lived, and my sister was there. Before we went, we talked about the fact that sometimes we may stop places where we are going to be viewed differently and that people might stare at us. Because my worst experiences have been in Nashville, compared to here. I didn't want to scare my kids. I don't want to make them feel like there is something they should watch for that's not there. But I also felt like I was grappling with the fact that we're viewed differently when the four of us go someplace. The whole idea was like, that was okay. It was kind of a neat thing, because then we would go into some place, and our son, who was probably nine or ten at the time, was sort of like, "Well, let's go to this Pizza Hut on the highway," rather than you know, . . . some little "Ma and Pa" restaurant. Your know, sort of like the idea of safety. Yes. I think it's sort of interesting where you start out viewing yourself as an individual and gradually you start to see

yourself as part of a group through the eyes of others. I think it's when you get that confrontation that you really start to think about it and start to think and reflect and take it for what it's worth.

Racial Majority in the Family. When the one-drop rule is implicitly applied or experienced within a family, it can change the racial proportions or composition of the household. A white family member can suddenly become aware of her whiteness or feel the minority within her household. In effect, she becomes aware of whiteness through the loss of some white privilege that generally allows her to experience herself as raceless.[6] Alberta, a woman of American Indian and white ancestry living in the Midwest, demonstrates how subtle this transformation can be:

> My folks went to a small college and my mother was about the only Indian. When we were growing up, my mother's parents were having hard times and came to live with us. When us kids came along, my father felt outnumbered. He felt "other" in a way he never expected. I didn't foresee that either, being young. It's taken a while for him to find other ways to identify in his life other than as a white man.

With the birth of mixed-race children, families must reconstruct race and even the racial designation of the family. As Wendy, a white woman married to a Japanese American man, put it: "The kids make it seem more interracial—an interracial family. They are growing up and they definitely are biracial and bicultural. With the kids, there are definite interracial members. With me and my husband, without kids, it's just the two of us."

In contrast, some parents of color worry that their children will not be able to relate to them as people of color, as race has increasingly been transformed from a caste status to class status. Lynn says, "Our daughter is reaching sixteen, that age, you know, where they don't want to come home and talk about stuff that's going on. But I think that whole thing about how she identifies, and that whole thing about who you date—I know my husband's mother will ask, 'Well, is she dating any black guys?' or 'We're worried that she is just going to do everything white.'"

Constructing Race. These narratives remind us that race is forever being constructed and reconstructed. The *What are you?* question posed to many persons of mixed heritage suggests that race is flexible, situational, context-driven, and generation-driven, and that notions of racial purity are fiction.[7] Social interactions that convey the importance of racial identification and racial affiliation construct race.[8] Below is a list of more than forty experiences that construct the meaning of race and racial identity for mixed-race people, taken from a questionnaire on racial experiences I gave to participants in my biracial sibling study.

- Told, "You have to choose; you can't be both."
- Your ethnicity is mistakenly identified.
- You're generally identified differently racially by phone than in person.
- Accused of not wanting to be Latino/black/Asian, etc.
- Told, "You don't look Asian/black/Latino, etc."
- Asked, "What are you?"
- People say things they wouldn't otherwise if they knew how you identified.
- Strangers look between you and your parent(s) to figure out the relationship.
- Told you do not "act" black/Chicano/Asian, etc.
- Told, "You look so exotic."
- Stared or looked at by strangers.
- Your choice of friends is interpreted as your "selling out" or being less than authentic.
- Accused of "wanting to be white."
- Your racial authenticity is based on your partner's race.
- Accused of "acting white."
- Have difficulty filling out forms that ask for your race/ethnicity.
- Your receive comments about your hair/hairstyle.
- Subjected to jokes about mixed-race people.
- Grandparent(s) or relatives reject you because of your parents' interracial relationships.
- Told, "You're a credit to your race."
- Feel competition between your parents/relatives to "claim" you for their own group.
- Told, "You think you're too good for your own kind."
- Told, "You have the best of both worlds."
- Told by strangers, "Mixed-race people are so beautiful."
- Asked about your racial heritage by strangers.
- Your surname does not match how people expect you to look.

- Told that you must be confused about your racial identity.
- People speak to you in foreign languages because of how they interpret your phenotype.
- Told, "Society doesn't recognize mixed race."
- Told, "You aren't really Asian American/African American," etc.
- Mistaken as your father's girlfriend.
- Thought to be related to a person of mixed heritage who does not resemble you.
- Told, "You must be full of self-loathing or hatred because of how you racially identify."
- Told, "You are a mistake."
- Identified racially differently depending upon who you are with.
- Identified racially differently in another part of the country or world.
- Your receive comments about your skin color.
- Identified differently by others from how you identify yourself.
- Your siblings identify differently as to race from how you do.
- Your parents identify you differently as to race from how you identify yourself.

Whereas these experiences are not all unique to persons of mixed racial heritage, the recurrence of themes of racial purity, foreignness, racial boundaries, and racial authenticity conveys the multiple ways in which race is constructed. These experiences are neither uniformly negative nor uniformly positive for people of mixed racial heritage.[9]

The question *what about the children?* has different meanings depending on who is asking and the context in which the question is asked. For some parents, it is a sincere question about the larger picture. And as some participants admitted, they did not have realistic views of the larger picture. Although intellectually they may have prepared themselves for their child's being teased, emotionally it was painful to experience the hurt of their child coming home crying. Other couples experienced the question as manipulative, pitting imaginary children against them. Garrett, a white man from Florida who grew up mostly among black people, had the following response to a focus group member whose parents encouraged him to think very carefully about children before he made a decision to marry.

We thought about it. My wife already had a child from a previous marriage. She's black and this child's father is black. We wanted more children and they have added to our lives. My father-in-law made me think that having a son was the biggest change in the family. So I think it's really an excuse people give, because I remember my wife's parents gave that excuse but now they've got a grandson. You never hear that kind of excuse or anything because they love him so much they'll do anything for him. If he had those problems they would fly up here and they would fight the school district; they would fight the governor to protect their grandson. I don't think they worried about somebody treating their grandson bad. I'm just saying my in-laws used the same excuse when they asked my wife, "What are you gonna do about the kids?"

The birth of children also serves as an impetus to consider how the meaning of race is constructed. Until recently, the one-drop rule, either implicitly or explicitly, socially and culturally determined the race of a person. It was rarely challenged only a generation ago that white men could produce white babies only with white women; white women can produce any-race babies, but only white women can produce white babies; black women can only have black babies; women of color produce babies of color and never white babies; men of color produce babies of color and never white babies; and black men can only produce black babies.

Although most people may not be able to articulate the one-drop rule, their ability to "know" how to classify mixed-race children if given only one racial option (i.e., black or Asian or white) illustrates how deeply ingrained this rule is. The one-drop rule affects how the family is viewed in public, which explains the anxiety of many families for whom race is a central defining feature of their status in society.

In order for children to learn how to identify the race of a person "correctly," they must learn how to distort color and other physical features to match popular views of race.[10] Those children with phenotypes that overlap with several ethnic groups gain much personal experience of racial construction through social interaction.[11] With each environment through which a person moves—work, school, religion, recreation—racial construction results from social discourse. For children, home, school, places of worship, and neighborhoods become significant places for learning about race.[12]

Approaches to Race

We are not a nation well equipped to talk about race, in part because
each of us is impacted by its traumatic past. But perhaps another, more
important reason is that in a predominantly white nation, those in
power do not perceive the need to talk about race. They construe
whiteness as the norm, and people do not tend to talk about what
is normative.[13] Some people therefore become very emotional and
defensive when talking about race, their emotions ranging from guilt
to sadness to anger. At the other extreme are people who do not relate
racial issues to themselves or have no strong feelings about these issues,
although they may clutch their purses when passing a black person
on the street or speak more loudly to an Asian or Latino who has
an accent. Then there are multiracial families, many of whom have
engaged in open dialogues with each other and eventually with their
children—a natural development when children reach the age where
they begin asking questions, such as, "Why am I a different color
from Mommy?" Early experience of racial discrimination from other
children is another natural entry point into discussion. As children
grow older and more mature, they are ready to hear stories of their
parents' courtship, including stories of family difficulties that arose as
a result. Children can then begin to understand why they never visit
one side of the family, or why they are treated differently from their
cousins, or why their multiracial family seems to make other people
uncomfortable.

Many participants in my study had developed certain skills for talking
about aspects of race. With those who had not, however, four problematic approaches to racial dialogue emerged:

1. We are all members of the human race;
2. Race is everything;
3. Don't make race an issue; and
4. We don't understand Americans and race.

We are all members of the human race. This is the colorblind approach,
which asserts that, essentially, race is not important. This approach
forecloses in-depth discussion about race and misses how race is about

power relations. The problem with this approach is not that it isn't true but that it neglects the reality that the term *human being* in this country historically meant *white people*. Regardless of the truth of the statement *we are all members of the human race,* race does make a difference in how people are treated. Some participants reported no history of racial or ethnic discrimination or said that when it did occur it was not traumatic. Some interviewees discussed how their parents influenced them positively to be open to people through taking this approach to race. But persons brought up in mostly white communities, where this approach was most common, discovered how naïve it had been when they later found themselves in hostile environments, unprepared to anticipate or fend off personal attacks.

Race is everything. At the other extreme is the race-is-everything approach, by which much of life is reduced to race. There may be much truth to this in some people's lives, since trauma does increase defensiveness against further psychological assault and colors our every experience. But under this model children grow up deprived by their parents of the opportunity to consider that many similarities and differences reside not in race but in environment, values, and differences of character and personality that have nothing to do with race.

Don't make it an issue. Race is minimized when parents are uncomfortable with the issue or feel unequipped to talk about it. Race was a often a volatile subject in their own homes as children; unresolved grief or anxiety from childhood colors their attitude as adults. Less common is the egocentric parent who does not judge people by race and therefore assumes that his or her child will simply do the same, that the child does not need help in contending with this source of malice in the world. That parents avoid the subject does not necessarily mean they have no awareness of race.

We don't understand Americans and race. A fourth approach is seen among immigrant parents who come from more racially homogenous countries; not being familiar with racism, they may not recognize it when it is directed toward them, particularly in its more disguised forms. These families do not talk about race, not because they deliberately avoid it but because they are unfamiliar with American racism. Racism experienced for the first time as an adult has less traumatic effects than racism experienced as a child.

Parenting Mixed-Heritage Children

I asked adult children from multiracial families, "Do you think your parents were prepared to raise mixed children?" Invariably and unsurprisingly, the answer was no, though the consensus was that white parents were less well equipped than parents of color.[14] More white mothers than white fathers were able to say they were naïve or unprepared for the job. Some persons asserted that nevertheless their parents had risen to the occasion. Participants over thirty often offered gracious and compassionate reflections on this question. They suggested that their parents' difficulties with questions of race stemmed from the limits of living in a culture that traditionally frowned on race-mixing, in a country where racial intermarriage was illegal for most of its history. As Elizabeth, a Latina-Indian woman in her forties, reflected:

> It was awful in so many ways. Maybe there were times in my life I blamed them for making a decision to have kids, but I also can't blame them, how they handled all this stuff [race]. Their parents didn't talk to them about race—they were both mixed. I guess this aspect of their lives was too painful. So I guess I've come to accept that they just didn't know how. As I grew up it was unspoken, like I knew this was a painful topic and I shouldn't bring it up. Almost as though, if they didn't talk about it, it couldn't be a problem. But then I was left to make my own conclusions, and my own mistakes—some that some conversations might have helped me avoid—like maybe a marriage or two. Oh well, I've worked a lot of it out on my own.

Parenting is challenging no matter what, particularly for parents of mixed-heritage children. These parents are told that they must discuss race in order to prepare their children to meet the world.[15] All of the fear about sex between races and the children these relationships produce yields some very ugly racial dynamics. How do parents equip their children, then, to defend themselves against the childhood taunts of oreos, coconuts, apples, zebras, and half-breeds? While a parent of color may have been subjected to name calling, what sets her or his children apart is that they may be called names by people from their own racial groups. Brad described the common dilemma of being caught between two worlds and having to defend himself from both sides.

> I have this friend of mine, and he was black and he was listening to this music on his Walkman. I also have this friend who is white and he

says, "What are you listening to?" And he was listening to Atlantic Star, I think, and it's like a black group. And my friend came up to me, and said, "Oh, nigger music," and I was thinking, well, I'm part black too, you know, and I guess that's when I realized that people didn't see me as black. And that was when I looked pretty Japanese. And that was about the same time as he called me Jappo. And I don't know why he said that, you know.

Are parents aware that their child may be put through the social ritual of hazing to prove allegiance to an in-group?[16] Are they aware that acutely sensitive children dealing with the usual adolescent angst need extra help in working through the sense of isolation that comes from being mixed and misunderstood by one's peers?[17] Or the hurt that comes from being a popular girl or boy, but one who has a difficult time dating because of peers' perceptions of their racial ambiguity?[18] Michael, a black Korean man in his twenties, reported that his mother insisted he date only Korean women, as other first-generation Korean parents tend to insist. But Michael sees the Korean community as very closed. Despite being as Korean, culturally, as his second-generation peers, he is not viewed as fully Korean because of his mixed racial heritage. In fact, his peers have taunted him, "You're everybody's nigger." Given his mother's expectation that he will marry a Korean woman, this young man may find himself in a terrible bind because of the discrimination he experiences in the Korean community.

Whereas parents may have some inkling that people assume a person's racial loyalties can be gleaned from his or her choice of partner, how will they talk about this with their child?[19] Does either parent truly understand the identity path their child may take in trying to understand what it means to be of mixed racial parentage in America at this point in history? Does a parent understand the depth of problem solving a child engages in when she or he goes through a phase of not wanting to be seen with a particular parent? Does the parent know that this is not only about being a teenager but may also be about the child's awareness of how that parent's race marks her or him racially (much as partner choice marks the mixed-race person)?[20]

The ethnic and racial legitimacy tests take many forms. They can be posed by questions about languages spoken in the home, holidays celebrated, foods eaten, churches attended, neighborhood, name, friends, and so on. These tests can be quite extensive. And the more one tries to prove one's legitimacy, the more power one gives to the racial system and the persons doing the testing, who can change the rules at whim.[21] Jim, a man in his late twenties of mixed black-white parentage, recalled how the rules were conveyed to him when he was a child.

> Every now and then you'll find yourself operating from that and because of the puzzled look on somebody's face or comment, you realize that you might be . . . another part of you is leaking out. This was really ingrained in me in school, interestingly enough, here in Seattle. I was in the busing program, and I was a kid from the south side of Seattle, which was a bit more mixed in race than the north side. I was bused up to the north side of Seattle to school. And being a kid that just wanted to be a kid and get along with everyone. But I found that I was kind of riding the bus with the black kids to the north end and part of me was wanting, you know, to associate with the kids on the north end just because they were kids doing something or whatever. And I was finding myself caught. I was finding I was going to hang out with the black kids and get, you know, "You're a white boy; you talk like a white boy." And, you know, "What are you doing?" So I would get this from the kids, both sides. White kids, black kids, both sides. I would see, feel, and hear white kids when they saw me hanging out with the black kids, you know what that's about. And vice versa on the other side. And I was always conscious of this because it was brought to my awareness and I was sensitive to it. And so from the get go, you learn to code switch, 'cause I didn't want to be labeled. I didn't like the fact that the white kids were labeling me as a black kid from somewhere else. And I didn't like the other label either. It constrained what I could do and what I felt in my heart of hearts, because I'm really both.

Jim's experience was echoed by other participants as well. Bill, of Korean and black parents, reported that black kids mocked his Korean side and Asians taunted him for his black side. But he was not mocked or taunted by whites or Hispanics. It was interesting that because Bill was a color/color mix, he did not threaten the border of whiteness and thus was not teased by white teenagers. Nevertheless, his ethnic and racial identity was constructed by his black and Asian peers.

Parents can help children defend themselves against childish taunts by talking with them about race. It seems that more than the markers of ethnicity, the sense of belonging and knowing to whom one is related gives a confidence that helps people cope with these challenges. Parents can accomplish this through talking about their experiences and sharing family stories. By talking about race, they can help their children to recognize what is going on in the name-calling process. The child then has more options and can decide how best to defend himself or herself and whether to take an offensive position with peers.[22] Parents often neglect to tell their children painful stories about race, but this can be detrimental to the child.

Silence, or palpable anguish, on the subject of race may explain why some children will not ask their parents for help in dealing with racial issues at school. They often feel protective of a parent, most often a white mother. Vivia, a college-age woman of black-white parentage, defended her white mother to a black male friend who called all white women "worthless whores." "So I tell him, 'So what does that make my mother, huh? You know she's white.' He says, 'Well, I make an exception for your mother.' I say, 'If you just saw her in a crowd of people, you wouldn't know she's my mother, so you would think that way about her.' He says, 'Maybe, then.' Then, I say, 'So what does that mean about me? I'm black and white. Where does that put me, what do you think about me?'"

Vivia had not related these interactions to her mother for years. She was clearly hurt by the comments of someone she considered a friend. However, this was not a new experience for her. She had had to learn how to protect herself from the ways in which her peers assigned meaning to race. While she and her black father did talk about race, she did not want to talk to him about these issues because she did not want him to think she could not fend for herself. It was important to her that he think she was competent to handle tough situations. She was reluctant to expose her vulnerability to anyone.

A child may protect a parent for several reasons. If race is not discussed at home, children may think that their parents do not understand the subject or do not know how to cope with racial insults. If a child brings up a racial incident at school and meets with an abstract response from her parents, such as, "We're all members of the human race," "Race doesn't matter," or "We all bleed the same color," the child gets no help from these pat answers and will be unequipped to deal with hazing, teasing, name calling, racial attacks, or other bullying. A child does not want a philosophy lesson when smarting from being told by peers that he or she was a mistake, or is an oreo cookie. Even if parents understand the complexity and hurt surrounding issues of race, if they were subjected to that hurt only in adulthood, they may not be able to translate their adult experience of it in a way that helps their child cope. It is possible that they will experience vicariously the psychological assaults their children suffer, and will toughen up simultaneously with their children—but they will have more emotional and intellectual resources for coping than their children do.

A child may also sense guilt in a white parent who is confronted by persons of color. Whereas many white parents develop experience and ways of coping with inappropriate and insensitive attacks for their choice of partner, their choice to have children, or their ignorance in certain matters (for example, how to deal with hair for children with African heritage), their children may not be aware of their competence. Many white persons have grown up feeling apologetic and guilty for the privileges conferred on them because of the color of their skin.[23] If their children have experienced their guilt, they may fear bringing more guilt upon the parent. In an extreme and dysfunctional scenario, the parent and child may reverse roles, with the child trying to reassure the parent and assuage the parent's guilt. Most children do not want to be confronted by their parent's lack of competence in an area in which they need a role model. In reality, many parents cannot provide the map the child needs for negotiating the world as a child of mixed heritage.

Does the parent of color know that mixed children are no longer automatically accepted by their peers of color, Asian, black, Latino?[24] Do parents know that siblings in the same family may identify themselves differently?[25] Do parents know that a child does not always identify himself racially in the way a parent thinks the child ought to, or even in the way that other people interpret the child's physical appearance?[26] Two brothers who were interviewed for the Biracial Sibling Project, similar in terms of phenotype, which was essentially white, identified themselves differently—one as white, one as American Indian. This was true of several siblings. One brother identified as white, the other as of mixed Asian descent. A sister identified herself as biracial, while her younger sister identified herself as black. In one family of three sisters, one identified herself as white, one as black, and one as mixed.

Do parents know that biracial kids and adults may fret more about their physical appearance than other people because of the questions and comments they have received, or that their racial appearance may have changed over time?[27] Brad, a young man of Creole and Japanese American heritage, described his experience:

Most people think my dad is Hawaiian so they probably think I am, too. But you know, like right now, if I look at my skin color though, it doesn't look as dark as sometimes I think it is. Sometimes I wonder if, like, if I, like, totally perceive myself different. Sometimes I look in the mirror and I'm, like, I'm shocked at what I see, sometimes. Like, sometimes I look darker than what I thought I did, but other times I am lighter and I don't know. I don't know if it's about being a brown person, or what. But I feel like sometimes my skin does look darker some days and some days it doesn't. That's, like, crazy to me. I was at my girlfriend's for Christmas and they're a white family. And we, like, have a good time there. They really like me. And they think I am cool. I can chat for hours. And I go to the bathroom and I see myself in the mirror and all of a sudden, I feel like I don't belong. You know, and I told her [my girlfriend] that, and she's, like, well, "Are you having a good time?" And I said, "Yeah. But these mirrors kinda get to me." And she's, like, "Why?" And I said, "When I realize what I look like, I don't really belong." So that maybe in essence, maybe I forget that I am a person of color until I look into the mirror.

The lack of dialogue on race may leave parents, regardless of color, unprepared to anticipate the racial issues that challenge their multiracial children. Can any parent truly be prepared to raise mixed children in this country? In hindsight, many parents readily admitted their naïveté. From white parents, most often mothers, there was a stricken look of grief and pain as they talked about how unprepared they had been and how hard it was for their children—how torn, teased, and rejected they felt—something most of them had not experienced unless they had been the subject of anti-Semitism or cruel taunts about weight or another aspect of physical appearance. Parents from racially homogamous countries felt bad for not anticipating how race relations would affect their children. Parents of color also expressed some regret about their lack of preparation for parenting mixed-race children. As persons of color, they knew what it was to be discriminated against; they even knew that it could be tough for their children, but sometimes they had trouble trying to straddle two (or more) worlds. In part this stemmed from a racial generation gap; their children had more choice about identification than their generation did. The increased freedom of choice available to their children stems from the greater numbers and visibility of children, adolescents, and young adults of mixed heritage. They are no longer so isolated in their experiences.

While many white partners were surprised by the prejudice and discrimination they faced in housing or employment or on the street after they married interracially, they tended to think that this affected only them and that they could deal with it. Parents were surprised when their children revealed that they did not feel welcome or wholly a part of a group, or that they were not accepted as a member of the parent's group, particularly when these children were well liked. Parents were equally surprised by the confusion some children experienced in trying to sort out who they were, perming or straightening or coloring their hair, trying to darken their skin in the sun, wanting to change their eye color. Parents were confused and even hurt when children declared a racial identity that did not include their own race.

All of the parents I interviewed realized that something was changing in racial identity politics. Whereas some black-white families raised their children to identify as black, not all the children did, which puzzled their parents and siblings. Some parents worried that a multiracial identity or insistence by a child that she was both black and white or Asian and black was an indication of self-loathing. But without public conversation on race and racial mixing, parents are not necessarily informed about how the young may be constructing their racial identities in ways that break the rules by which their parents were socialized.[28] Cathy, who identifies herself as American Indian on her father's side, described her racial situation:

> I do act different and I am different at home with my husband than I am around my parents just because it's more of . . . I don't know how to say it. I don't even know . . . at home it's different just because, you know, I feel the same, but I feel more proud when I'm in a situation where I can be thought of as something different, because at home with my husband it's just not anything. I'm not an Indian, I'm just a woman. But when I'm at somewhere else like with my parents or something, you know, I'm Daddy's little girl. I'm, you know, Indian. Like at powwows and stuff. It gives me a sense of self, an *oomph* and connection and I am somebody. . . . My son, I make sure he goes to powwows with me and knows the traditions.

The Asian-heritage children in my study sometimes identified as Asian, sometimes not. Multiracial persons of Asian ancestry in some families and in isolated communities experienced themselves as raceless in the way that white people often do. In doing so, they inevitably identified as white without denying their racial or ethnic heritage.[29] In these cases, ethnic heritage was viewed as an interesting aspect of themselves but had little meaning; there was little attachment to the ethnic culture.[30] Thus ethnic heritage, which has also been synonymous with racial disenfranchisement, is now reduced to symbolic status, much as white ethnic groups in America may note they are of German, Scottish, or Danish heritage but have no particularly emotional or cultural attachment to it.[31] This experience was not unique to Asian-heritage persons, but it was more common among them than among persons of black-white heritage.

Parents found it even more confusing when their children experimented with identifying ethnically and racially with groups with which they did not share a history, for example, Puerto Rican, Indian, Samoan, Hawaiian, Egyptian, and so forth.[32] Some parents provided cultural exposure on a consistent basis, but this did not guarantee that their child would identify in the way the parents desired or expected. Take Aki, Brad's older sister, a married woman of Creole and Japanese American heritage in her mid-twenties, who discussed symbolic identity. I asked her, "What are your racial or ethnic community or communities?"

> Identity? I don't think I really had much of one, an identity in community. Um, we do have a group of friends that are primarily Japanese that we run around with every once in a while. That would be my only sense of community, I guess. Us kids grew up together. I don't really feel like I have a racial community. I just, you know, run around with whoever and I just don't belong to any specific group, racially. . . . I, we, go to the Bon Odori and the Buddhist bazaars. I mean we do things that, you know, are affiliated with the JCL [Japanese Citizens League], but we don't necessarily belong. It's something everybody can go to and do without being members.

Immigrant parents unfamiliar with how the racial system works but nevertheless internalizing some of it may give their children very mixed messages. Tessie, a young Filipina American, recounted how her aunt married a black man and had children, but forbade her daughter, who is of Filipino and black heritage, to date black men. Tessie could not understand this. In contrast, John and Karen, siblings of Korean and African American heritage, spoke of how well their parents equipped them to negotiate issues of race.

A child's understanding of race may be derailed if a family is unstable and the dysfunction becomes racially encoded.[33] Both the Biracial

Sibling Project and the Multiracial Families Project highlighted similar forms of family dysfunction: addiction in one or both parents, abandonment, family violence (battering of a parent, physical, sexual, or emotional abuse of a child), emotional instability, or mental illness. Repeated negative events combined with emotional criticism or trauma by a parent may become entwined with race. This can happen even when parents do not verbalize directly negative messages about race, because society provides the messages of stereotypes. Thus, if a child hears her white mother calling her black father "a lazy, no good, pimp," or hears her father or in-law telling her Asian mother "I just wish you'd go back to where you came from," she may encode this fight as a racial one because of the abundance of racial stereotyping available outside the family. Without family discussion there is less chance to disentangle the meaning the child invests in such words. More subtle messages may come from one parent frequently correcting a partner's language use or seeming not to understand the partner. In this way, the partner is repeatedly defined as deficient and inferior. If a child identifies with the parent being denigrated, the child may color-code these interactions. Some participants in my study who had been treated cruelly by a parent, or who saw that parent treat other people cruelly, color-coded this experience and stayed away from people who resembled that parent racially.

Tessie was angered by both parents' racial stereotypes of all groups except whites and links their behavior to her color-coding, which she turned against her sister. "I kinda thought my sister was kind of whitewashed. . . . I used to insult her that way and say, 'You're so whitewashed. You want to be a white person.' I was really mean to her when I was little, you know. . . . I think it was from my dad—that he was so accepting of white people, but so unaccepting of black people, that I did the opposite."

Essentially, Tessie encoded her father's alignment with whiteness at the expense of people of color with whom she identified. Consequently, she attached negative emotional affect to whiteness. In wanting to be different from him in this way she rejected whiteness out of hand. Her parents' discriminatory attitudes, in addition to growing up in the 1980s in the very diverse community of Oakland, California, made her open to male partners—except white ones. As she grew and matured, she was gradually able to untangle some of the color-coding she was using to express her anger toward her parents.

A very small number of people in my study believed that their parents had been irresponsible to have children, given how messed up society was. As one respondent said, "Fine if they make a choice that is difficult for them and doesn't affect helpless people, but children are helpless, at least initially." This bitterness reflected the view of a small minority; most of the people in my study and in others would not go so far as to say that they wished they had not been born.

Wishes for an Easier or Happier Life

Finally, I asked survey participants, "Is there anything that you wish could have been different growing up, that would have made your life easier, happier, or better?" Though the answers to this question were varied, women generally wanted to lose weight; men wished to be taller or more muscular. Race-related wishes included wanting parents to have talked more about race, about why people acted the way they did and how they might respond. Several people expressed the desire for more contact with relatives of an absent parent, so that they could understand the culture of the parent by which they were physically marked but from whom they were psychologically estranged. Wishes to have attended more diverse schools or to have been around other persons of similar heritage also figured prominently.

Then there were answers that had more to do with racial politics outside the family. Not uncommon were wishes for darker skin, more obviously Asian features, wishes that the parents had passed on Spanish so that they could fit in with the Chicano, Puerto Rican, or Mexican American community. These were very different desires from what mixed-heritage people wanted, or are assumed to have wanted, in the past, or what most people assume they would want today. As Brad put it,

> I think I'd like to be darker. Like during the winters and stuff, I feel like I get pretty lighter. I just feel like I look a lot healthier when I'm darker. And when I went to Jamaica, and when I came back from there, I like it. Felt like I looked pretty good. You know, clothes just looked better on me, and yeah, I think I'd rather like that. Plus, that way, I wouldn't have to try to explain myself so much when people asked me what I was. 'Cause, like, a lot of ignorant people, that's all they look at, is skin color, you know. But, like, black comes in many shades. So it would save me a lot of explaining if I was darker. You know, if I was white, but

had the same skin color that I have now, I would wish I was whiter so I wouldn't have to explain that I'm white. Guess I feel I would look like I was whatever I was.

Some desires were more subtly fueled by race. Jim wished that his mother had not been so self-conscious of their difference as a family. "My mom was very controlling. Going back, she had that thing about, you know, we weren't going to be seen as any kind of stereotype [black kids]. So I mean the phone skills, the table skills. I was probably one of the most polite children ever. And so she's very domineering."

Their various wishes notwithstanding, the adult children of interracial marriages that took place between 1940 and 1980 rarely wished to deny or dispossess themselves of their heritages. This confirms the findings of psychologist Christine Hall and sociologist Teresa Williams, who studied persons of Asian-black parentage and Asian-white parentage.[34]

Many participants expressed sentiments similar to those of Cathy, of white-Native American heritage. "I think we had a really good childhood. There really wasn't anything that they did that I didn't think was right. Everything that they did was always there to help us. They always encouraged us. Never put us down for anything. Even if we did really bad. I mean they'd still, you know, get on you for, if you didn't try hard, but they wouldn't just say, 'Oh, you can't do that.' You know, they'd always say "You can do it," and they were really good parents. There wouldn't be anything I would change. No."

Generation Gaps

Several generation gaps were apparent in both the Multiracial Families Project and the Biracial Sibling Project. A large generation gap was apparent in the racial attitudes of people who grew up in the 1960s and 1970s and their parents. This gap has been analyzed by Gallup polls on attitudes toward interracial marriage from 1968 to 1991, by Tenzer's poll of white women on the subject of interracial dating, and by various magazine and newspaper polls. The gap is even larger between the pre-civil rights generation and their grandchildren. A different type of generation gap now exists between some parents who have been in interracial marriages or relationships and their teenage and young adult children, because the identity options for persons of mixed heritage have changed in the last ten years.

Several years ago, I developed a "Bill of Rights for Racially Mixed People" that summarized the controversies and conflicts of race that exposes these gaps and promotes conversation.[35]

Bill of Rights for Racially Mixed People

I have the right . . .
> *Not to justify my existence in this world.*
> *Not to keep the races separate within me.*
> *Not to be responsible for people's discomfort with my physical ambiguity.*
> *Not to justify my ethnic legitimacy.*

I have the right . . .
> *To identify myself differently than strangers expect me to identify.*
> *To identify myself differently from how my parents identify me.*
> *To identify myself differently from my brothers and sisters.*
> *To identify myself differently in different situations.*

I have the right . . .
> *To create a vocabulary to communicate about being multiracial.*
> *To change my identity over my lifetime—and more than once.*
> *To have loyalties and identification with more than one group of people.*
> *To freely choose whom I befriend and love.*

This Bill of Rights provides a foundation for parents to discuss race among themselves and with their children. I thought of it in terms of a process of change with which couples and children of mixed-race unions contend, but it is useful for anyone who wants to examine the assumptions they make about race. The Bill of Rights captures the resistance to hypodescent, choose-just-one orders, and static concepts of race. It is clear that people who marry interracially and have children ensure the continuation of the quiet revolution. Resistance and revolution provide the foundation for continuing to think about the process of change.

The first four rights assert psychological choices and all twelve resist the illogic of race as it has been dictated for centuries in this country. Mixed-race persons, until recently, have been often thought of as products of rape, concubinage, or one-night stands. An example of this thinking came to national attention in 1994. A Wedowee, Alabama, high school principal threatened to cancel a school dance if any students showed up as interracial couples. Revonda Bowen, a student of black-white parentage, asked with whom she was supposed to go to the dance.

The principal's retort, "You were a mistake," although it expressed the sentiments of many others, led Revonda's parents and other parents to lodge a complaint with the school board, and much negative attention was focused on this small town. Revonda's simple question reflected the changing politics of race. Attorney Carlos Fernandez, in a legal analysis of her case, raised the question: Were her legal rights protected by civil rights laws?[36] Do mixed-race people fall between the cracks? Revonda's case was settled before trial, so this question remains unanswered.

Law professor Deborah Ramirez observes three obvious demographic trends that necessarily change our national dialogue on race, forcing us to reconsider how we try to remedy the racial injuries of the past: The percentage of people of color has increased and this increase is sizable; the number of non-black minority persons has increased significantly—we are no longer a nation of black and white; and the number of people identifying as multiracial has increased substantially.[37] This last trend alone creates a visible adult cohort that has come of age and speaks for itself. These issues gained center stage with the issuing of the 2000 U.S. Census, which included the option of checking more than one race. Increasingly, too, the mixed heritage of children is recognized in school.[38] This change alone is already creating a revolution in our thinking about race. Even persons who are not of mixed heritage are increasingly exposed to the concept that someone can be both or all.

A twenty-something study participant named John described the ambiguities inherent in being of mixed race:

> Just by the fact that by telling someone that I was black would be almost a joke. So I would have to say, you know, I'm black and white. And so that has always been my statement. I'm black and white. I remember when I went into the Marine Corps and I was going through processing and they asked me what my race was, you know? I said, "Well I'm black and I'm white," and people started laughing. And they said, "Oh, we're gonna take care of that funny side of you." They didn't believe me. That was in the North. But down South, I was checking out at the station in Memphis and I had my hands on the desk . . . and there was a black sergeant, and being a sergeant in the Marine Corps he never even looked at my face. He was just stamping paperwork. And he looks at my hand and then he looks up at me. He goes, "You must have black in you." They can tell more in the South.

In the Biracial Sibling Project, it was clear that society's rules and behaviors around race had a major influence on identity, but individual personality, family experiences, friends, and phenotype also had a tremendous amount of influence.

In earlier research, I identified four ways in which people might identify themselves racially, which depended in part on age, or generation, and geographical region. In general, people either (1) accepted the identity society assigned them, which usually invoked hypodescent rules; (2) actively chose to identify with a single heritage; (3) identified multiracially; or (4) identified as a new group.[39] The last option was illustrated vividly in anthropologist Karen Leonard's work on the offspring of Mexican mothers and Punjabi fathers in California's Imperial Valley.[40] The results of the Biracial Sibling Project offer a fifth possibility, that of symbolic race or ethnicity. Waters has described this as a process that transforms white persons' ethnicity over generations, where there is a recognition of links to a cultural heritage but where one is not necessarily culturally or ethnically competent or attached.

What seems most difficult and revolutionary for people to grasp is that people may identify differently in different situations. Various therapists and researchers have referred to this as situational or simultaneous or dynamic ethnicity. Sociologist Cookie White Stephan notes that with the mixed-heritage people in her studies in Honolulu and Albuquerque, she can clearly document situational ethnicity.[41] Different elements of ethnicity, frameworks for behavior, may serve one differently in different situations. John, who identified himself as both black and white when he entered the Marine Corps, elaborated on the theme of situational identity.

> My communities would be both African American and white, if you will—and both, at any given time, or one or the other. I mean literally. [So how does that work? I asked.] Well, you know what instantly comes to mind is, like, when I go visit extended family. On the white side, I don't act a certain way, you know, on a conscious level. I just try to make people feel comfortable within what they know and who they are. And on the white side of my family, they, my grandmother and my grandfather specifically, were prejudiced people. And when I was born they threatened to flush me down the toilet. And there was a real, you know, there was a big division. They would call my black grandparents and cuss them out for polluting their daughter. This really goes back

to this real hatred that's this real hate, you know, filled prejudice. So anyway, through growing up this was all reconciled. And I think some of it had to do with my [white] grandparents. . . . I always had this feeling in the back of my head that the fact of me coming out white—I think it was easier for them to accept the situation given that I [look] white. So anyway, when I went on the white side of the family, my identity is their identity. The sort of values, the talk, the conversation is different. You know, everything. So I'm there and I fully identify on that measure. [What about the African American side and community?] Interestingly enough, I can bring more into that community when I go. I'm thinking over holidays just recently here. On my grandmother's side I act who I am. [Which is?] African American and white. And which is, you know, a Washingtonian and American citizen, and it's just me. . . . All these things combine and I'm there. And my speech changes. I do code-switch, as they call it, a little. But it's not to make them feel comfortable at that point. It's because I feel comfortable. I feel more comfortable in that setting to be me than I do in the white setting . . . I feel like I'm at home in the black family community . . . I would have to say that in my heart of hearts the more endearing side would be the African American side. And I'm not saying one is better than the other—that's just where my heart is. I can code-switch and I can do one or the other, but everything is interwoven.

One of the signs that something is changing in racial matters is the difference in experience between older and younger mixed-heritage persons, though I do not know at what age I would divide these groups. Whereas some of the younger persons sometimes identify as white or feel no different from their white peers, and may have not experienced real discrimination, older persons of mixed heritage seldom share this experience. Racial rules were much more rigid even twenty years ago, and racial oppression and discrimination much more severe in general. It was almost impossible openly to identify as white without difficult public consequences. Older, Korean War–era persons of mixed Asian heritage were not identified as multiracial both because of racial construction as Asian but also because their mothers were foreigners from a non-white country.

Thanks to years of resistance and revolution, the racial rules are changing. People were developing new vocabularies for naming themselves long before Tiger Woods came up with his self-defined childhood identity of *Cablinasian*. Parents speak of multiracial children as

Chicanese (Chicano and Japanese), Indopino (Indian and Filipino), melange, hapa, and Latinegra.[42] And with the growth of blending and multiplicity, it is easier for people to change identities during a lifetime, not for mercenary reasons but because of psychological fit and accuracy.[43] This identity may go from nothing to Asian to black to mixed to AfroAsian to "citizen of the world." With the increased geographic mobility of people both within the nation and between nations, anthropologist Jan Weisman suggests that other salient identities may emerge that are critical to functioning in an increasingly technological world.[44]

Today we see the first generation of mixed-heritage people to grow up in a visible cohort. With the impact of numbers, combined with the changing proportions of visible ethnic groups in the nation, they speak about their own identity, subvert people's assumed notions of race, and nonviolently wage acts of resistance that challenge us to engage in broader dialogues about race. This ability to shift belonging and perspective is not necessarily synonymous with a shifting of loyalties, as John illustrated. It does, however, challenge us to take different perspectives in life that may leave us less judgmental about other people's alliances in friendship and love.

It is through this evolution that we realize some of Martin Luther King, Jr.'s wish, when he said, "I have a dream that my four little children will one day live in a nation where they will not be judged by the color of their skin but by the content of their character."[45] Race makes a difference in what we experience, but it does not necessarily make a person. The American writer Peter de Vries made an observation that is fundamental to the quiet revolution when he wrote, "The value of marriage is not that adults produce children, but that children produce adults."[46]

8

Ten Truths of Interracial Marriage

n 1944 the Swedish sociologist Gunnar Myrdal published his classic study of race relations, *An American Dilemma: The Negro Problem and Modern Democracy*. In identifying race as the American dilemma, Myrdal echoed W.E.B. DuBois's observation half a century earlier that the color line would be the problem of twentieth century. At the dawn of the twenty-first century, with Jim Crow laws and other legal barriers gone but not forgotten, we still struggle with the problem of race in America. And while race is no longer an issue only for black and white Americans, it remains defined by a long history that constructed black and white relations. This explains why even though only one-quarter of interracial marriages take place between black and white partners, intermarriage still predominantly conjures up images of black and white. Ironically, some of the younger participants in my study, who had not learned all the old, harmful rules of race, did not see their relationship as interracial because it was not black and white.

One of the obstacles to progress may be that racism and sexism, and the power struggles within each sphere, have been regarded as separate. Psychologist Aida Hurtado observes that the difficulties of feminist theory in analyzing gender subordination are similar to the difficulties of race theorists analyzing race. Whereas both are analyzed as evidence of institutionalized imbalances in structural power, they are not constructed simultaneously.[1] Sociologist Abby Ferber[2] and philosopher Naomi Zack[3] also observe how imperative it is to understand the simultaneous influences and intersections of race and gender. My study demonstrates that when we see race and gender as master statuses connected by sex and fear of interracial sexuality, we gain a better understanding of the ways in which race and gender are constructed. This finding helps us understand why interracial marriage is not more common and why we seem to be moving toward increased possibilities of interracial intimacy, dissolving centuries of racial apartheid in intimate relationships and kinship networks.

Interracial relationships, and particularly interracial marriage, leave a permanent record of a transgression against what has been considered normal, "sticking with your own kind." They challenge the privilege and property of whiteness and any other rigid category of race—or gender. Some people fear that opening the way to interracial marriage might open the door to same-sex marriage and violate other cultural norms. Thus interracial marriage is a vehicle for examining race and gender relations as well as the structures that shape them. Anthropologist Roger Sanjek notes that "Race, sex and power remain the essential ingredients of the continuing 'American dilemma' of the United States . . . the power of race has long been expressed and mediated through sex. Rape, forced disruption of black conjugal ties and kinship networks, sexual mythology and fear, and legal bars to interracial marriage, and the overriding of kinship by race are historic features of the race-sex-power equation."[4]

Although the "colors of race" have expanded through imported labor and immigration, we see that race has achieved a more rapid transformation from a fictional category based on real or imagined physical features, essence of character, and capabilities to ethnicity for virtually all groups except blacks. And with this transformation from a racial caste category to an ethnic class category, objections based on "essences" recede. Thus, although there are objections to all forms of intermarriage, the strongest objections still pertain to black-white marriage.

Participants in my study repeatedly illustrated the point that race is a social and cultural invention, a make-believe tale that is hard to stop believing. Americans even today have countless devices that we use to convince ourselves that race is more than a fiction, that it is a real division between people that must be observed and respected. Afro-American Studies Professor Henry Louis Gates lists these devices that proclaim race to be real: birth certificates, biographical sketches, treatises, certificates, pamphlets, and so on.[5] The result is that race becomes very confusing, its boundaries simultaneously real and unreal. The meaning placed on interracial marriage, biracial children, or multiple and simultaneous racial alliances is part of the struggle to come to terms with the race fiction Europeans and Americans invented. President Clinton's Race Advisory Board chairman John Hope Franklin wrote, "stereotypes remain because Americans cling to the idea that it is best to try to ignore race. That, in turn, forces people to bury—and therefore harbor—beliefs they form from stereotypes heard at school, in the media and from family members."[6] In the public discussions hosted by this advisory board, comments on interracial marriage and the classification of multiracial children were conspicuous for their absence. The board contained no representatives of the various multiracial groups in this country. Even in a progressive attempt to discuss race, race was bounded and bordered, creating a fiction that race mixing is inconsequential to the American landscape of race, gender, and politics despite a history of legislative struggle for civil rights against a backdrop of fear.[7] Bigotry, fear, and denial are still formidable forces in this country's racial culture. Lynnette, a white woman, reflected on how racial boundaries were reinforced by her black husband, even in her own interracial family:

> I think it is the way we view ourselves as interracial. My husband, though, is not very accepting of white people. He doesn't view me as white, he never really kinda has. I don't know what kind of perception he has. So in some ways that has been a split in providing some more unity to the family. He's very color conscious. He says a lot of things at home that could be divisive and the kids don't feel comfortable with . . . my daughter will go around and tease him with things like, "I'm going to marry somebody white, and know the color of this family."

This husband probably had no intention of creating an interracial family. But, ironically, by in effect using the one-drop rule invented to serve white male privilege, his family becomes a black family and he remains authentically black. He has also applied male privilege in denying his wife's racial identity, knowing that his racial identity will dominate hers, rather than the other way around. The experience of the younger generation, raised in the aftermath of civil rights reforms, confirms that race is socially constructed by the majority.

Families are the initial socializing agent, in questions of race as in everything else. As a psychologist, my prime interest in developing this study was to understand the process of political, social, and spiritual transformation that interracial marriages instigate in families. It seems that the theories of the past were limited by the attitudes of the era in which they evolved. Female gender roles in this American drama were either passive roles or victim roles, pawns rather than agents. Women have always been central to the creation and maintenance of families, and my research strongly suggests that current theories must make the role of women central in race relations, racial construction, and interracial marriage. A year after her daughter's wedding to a black man, Ann, a white woman from Seattle, had gained new respect for her daughter's ability to make independent decisions and saw her as an embodiment of the changing roles of women.

> Probably extended family members would have more concern than her own parents, since we know her well. In a sense, we were more surprised than upset about the dating going on. But she has also, for two summers, gone fishing on a commercial fishing boat, so what I am saying is she's probably broken ground in other areas by being the first. . . . My sisters and I would never have been on a commercial fishing boat with four or five men. But a new generation. I guess she is more of a risk taker than perhaps myself. . . . We had visiting students in our home where we raised our kids. So I think that added to her feeling she could come to us and share this. Our home was open. So I was surprised, but I wasn't offended. I didn't go home or cry or stew or anything. I think probably behind doors some of our extended family did. For example, we had a grandpa who was in his eighties, and so there may have been some rolling of the eyes, so to speak. But my husband and I were anxious to meet him . . . [and] he is wonderful. They were married about a year ago. He enhances our family, and if the others don't see it, that's their problem. But they came to the wedding, and grandpa came.

One of main questions I sought to answer was what distinguished families who could take in a racially different family member from those who could not. Distilling the answers led me to summarize the results in terms of the closed- and open-family systems discussed in Chapter 5. As T. W. Adorno and his colleagues showed, the definition of who can belong to a family and who cannot is a way of asserting and maintaining authority and privilege. But in order to do this, tremendous self-deception must be practiced, for it involves the rewriting of the character and contributions of whole groups of people.[8] It became clear in thinking about families as variations of closed or open systems that the key element in distinguishing these families was the degree to which racial reproduction was considered a significant product of the family. This led me to realize that even in modern America, families are about business: mergers, franchises, and acquisitions. And when one becomes a liability to the business of family, the pain and rejection that follow can cause deep and lasting wounds. Regardless of what happens to a marriage, whether it is a lifelong success or a short-lived fiasco, one cannot go home the same person who was banished from the original corporation.

The dynamics that prevailed in closed, pseudo-closed, and even pseudo-open families had the elements of psychologist Gordon Allport's ten sociocultural laws of prejudice.[9] Allport noted that at the root of discrimination, ten conditions fed and sustained prejudice. The more conditions that were present in any particular place or time, the more likely we would be to see prejudiced personalities. Allport defined these conditions as follows:

Where the social structure is marked by heterogeneity;
Where vertical mobility is permitted;
Where rapid social change is in progress;
Where there are ignorance and barriers to communication;
Where the size of a minority group is large or increasing;
Where direct competition and realistic threats exist;
Where exploitation sustains important interests in the community;
Where customs regulating aggression are favorable to bigotry;
Where traditional justifications for ethnocentrism are available; and
Where neither assimilation nor cultural pluralism is favored.[10]

Allport's conclusions are important to this study. We live in a period of rapidly changing gender roles, technological development and expansion, and increased global and cultural exchange—in an increasingly competitive world. Many of Allport's conditions prevail now. Simultaneously, we have a young generation of people operating under some changing principles of competition, discrimination, and gender role expansion.

Discussions of interracial marriage through the past century have replicated the very dynamics that are central to it; that is, they usually take place intraracially rather than interracially. The black feminist scholar bell hooks notes that racial reality looks quite different when constructed from a white perspective than it does from a black perspective.[11] Historian Paul Spickard's research on intermarriage documented the significant protest in communities of color against aspects of integration and miscegenation.[12] In the course of his work as an attorney for the NAACP before his appointment to the U.S. Supreme Court, Thurgood Marshall noted that the difficulty with repealing Jim Crow laws and reversing *Plessy v. Ferguson* was the opposition from black communities.[13] The audible voice of protest, whether white or non-white, has been male. The voices of people of color and women have been muffled and marginalized, though they are so central to the phenomenon.[14]

Racial intermarriage looks quite different from a male perspective than from a female perspective. Women's primary responsibility for childbearing and child rearing makes them central to any discussion of interracial mixing. In these discussions, women and their bodies have historically been seen as the property of men. Rod, a black man in his thirties, provided a glimpse of this double standard in black families and communities when I asked him how his family was likely to react if his sisters married interracially. Rod was married to a white woman.

Well, you know, honestly, they would probably not be accepted. We're all educated and cordial, but then again, when our family gets together, there's no telling who's going to say what or who's going to do what and if there's something like this introduced that's upsetting, anything can happen. You know, a person might, he might be called a white boy or he might be caught in a deep conversation that you're not normally exposed to black perception—real black perception. And it's oftentimes difficult for someone of a different race to socialize with the family because those real realities come and so that's uncomfortable. So for the men, most of the men, we have had relationships, have brought the women to a family gathering, but not for my sisters. Too much negative response from the family. I believe that a lot of that has to do with how the women's role is perceived by the men in our family and that the

rules [for] women [with] regard to interracial relationships is generally
not something the men in our family saw. The history of white men
using black women. We're suspicious.

My research has led me to conclude that women will become central gatekeepers of race and racial construction, reconstruction, and
deconstruction. Women, rather than being pawns, are central figures
in the growth of interracial marriage. Increased female financial independence, access and options for birth control—even abortion—as
well as geographic mobility and relocation, provide more control over
a woman's choice of partners. Already intermarriage rates for Asian
American women, Hispanic women, and American Indian women are
substantial, and often higher than for their male counterparts. With
the sex-ratio imbalances in the African American communities across
the country, with more women of marriageable age than available
men; with the advanced education of a growing number of African
American women; with the inscription of blackness on mixed-race
children regardless of the sex of the parent who is black; and with the
assignment of child cultural socialization to women, African American
women will become significant to the discussion on interracial marriage
as their rates of intermarriage increase. This will be a direct contrast to
their forced interracial experiences in previous eras.[15] I believe that the
current reconstruction of black femininity will be related to continued
examinations of race and gender and their intersection through sex
and interracial relationships and marriage. White women will continue
to make choices across color lines; when both gender and race are
taken into account, white women's power in its totality is not that
different from that of men of color. Thus, the potential outcome of
such transformations may be that discussions of race will increasingly
have a female voice.

Sanjek suggests that the transformation of race to ethnicity will likewise allow some people of color to assume privileges that were previously
reserved for whiteness. Recall that Roberta, the white grandmother
introduced earlier, has a biracial Asian-white grandson. When I asked
if she now saw her family as an interracial or mixed family, she replied,
"Oh, yes. . . . We're all white." By defining race in black and white
terms—even though her Japanese son-in-law is not considered white by
U.S. racial classifications, and her grandson is not considered "really"

white by those who patrol the borders of whiteness—Roberta makes her daughter's marriage less objectionable. Her answer, ironically, can be seen as a way of reconstructing race by broadening the boundaries of whiteness. But can these boundaries be broadened to include mixing with the black population? Without this expansion, we will not accomplish true racial deconstruction but only the reconstruction of whiteness. Attempts to retain a white ethnic identity—for example, Polish American, Irish American, Italian American—do not have to feed white supremacist notions or reinforce the fiction of race. Unfortunately, whiteness as race in the U.S. seems to tolerate only symbolic ethnicity, particularly for newer immigrant groups.[16] Perhaps this is also part of the explanation for the distance between black and white—that many if not most blacks will not willingly give up their African American identity.

Though they make strange bedfellows, love and prejudice can coexist between partners, as I saw again and again in my research. Sometimes this was manifested in acts of collusion in which partners left their spouses standing alone to take their family's racial prejudice and abuse. I doubt that intermarriage is the solution to all of America's race problems in America. But it does provide one avenue for the challenging of stereotypes, particularly when it involves an extended kinship network of different-race and mixed-race kin. It is an opportunity to move into a different dialogue about race, a dialogue in which the voices of multiracial adult children and women and people of color can also be heard. Intermarriage will soon affect a substantial portion of Americans of all colors.

Individual and family identities may be transformed through these marriages. In her recent work, bell hooks has emphasized love as action and attitude that can inspire us to end oppressive practices. Whereas Martin Luther King, Jr. and others stressed the political uses and meanings of love, we hear love discussed less frequently in these terms as a powerful and transcendent force.[17] Joseph Campbell spoke to the transformation that marriage heralds when he wrote, "Marriage is not a simple love affair, it's an ordeal, and the ordeal is the sacrifice of ego to a relationship in which two have become one."[18] Campbell's statement is reflected in Martin Luther King, Jr.'s observation that "all men [and women] are caught in an inescapable network of mutuality, tied in a single garment of destiny. Whatever affects one directly affects all indirectly."[19] At its most intense, love provides a reminder that two people have merged their lives and that they are having to negotiate some new boundaries and definitions of self. In the case of interracial love, some fictions around race must be challenged. People are resilient when they are deeply in love. They are open to new ideas and experiences because their love can override fear. Thus they promise hope of transformation in attitudes. The partnership between individualism, so highly prized by American culture, and romantic love makes interracial marriage an increasing possibility for most families now that legal barriers have been removed.

The psychologist Robert Sternberg found that three components form romantic love, the major motivating force in the marriage decisions of almost all of the participants in my study. The degree of their presence determines the quality or definition of love in a relationship.[20] First, he notes that there is an intimacy component from which connectedness arises. The intimacy involved in a lasting love relationship has several dimensions that are neither defined nor limited by race. Prager observes that intimacy can occur at different levels: (1) the frequency of personal sharing; (2) the depth and risk involved in the sharing; and (3) the amount of sharing that takes place and continues over time.[21] Conversations about racial experiences, culture, gender, and class were part of the experiences that provided a depth to the intimacy many participants had with their partners.

Second, there is a passion component that drives the initial physical attraction and sexual desire. In stereotypes of interracial relationships, the first component—intimacy—is often dismissed and only sexual desire and attraction are given credence as motivating forces. The third component is commitment, which requires a person to distinguish between liking and loving, infatuation and love, and lust and love.

When an interracial marriage or engagement is met with hostility, its opponents assume that the individuals involved lack the capacity to make the commitment that is Sternberg's third component of romantic love. Instead, interracial love is constructed as an immature form of attachment motivated by anger, rebellion, and pathology, rather than as an engulfing, embracing form of love that John Welwood describes as a soul connection. Two people come together to realize their deepest potential—to be the best people *they* can be.[22] When motivations and individuals are stereotyped in a dismissive way, all individuals who love across color lines are seen as more similar than dissimilar. But research offers little data to support the notion that there is a consistent profile or type that is more inclined than others to intermarriage.[23]

In one of the few empirical studies designed to examine profiles of persons who intermarry, a longitudinal family study in Hawaii, Johnson and colleagues found few differences between groups. Among women who intermarried and women who did not, Asian American women who married interracially tended to be more independent than Asian American women who did not. Men who intermarried were less domineering than men who did not.[24] Even though this study was conducted almost twenty years ago, it captured an important aspect of flexibility in gender roles that I think contributes to the possibility of intermarriage. Many of the white men married to women of color in the study seemed willing to give up some aspects of white male privilege. Many were willing to be minorities in racial or ethnic communities. While I do not suggest that a white man in a black or Asian or Hispanic community suffers the same discrimination that a black or Asian or Hispanic or Indian man does in a white community, Johnson's findings suggest that these white men had less investment in maintaining a special sense of self through their whiteness.

With flexibility to redefine masculine and feminine roles in relationships, the heart of what might be exchanged between people may be more difficult to pinpoint. Such changes may also redefine standards of physical attractiveness. For example, an attractive man does not have to be tall; an attractive woman does not have to be small or thin. If standards of attractiveness can extend beyond European standards of beauty, so, perhaps, can our motivation to know persons who would otherwise not be of interest. If our culture ever reaches the point where height is not associated with power, we might also see more frequent exceptions to one of the rules of heterosexual coupling, that is, that the male is supposed to be taller than the female. The ability to break this rule would reflect an expansion of the definitions of masculinity and femininity. Just as we have invented fictions about race and gender, we maintain many fictions about physical attractiveness as well. Race, ethnicity, and class influence what we consider acceptable and desirable gender roles. Living in a more pluralistic way could make physical attraction that much more mysterious, because we would become that much more aware of how socially and culturally conditioned attraction is.

It is no wonder that love is difficult to study. Although it can be a psychological state of mind, a judgment, an action, or an orientation, the meaning of love can be so individualistic as to make its study frustratingly complicated. Seldom is the love that binds people together the subject of studies of interracial marriage. Yet I observed that despite cultural, class, gender, religious, and racial differences, people satisfied essential needs through their partners that seemed to transcend these categories.

Despite the human drama that accompanies every search for love, companionship, and understanding, interracial marriage is most often depicted as foolhardy and irrational rather than heroic. At some level it seems easy for many people to dismiss interracial love as irrationality, infatuation, curiosity, or immaturity—a stage that will pass. Or else it is simply fetishized—she has a thing for black men, he has a thing for Asian women.

The irrationality of love has been associated with "addiction" or "fatal attraction"—and interracial love has certainly been depicted as irrational, addictive, even fetishistic. Fortunately, Peele and Brodsky untangle these issues in their book *Love and Addiction*.[25] They offer eight ways that infatuation and sustained love can be distinguished. In contrast to addiction, love is

1. an expansive experience rather than total focus on another person;
2. a helping relationship rather than idealization of another person;
3. an opportunity for enhanced growth rather than retreat to a private world;
4. the intensification of pleasure in life rather than intensification of pain;
5. a productive and beneficial experience rather than an incapacitating one;
6. a natural outcome of one's self and life rather than purely accidental and tentative;
7. an experience that continues and intensifies friendship and affection rather than an all-or-nothing experience; and

8. a responsibility that has an attendant heightened awareness rather than an uncontrollable urge or unconscious motivation.

The participants in my study all spoke of love as a motivating force for their choices. Although some divorced and some married persons reflected on their naïveté or youthful optimism at the time of their marriage, these marriages were about love. Participants referred to the psychological needs they thought their relationships provided. When both partners had the ability to work, emotional and relational needs took precedence over instrumental needs.

The hundreds of hours of interviews and background research I conducted can be distilled into what I call "Ten Truths About Interracial Marriage."

1. The civil rights movement and subsequent patterns of racial desegregation created opportunities for people to interact in meaningful ways, which has resulted in an increased rate of interracial marriage.
2. In the past twenty-five years, women's decreased financial dependence on their families has given them freedom to choose mates regardless of family approval.
3. Love, shared vision, and common values compel an interracial couple to marry, just as they do other couples.
4. The motives behind interracial marriage seldom include the desire to rebel or to make a political or social statement.
5. Families that reject an interracial marriage value the reproduction of their race over love, integrity, and commitment.
6. In order to live in an affirming emotional climate, an interracial couple may have to replace estranged blood kin with a fictive family of friends.
7. Conflicts within interracial marriages are more likely to arise from cultural, gender, class, social, and personal differences than from racial ones.
8. Irreconcilable differences within interracial marriages are similar to those within same-race marriages: loss of respect, unwillingness to compromise, hurtful actions, lack of responsibility, dishonesty, and conflicting values.

9. The rate of divorce for interracial marriages is only slightly higher than for same-race couples in the continental United States; the gap is quickly closing as divorce rates rise for all marriages.

10. Interracial couples can and do produce healthy, well-adjusted children.

In Puccini's last opera, *Turandot,* set in legendary Peking, the Chinese princess Turandot declares that she will accept the hand of the suitor who can answer three riddles. Those who try and fail will be executed, allowing Turandot to avenge an ancestor who was raped and murdered by a Tartar prince. Unbeknownst to her, one of the suitors, Prince Calaf, is the son of the exiled king of Tartary. Turandot lives in the past and Calaf in the future, as she reminds him that failure to solve the three riddles result in death and he reminds her of the possibility of life. "Turandot poses the first enigma: what rises at night, invoked by all the world, only to die at dawn reborn in the heart? Calaf rightly answers: hope. The second riddle is: what darts like a flame but is not a flame, that grows cold with death yet blazes with dreams of conquest? Turandot is furious when Calaf solves it with the answer: blood. Thirdly she demands what inflames you, white yet dark, that enslaves if it wants you free, but in taking you captive makes you king. Calaf, after hesitation, answers: Turandot."[26] Seeing her fear and fury at losing her superior position, he offers her his head nonetheless if she can discover his identity by dawn. No one in the kingdom sleeps that night as his identity is sought. Just before dawn, his father and his attendant, Liù, are brought before her. Liù, protective of the exiled king and pressed by Turandot to explain why she would endure torture or even death for him, answers "love." The concept is foreign to Turandot, but she is nevertheless moved momentarily. She soon recovers herself, however, and has Liù's tongue cut out. Calaf appears and reveals his identity as the son of the exiled king. Turandot believes she has turned the tables and has restored her power over him. Fearless in the face of death, he kisses her as a challenge to experience his love. With his identity in her possession, Turandot surprises all. She opens her heart after years of lovelessness and reveals Calaf's name to the court as Love, thus sparing his life and starting hers anew, freed from her fear and hatred of Tartars.

Whereas the riddles are solved with the answers hope, blood, and love, these are indeed real-life enigmas when it comes to discussions of interracial marriage. Interracial marriage gives us hope that love can transcend some of the barriers that legislation has not. Its power to transform us, one at a time, cannot be underestimated, allowing us to release the hate, fear, and guilt of the past and move into the future with love as a political device. Despite some almost universal propensities for stratification, competition, and ethnocentrism, I believe that with stealth and persistence the people in my study demonstrated that love has the capacity to erode the fear and hate that have blemished many a participant's family landscape. Interracial marriage and its children provide an opportunity for a different discussion of race relations within the power matrices formed by race, gender, and ethnicity. Today's children are tomorrow's adults. I hope we teach them well.

Appendix
Trends in Interracial Marriage

Trends in interracial marriage have been deduced by looking at the number and rates of intermarriage over each decade since 1960. U.S. Census reports, Public Use Microdata Samples, and regional surveys were used for most of these figures, or, where cited, figures were obtained from other sources; this explains the slight variations between figures.

The 1960s

Prior to the repeal of anti-miscegenation laws, the Census of 1960 counted 148,000 interracially married couples.[1] Of these, 51,000 were black-white couples evenly divided between black husbands/white wives (25,000) and white husbands/black wives (26,000).

Prior to 1960, due to immigration restrictions, the presence of Asian Americans was very small and the largest American-born group was Japanese American. There were few Filipinos, Koreans, or Chinese in the country, and Asian intermarriage was infrequent. Blacks and whites who intermarried therefore usually married each other. Of white intermarriages with other than black partners, white men intermarried most frequently with Asian and American Indian women. Intermarriages between white men and non-black women in the 1960 census were: Japanese (21,700), American Indian (17,300), Filipina (4,500), and Chinese (2,900). A large proportion of the Asian women were foreign-born. Thornton notes that from 1945 to 1959, over 72,000 foreign spouses of Asian origin married to U.S. citizens immigrated to the

179

United States.[2] The majority of these foreign spouses were women; the majority of them married white men. White men also intermarried with 9,000 other women who were listed by the 1960 Census as "other race."

White women intermarried with black men more frequently than with any other group (25,000). The next largest groups married by white women were Filipinos (11,200) and American Indians (12,000), followed by Japanese (3,500) and Chinese (3,500) men. Whereas all groups may have some cultural similarity with white women, American Indian men would have had the fewest cultural prohibitions compared to Japanese and Chinese men. Filipino men would still have been in more abundant supply than Filipina women. This sex-ratio imbalance, coupled with the impact of American colonization of the Philippines, may explain the difference in the pattern of white female intermarriage with Filipinos compared to general patterns of white male intermarriage.

Black men partnered with other than black or white women were most frequently partnered with American Indian women (2,200) and Japanese women (1,700). They were rarely partnered with Filipinas (500) or Chinese women (less than 100), groups that were still very small in the United States. It would be reasonable to explain these patterns by the sex-ratio imbalances in the Asian American communities that led to competition for Filipino and Chinese women.[3] However, the prevailing colorism within the Asian countries, with a definite preference for light skin, made black men less acceptable marriage partners than white men, who were less acceptable than Asian men.[4] There were 565 other partnerships of white women in which the race of the man fell into the category of "other."

Black women intermarried with other than white partners were most frequently married to American Indian men (1,100). Rates of intermarriage were much lower with the Asian American groups: Filipinos (500), Chinese (300), and Japanese (less than 100). There were 324 "other" intermarriages of black women.

While figures on intermarriage for people of color other than black are rarely posted for public consumption, they follow the same pattern as with black intermarriage. Much of this has to do with sheer numbers and availability of white partners. Thus in 1960, all the above groups intermarried more frequently with white persons than with other people of color by a substantial majority. The second most frequent type of intermarriage was with black partners, except for Chinese women, who coupled with black (80) and American Indian men (40) least frequently. American Indian women partnered least frequently with Japanese (20) and Chinese men (20).

Patterns of Puerto Rican marriage followed immigrant patterns and were very low at the time of the 1960 Census.[5] In contrast, 40 percent of Mexican Americans in Los Angeles County were intermarried in 1963.[6] Younger men, as a group, had the greatest tendency to intermarry.[7]

A small but significant number of men (26,400) and women (32,200) classified as "other" most frequently married each other (18,300). Besides partnering with other "others," the next most frequent likelihood was a partner of Asian heritage. "Other" women most frequently married white husbands (9,000), followed by Filipinos (2,100), Chinese (1,200), and Japanese (1,100). The men classified as "other" most frequently married white women (4,700), followed by Japanese (1,400), Chinese (900), Filipino (620), black (300), and American Indian (200). These "others" were probably people whose racial heritage defied U.S. Census Bureau classification.

Few data were available on Asian American intermarriage during this decade. Using Los Angeles County data, Tinker found that for 1960 and 1961 the interracial marriage rate for newlywed Japanese Americans was 67.9 percent, with women having higher rates of intermarriage than men.[8] The internment of Japanese Americans during World War II, the pressure to assimilate into American society, and the immigration of Korean War era brides were all probable factors in this increase in intermarriage for Japanese American women. Few data were available for Korean American intermarriage before 1970, though intermarriage began to be significant after World War II and the Korean War. Few data exist on Filipino intermarriage, which had been legal up until 1933, when Filipinos were reclassified as Malays in California and included in anti-miscegenation laws.

Data from Hawaii for the 1960s suggest high rates of intermarriage for men.[9] Interethnic and interracial marriage cannot be distinguished from the available data, but Koreans had the highest rates of outmarriage (79.3 percent), followed by Chinese (59.9 percent), Filipino (49.3 percent), and Japanese (24.1 percent).[10] The rates for women were always higher than for men, but the two rates were close except in the case of the Japanese.

During this decade, shortly after changes in immigration laws in 1965, the number of immigrating Asian spouses substantially increased. From 1960 to 1969, approximately 98,000 Asian spouses (compared to 146,000 European spouses) entered the United States.[11] This represents more than a 50 percent increase in Asian spouses from the previous decade of the 1950s (61,000). From 1960 to 1969 almost 58,000 spouses came from Japan. Germany, Italy, and England provided the largest numbers of European spouses. Mexico, although it became a major source only a few years later, provided less than 7,000 spouses per year in the years 1960 to 1969.

The 1970s

Racial intermarriage was decriminalized and legal prohibitions were removed in 1967. Within a decade the number of racial intermarriages doubled.[12] The rate of white intermarriage with persons other than blacks increased by 250 percent, while the rate of black intermarriage with persons other than whites rose by 170 percent. Black-white intermarriages increased but only because of an increase in the number of black husbands and white wives (41,000). The number of black wives and white husbands reflected in the 1970 Census was approximately the same as in 1960 (26,000).

New York City data gathered by researchers at Fordham University show intermarriage trends for persons of Latino or Hispanic heritage. Fitzpatrick and Gurak found that older age was associated with intermarriage among Hispanics.[13] This finding stands in contrast to a previous study by the same researchers, which showed younger Mexican American men in Los Angeles intermarrying at significant rates. The rate of Puerto Rican intermarriage was the lowest for Mexican American or Chicano, Cuban, and Puerto Rican groups, at 29.5 percent.[14] This might be due to the tendency of Puerto Ricans, even now, to return to Puerto Rico for their mates. Among Hispanics, Cubans were the most likely to intermarry. Higher rates of Cuban intermarriage were attributed to sex ratio imbalances, specifically a greater supply of women than of men, which motivated Cuban women to seek other mates.[15]

Asian American intermarriage continued at high rates during the 1960s and 1970s. The rate of interracial marriage for urban and rural Chinese men based on the 1970 U.S. Census was 13 (urban) and

14 (rural) percent. Urban Chinese women had a similar rate of 12 percent. However, when the rural groups were divided into farm and non-farm residents, non-farm intermarriage rates were substantial for both men (33 percent) and women (38 percent). Similar rates of intermarriage prevailed in all parts of the country except New York, where sex ratios were still uneven and the rate for men was double that for women.[16]

Using a similar urban/rural breakdown, patterns for Japanese American intermarriage showed that women intermarried at approximately three times the rate of men. Urban male intermarriages were at 12 percent compared to 33 percent for women. The rural non-farm figures were 14 percent and 42 percent for men and women, respectively.[17] Various research reports using California data yielded similar patterns. The rates of intermarriage were significant and women intermarried more frequently than men in Los Angeles County[18] and Fresno County.[19]

According to the U.S. Census, rates of intermarriage for Filipino men and women were similar to each other, though men intermarried slightly more frequently than women did. This was an exceptional pattern compared with other Asian American groups. The urban sample and rural non-farm samples yielded similar rates of 28 percent for women and 33 percent (urban) and 35 (rural non-farm) percent for men.[20]

Korean intermarriage in Los Angeles County for the years 1975 to 1979 ranged from 26 percent in 1975 to 34 percent in 1979, with women interracially marrying often at more than twice the rate of men.[21] No data were reported for Vietnamese, still a small group at that time.

Between 1970 and 1979, a period when the 1965 Amendments to the Immigration and Nationality Act were in effect, Asia overtook Europe as a source of spouses (193,000 compared to 142,000), a pattern that continued through at least the mid-1980s. Spouses immigrating from elsewhere in North America increased tenfold from the previous decade (to 230,000). As a country, Mexico became the leading source of foreign spouses (125,000) for the period 1970–1979. The Philippines became the second leading source of spouses (57,000). These figures stand in stark contrast to the period 1960–1969, when Germany was the leading source of spouses (112,000); in the following decade, Germany provided only 30,000.[22]

The 1980s

By 1980, the number of interracial marriages had tripled over 1970 figures and was more than six times higher than the 1960 figures.[23] While all groups contributed to the increase, the surge in Asian and black intermarriages with whites accounts for most of it. Asians had the highest percentage of interracial marriages (23 percent) compared to other groups: blacks (2 percent), Hispanics (13 percent), and non-Hispanic whites (1 percent).[24] Nevertheless, intermarriage remained infrequent, with only 1.3 percent of married couples over fourteen years of age considered interracial. Of these, 27 percent were black-white marriages.

Marriages between black men and white women more than doubled from the figures in the 1970 Census (41,000), to 94,000. In contrast, the rate of marriage between white men and black women remained similar, increasing numerically by 1,000 to 27,000.

White intermarriage with non-black partners more than tripled from 1970 (to 785,000), and black intermarriage with non-white partners almost quadrupled (to 47,000). This increase reflects marriages with all other groups, but particularly with Asian Americans. Glick reports that 40 percent of marriages involving a Japanese-heritage wife were interracial; the corresponding figures for Chinese and Filipina wives were 10 percent and 23 percent, respectively.[25] Rates varied depending on the geographic region of sampling.

Intermarriage in the American Indian and Mexican American and Latino communities continued at significant rates. Analysis of 1980 Census figures reveals that American Indian men and women married white partners about equally, at 48 percent and 48.3 percent.[26]

In the most comprehensive Census analysis of Asian American inter-marriage, Lee and Yamanaka used a 5 percent Public-Use Microdata Sample from the 1980 Census to examine these trends. They had a large enough sample to examine patterns for Chinese, Filipino, Indian, Japanese, Korean, and Vietnamese groups. They divided these groups by gender and took an additional one percent sample to have a non-Asian comparison sample, which they similarly divided by gender. For all Asian groups, interracial marriages comprised 23 percent of marriages. Younger people intermarried at higher rates than did older people, with the exception of South Asian men, and American-born Asians had higher rates of intermarriage than did foreign-born Asians. Education, income, and occupation did not offer a consistent pattern to explain intermarriage.

In general, when Asians married interracially, they tended to marry non-Hispanic whites or Hawaiians, the former pairing being the most frequent. After these two groups, intermarriage tended to be interethnic with other Asians. Of the Asian groups, Filipinos had the most open pattern. They intermarried most or next-most frequently with all the other non-Asian groups used for comparison: non-Hispanic whites, blacks, Hawaiians, others, and Hispanics. After intermarriage with whites, the rates of Filipino-Hispanic and Filipino-Hawaiian marriage were highest among Asian groups.

Without exception, Asian American women intermarried at significantly higher rates than men. The rates at which Asian American men intermarried was relatively low, with Vietnamese and Korean men intermarrying least frequently (at rates of 4.5 and 4.6 percent, respectively). The Filipino and Japanese groups had the highest rates for men, at 18.2 and 15.1 percent, respectively. These groups in general had longer histories in the United States and therefore a greater chance of being native-born. Chinese men were intermediate to these groups, intermarrying at a rate of 9.3 percent.[27]

Regional rates varied significantly. Kitano et al. documented much higher rates of intermarriage for women and men in a Los Angeles County sample using marriage license data for 1984 and 1989, though these figures also include interethnic marriages among Asian groups. For the decade of the 1980s in Hawaii, they find high rates, ranging from 44.8 percent for the Japanese to a high of 67.4 percent for Koreans. However, these figures include interethnic marriages among Asian groups. These regional differences may be explained by immigration patterns. A substantial number of Asian Americans in Los Angeles County are second generation or more, compared to more recent patterns of immigration from Asian Indians and Filipinos to the East Coast.

In 1982, the results of a study using Los Angeles County marriage data were released.[28] Marriages of Chinese Americans in Los Angeles County showed high rates of outmarriage for both women (46 percent) and men (35.7 percent) in the under-25 age group. These results confirmed those of a previous study using a different methodology and using

1970 Census data rather than county marriage licenses. The earlier study concluded that youth was associated with a tendency toward intermarriage, as Lee and Yamanaka also found.[29] Sung also found this result across cohorts in her study of Chinese American intermarriage in New York for 1982,[30] though within the younger cohort she found that both brides and grooms who married interracially were slightly older than their peers who married other Chinese. This finding suggests that increased age may result in more independent choices and less bowing to parental pressure. In comparing 1972 with 1982 marriage license information, Sung also found that brides and grooms in 1982 who married someone other than Chinese were even older than their counterparts a decade earlier. They also tended to have more education and hold higher-paying jobs.

In a 1986 interview study, Min found that of 560 Korean immigrants to California's Los Angeles and Orange Counties, 4.6 percent married interracially. When the outmarriage rate included other Asians, it rose to 8.2 percent. Although she interviewed only immigrants with a single clan surname, she suggests that the discrepancy between her figures and the much higher estimate of 16.5 percent made by Kitano (using Los Angeles County marriage records a few years earlier), might be due to some sampling errors in Kitano's study. She estimates that the actual figures rest somewhere between the two studies.[31]

Murguia summarized the results of several regional studies of Chicano intermarriage in Albuquerque, Los Angeles, San Antonio, and California.[32] He found that intermarriage was definitely increasing for this population and that the later the generation in the United States, the greater the likelihood of intermarriage. He found that in the three southwestern states with the highest proportion of Mexican Americans, the rates of intermarriage varied greatly, from a low in Texas (9 to 27 percent), to a middle range in New Mexico (27–39 percent), to a high in California (51–55 percent).

Fernandez and Holscher examined marriage license records in eight of the fourteen counties of Arizona containing 45 percent of the Mexican American population for 1960, 1970, and 1980.[33] They found a significant increase in the rate of intermarriage over twenty years, from 28 percent in 1960 to 39 percent in 1970 to 44 percent in 1980. These rates were higher than the rates found for a similar time frame in New Mexico.[34]

The 1990s

The 1990 Census gives us the most dramatic snapshot of our trajectory as a mixed-race nation.[35] The number of black-white marriages nearly doubled from the previous decade (121,000) to 213,000 couples. What was different in this ten-year growth pattern was that the rate of intermarriage for black women with white men, which had stayed fairly constant from 1960 to 1980, doubled, jumping to 54,000. Black husbands with white wives increased significantly, too, from 94,000 to 159,000 couples. An estimated 9.5 percent of black grooms married white brides.[36]

Other intermarriages also increased dramatically. White intermarriage with non-black partners increased from 785,000 to 1,173,000 couples, while black intermarriage with non-white partners increased from 47,000 to 75,000 couples. The statistics for black men and Asian women showed similar patterns. Almost three-fourths of intermarriages for African Americans and Asian Americans are comprised of black male-white female and white male-Asian American female pairings. These unbalanced patterns of gender and race generate several antagonisms between Asian American men and women, black men and women, black women and white women, and Asian men and white men. These antagonisms often are articulated in terms of stereotypes of race and gender and involve the displacement of blame and resentment. Balances and imbalances of sex ratios drive intermarriage to a significant degree and explain the surge in intermarriage of white men with black women in the 1990 Census.[37] Except for black women, the availability of marriageable partners within groups is fairly even.

The statistics can be misleading, depending on whether all marriages are looked at or only first-time marriages. Those who want to downplay the impact of these marriages on the American demographic landscape tend to look at all marriages together, regardless of whether they are first, second, or third marriages. For example, in 1990 blacks who were interracially married accounted for 6 percent of all married couples involving a black spouse (including same-race black couples). This change in itself is a dramatic increase from 3.4 percent in 1980, 1.9 percent in 1970, and 1.7 percent in 1960. However, if only first-time marriages are considered, 1990 figures show that 10.8 percent of marriages in which one partner was black were interracial. According to Besharov and Sullivan, in 1993 the percentage of married couples involving one black partner had doubled from the 1990 figure of 6 percent to 12.1 percent.[38] More than one in ten marriages for African American persons will be interracial. This rate of intermarriage will undoubtedly present a challenge to both black and white communities, although the most recent Gallup poll suggests that the overwhelming majority of white and black Americans approve of intermarriage.[39]

As of 1995, a Current Population Survey showed a doubling of the number of black women married to white men (122,000) compared to a decade earlier (61,000). Numbers have increased for black men and white women as well (206,000 in 1995 compared to 150,000 in 1990).[40] This trend is significant because of the dramatically decreased disparity of intermarriage between black men and women with white partners. It corroborates research findings predicting that intermarriage for black women will increase because of changes in attitudes, imbalanced sex ratios, and less emphasis on the need for similarity in class, race, or ethnicity.

David Hayes-Bautista and Gregory Rodriguez, writing for the *Los Angeles Times* in 1996, offered statistics on newlyweds in Los Angeles County that suggested a compelling trend toward mixed marriages. They note that approximately one out of five Los Angeles County generation X-ers are intermarried. They note that a white (non-Jewish) male in his twenties is four times more likely than his father to marry interracially. They also note that the rate of intermarriage for African American men in their twenties was even higher than the national average, at almost one in five marriages. One-quarter of U.S.-born Asian American women and U.S.-born Latino newlyweds in Los Angeles County have married interracially. Because of the large Latino population, Hayes-Bautista and Rodriguez find it no surprise that more than two out of three intermarriages included a Latino partner.[41]

Notes

Chapter One

1. John Welwood, *Love and Awakening: Discovering the Sacred Path of Intimate Relationship* (New York: Harper Collins, 1996).

2. See C. Harris, "Whiteness As Property," in *Black on White: Black Writers on What It Means To Be White*, ed. D. R. Roediger (New York: Shocken Books, 1998), 104–18; P. R. Spickard, *Mixed Blood: Intermarriage and Ethnic Identity in Twentieth-Century America* (Madison: University of Wisconsin Press, 1989).

3. H. L. Kitano, D. C. Fujino, and J. T. Sato, "Interracial Marriages: Where Are the Asian Americans and Where Are They Going?" in *Handbook of Asian American Psychology*, ed. L. C. Lee and N. W. Zane (Thousand Oaks, Calif.: Sage Publications, 1998), pp. 233–60.

4. See, e.g., Kitano et al., "Interracial Marriages"; Spickard, *Mixed Blood*; and M. C. Waters, *Ethnic Options: Choosing Identities in America* (Berkeley: University of California Press, 1990).

5. Hawaii boasts the highest proportion of intermarriages. However, it is a small state, and the number of these marriages is small in absolute terms compared to these other five states with large population bases.

6. Spickard, *Mixed Blood*, p. 374.

7. D. J. Besharov and T. S. Sullivan, "One Flesh: America Is Experiencing an Unprecedented Increase in Black-White Intermarriage," *New Democrat* (July/August 1996).

8. Spickard, *Mixed Blood*.

9. Michael C. Thornton, "The Quiet Immigration: Foreign Spouses of U.S. Citizens, 1945–1985," in *Racially Mixed People in America*, ed. M.P.P. Root (Thousand Oaks, Calif.: Sage Publications, 1992).

10. M. Guttentag and P. F. Secord, *Too Many Women? The Sex Ratio Question* (Beverly Hills: Sage Publications, 1983); D. L. Pagnini and S. P. Morgan, "Intermarriage and Social Distance among U.S. Immigrants at the Turn of the Century," *American Journal of Sociology* 96 (2) (1990): 405–32.

11. P. M. Blau, T. C. Blum, and J. E. Schwartz, "Heterogeneity and Intermarriage," *American Sociological Review* 47: 45–62.

12. R. Adams, *Interracial Marriage in Hawaii* (New York: Macmillan, 1969).

13. P. L. Taylor, M. B. Tucker, and C. Mitchell-Kernan, "Interethnic Marital Attitudes and Dating Patterns in Twenty-One Cities," unpublished manuscript in possession of the authors, 1998.

14. D. Fujino, "Extending Exchange Theory: Effects of Ethnicity and Gender on Asian American Heterosexual Relationships," Ph.D. diss., University of California, Los Angeles, 1992.

15. Y. L. Espiritu, *Asian American Women and Men* (Thousand Oaks, Calif.: Sage Publications, 1997). See also S. Sue and J. K. Morishima, *The Mental Health of Asian Americans* (San Francisco: Jossey-Bass, 1982).

16. P. S. Paset and R. D. Taylor, "Black and White Women's Attitudes toward Racial Marriage," *Psychological Reports* 69: 753–54. However, recent trends in black female intermarriage suggest significant increases. A recent Current Population Survey shows that the number of black women married to white men doubled between 1990 and 1995. Taylor et al. also found black women more open to intermarriage than in previous studies.

17. b. hooks, "Representations of Whiteness in the Black Imagination," in *Black on White: Black Writers on What It Means to Be White*, ed. Roediger (New York, NY: Schocken Books, 1999), pp. 38–53.

18. Z. Qian, "Breaking the Racial Barriers: Variations in Interracial Marriage between 1980 and 1990," *Demography* 34: 263–76.

19. Root, ed., *Racially Mixed People in America*.

20. For example, see M. B. Tucker and C. Mitchell-Kernan, *The Decline in Marriage among African Americans* (New York: Russell Sage Foundation, 1995); W. R. Johnson and D. M. Warren, eds., *Inside the Mixed Marriage: Accounts of Changing Attitudes, Patterns, and Perceptions of Cross-Cultural and Interracial Marriage* (Lanham, Md.: University Press of America, 1994); B. L. Sung, *Chinese American Intermarriage* (New York: Center for Migration Studies, 1990); Spickard, *Mixed Blood*; P. C. Rosenblatt, T. A. Karis, and R. D. Powell, *Multiracial Couples: Black and White Voices* (Thousand Oaks, Calif.: Sage Publications, 1995); L. R. Tenzer, *A Completely New Look at Interracial Sexuality: Public Opinion and Select Commentaries* (Manahawkin, N.J.: Scholars' Publishing House, 1990).

21. For example, J. Crohn, *Mixed Matches: How to Create Successful Interracial, Interethnic, and Interfaith Relationships* (New York: Fawcett Columbine, 1995);

H.J.B. Hamilton, *Christmas and 33 Years Inside an Interracial Family* (Self-published, 1990); F. Prinzing and A. Prinzing, *Mixed Messages: Responding to Interracial Marriage* (Chicago: Moody Press, 1991).

22. P. H. Collins, "It's All in the Family: Intersections of Gender, Race, and Nation," *Hypatia* 13 (3): 62–82. Collins argues that family is the site of original socialization to knowing one's place in several hierarchies: age, race, gender, sexual orientation, class, and so on. These variables are reflected in how we organize ourselves as a nation and in the "natural" disenfranchisement of certain groups of people.

23. I conducted all interviews prior to 1996; in 1996 two research assistants joined the project, Jaslean LaTaillade, and Valerie White, both graduate students at the time completing their doctoral degrees at the University of Washington. They conducted most of the interviews through 1997 and helped facilitate many of the focus groups for the Multiracial Families Project. Ms. White conducted most of the semi-structured interviews for the Biracial Sibling Project. In accordance with psychology ethics in research, all names and significant identifying information have been changed to protect the confidentiality of participants. These changes were made despite my knowledge that some participants would be proud to have me to use their real names. All interviewees gave written permission for their interviews to be included in this study.

24. Many couples deliberately moved to metropolitan areas where there were more interracial families.

25. There were two exceptions made in Seattle. A husband and wife participated together in one group and a lesbian couple, previously married interracially to male partners, participated together in another group.

26. They either grew up or lived in a state for an extended period of their adult life.

27. Persons were excluded who defined their relationship as long-term dating or cohabiting without a major commitment.

28. I had not made this a focus and did not feel my research was extensive enough to offer more analysis than I do. However, these interviews were immensely helpful in sorting out the conventions of marriage, the damage that betrayal and withdrawal of parental love causes to a person, and the power of love.

29. The National Spiritual Assembly of the Baha'is of the United States has been very forthcoming about racism as a "disease of the spirit" that jeopardizes all of us as citizens of the world. National Spiritual Assembly of the Baha'is of the United States, *The Vision of Race Unity: America's Most Challenging Issue* (Wilmette, Ill.: Baha'i Publishing Trust, 1991).

30. F. M. Ahern, R. E. Cole, R. C. Johnson, and B. Wong, "Personality

Attributes of Males and Females Marrying within vs. across Racial/Ethnic Groups," *Behavior Genetics* 11 (3): 181–94; Spickard, *Mixed Blood*.

31. C. Hernton, *Sex and Racism in America* (New York: Doubleday, 1965; 1988).

32. Prinzing and Prinzing, *Mixed Messages*; Crohn, *Mixed Matches*; B. Wehrly, K. R. Kenney, and M. E. Kenney, *Counseling Multiracial Families* (Thousand Oaks, Calif.: Sage Publications, 1999).

33. Harris, "Whiteness as Property"; b. hooks, "Representations of Whiteness"; G. E. Wyatt, *Stolen Women: Reclaiming Our Sexuality, Taking Back Our Lives* (New York: John Wiley, 1997).

34. Harris, "Whiteness as Property."

35. Southern Poverty Law Center, "All in the Family," *Intelligence Report* 95: 12–19.

36. Taylor et al., "Interethnic Marital Attitudes."

37. M. L. King, Jr., *Strength to Love* (New York: Harper & Row, 1963), p. 104.

38. J. D. Forbes, *Black Africans and Native Americans* (New York: Basil Blackwell, 1988). See also G. R. Daniel, "Passers and Pluralists: Subverting the Racial Divide," in *Racially Mixed People*, ed. Root (Thousand Oaks, Calif.: Sage Publications, 1992), pp. 91–107; T. P. Wilson, "Blood Quantum: Native American Mixed Bloods," in *Racially Mixed People*, ed. Root, pp. 108–25.

39. *Time Magazine*, Special Issue, fall 1993.

40. K. S. Peterson, "For Today's Teens, Race 'Not an Issue Anymore,'" *USA Today*, November 23, 1997, 1A.

41. This figure does not include other interracial pairings such as Filipino and American Indian, Vietnamese and Puerto Rican (if they counted themselves as "other" on the race question), etc.

42. D. E. Hayes-Bautista and G. Rodriguez, "L.A. County's Answer for Racial Tensions: Intermarriage," *Los Angeles Times*, May 5, 1996, M6.

43. Besharov and Sullivan, "One Flesh."

44. This insight is similar to an observation made by James Baldwin in *Notes of a Native Son* (1955): "Our dehumanization of the Negro then is indivisible from our dehumanization of ourselves; the loss of our own identity is the price we pay for our annulment of his." (Quoted in E. Ehrlich and M. De Bruhl, eds., *The International Thesaurus of Quotations* [New York: Harper Perennial, 1996] p. 58.)

45. Quoted in ibid., p. 586.

Chapter Two

1. Spickard, *Mixed Blood;* Tenzer, *A Completely New Look.*

2. Back cover of May/June 1992 issue of *Interrace Magazine.*

3. Prinzing and Prinzing, *Mixed Messages,* pp. 93–96.

4. A. Lewis, "What Does the Bible Say about Mixed Marriage?" *The Standard,* June 1997, p. 8.

5. R.J.C. Young, *Colonial Desire: Hybridity in Theory, Culture and Race* (New York: Routledge, 1995); see also L. A. Stoler, *Race and the Education of Desire: Foucault's History of Sexuality and the Colonial Order of Things* (Durham: Duke University Press, 1995).

6. A. L. Ferber, *White Man Falling: Race, Gender, and White Supremacy* (Lanham, Md.: Rowman & Littlefield, 1998), p. 29.

7. R. V. Guthrie, *Even the Rat was White* (New York: Harper and Row, 1976).

8. Darwin published his seminal work, *The Origin of Species,* in 1859. His arguments were later distorted by the Social Darwinists, who used his theories to ends for which he never intended them. Darwin wrote that "degrees of hybridity meant that species could no longer be regarded as absolutely distinct" and that varieties within a species were just that—varieties, not distinct species. Quoted in Young, *Colonial Desire,* p. 11.

9. Ibid.

10. Gobineau would further suggest that the Aryan population's tendency toward intermarriage with other populations reflected a civilizing instinct to better "lesser" races of people. Young, *Colonial Desire;* Ferber, *White Man Falling.*

11. Ibid.

12. Ferber, *White Man Falling,* p. 31.

13. Prichard noted that, if anything, there was evidence of hybrid vigor when populations mixed. He used the example of the West Indies as a geographical region in which much mixture had taken place and no evidence of infertility due to race mixing existed. Young, *Colonial Desire,* pp. 10–11.

14. Ibid., pp. 9–10. Huxley is credited with this unsupported conclusion in 1863.

15. Ibid., p. 16. Broca, reluctant to give up the hybridity theory of inferiority, proposed degrees of fertility based on the relatedness of races.

16. Although Prichard's work was less subject to prevailing pressures, subsequent editions of *The Natural History of Man* (1843) had to retract some of his conclusions. Young asserts that "degeneration was thus the final, and undoubtedly the most powerful, retort to any apparent demonstration of the fertility of mixed unions. Its triumph is marked by the fact that in 1855 the fourth edition of Prichard's *Natural History of Man* was corrected with an 'Introductory Note' on race by Edwin Norris and made consonant with Knox and Edwards' laws of 'decomposition' and of diminished fertility between dissimilar races." Ibid.

17. S. Chan, *Asian Americans: An Interpretive History* (Boston: Twayne Publishers, 1991).

18. R. Daniels, *The Politics of Prejudice: The Anti-Japanese Movement in California and the Struggle for Japanese Exclusion* (Berkeley: University of California Press, 1962), p. 49.

19. Tenzer, *A Completely New Look;* Spickard, *Mixed Blood.*

20. Spickard, *Mixed Blood*, p. 374.

21. Whether such a relationship was a mutual marriage or strictly a business arrangement to advance the agenda of England should be critically examined. The latter explanation is in line with colonial strategies for occupying lands settled by indigenous people. See Tenzer, *A Completely New Look.*

22. Chan, *Asian Americans*, pp. 116–20. In 1880, Chinese were included in California's anti-miscegenation laws along with persons of African heritage to at least three generations if there was mixture. Twenty-five years later, due to a loophole in one of the laws and the influx of Japanese, laws were amended to prohibit intermarriage between whites and Mongolians, which included Chinese, Japanese, and Koreans. From the 1920s through the 1930s, Filipino intermarriage occurred but was protested. Court challenges such as *Roldan v. Los Angeles County* declared that Filipinos were not Mongolians and were therefore not subject to the anti-miscegenation laws. Strong anti-Filipino sentiments resulted in an eventual inclusion of Malays to the register of people to whom anti-miscegenation laws applied. Filipinos were thus prohibited from intermarriage with whites.

23. C. Fernandez, personal communication.

24. Harris, "Whiteness As Property."

25. K. I. Leonard, *Making Ethnic Choices: California's Punjabi Mexican Americans* (Philadelphia: Temple University Press, 1992).

26. Daniel, "Passers and Pluralists"; J. D. Forbes, "The Manipulation of Race, Caste, and Identity: Classifying AfroAmericans, Native Americans, and Red-Black people," *Journal of Ethnic Studies* 17: 1–51; Forbes, *Black Africans;* W. L. Katz, *Black Indians.* Katz notes that historian Carter G. Woodson "wondered if Africans did not find 'among Indians one of their means to escape' from slavery," p. 5. Daniel and Forbes also emphasize that for some Indian bands, racial intermarriage was a means of survival of lineage, as numbers had dwindled.

27. F. Cordova, *Filipinos: Forgotten Asian Americans* (Dubuque, Iowa: Kendall/Hunt Publishing Co., 1993).

28. R. L. McCunn, *Wooden Fish Songs* (New York: Dutton, 1995); see also J. W. Loewen, *Mississippi Chinese: Between Black and White* (Cambridge: Harvard University Press, 1971); Cordova, *Filipinos.*

29. Chan, *Asian Americans.*

30. Tenzer, "A Completely New Look."

31. Wyatt, *Stolen Women.*

32. b. hooks, "Representations of Whiteness."

33. C. C. Hernton, *Sex and Racism in America* (New York: Doubleday, 1965; 1988).

34. Ferber, *White Man Falling.* Ferber provides a cogent and well-illustrated analysis of white men's vigilance and the ways in which it continues to support white supremacist thinking and activity. *The Turner Diaries,* published by a white supremacist, provide a terrifying, uncensored window into white supremacist thinking on interracial alliance. It is riddled with paranoia, white privilege, anxiety, and evil paralleling the content abundant in white supremacist newsletters. See A. Macdonald, *The Turner Diaries* (New York: Barricade Books, 1978; 1996).

35. Quoted in R. Andrews, *Concise Columbia Dictionary of Quotations* (New York: Avon Books, 1987), p. 219.

36. Food references are also common in derogatory comments to and about mixed-race persons, e.g., apples, oreos, mixed nuts, milkshakes.

37. M. L. Wong, "An Act of Revenge: Toying with Race, Passions, Desire and Danger" (paper presented at the annual meeting of the American Psychological Association, Toronto, Canada, 1994).

38. Tenzer found that a significant number of white women in his survey felt that white men had irrational conclusions about their sexuality in reference to black men. White women who had dated black men thought that there was a significant myth built around black men's sexuality. See also F. Fanon, *Black Skin, White Masks* (New York: Grove, 1967).

39. Hernton, *Sex and Racism.*

40. S. J. Whitfield, *A Death in the Delta: The Story of Emmett Till* (New York: Free Press, 1988).

41. Of course, violence to prevent border crossing continues today in a much less visible way. Hernton notes that when President Clinton's confidant, Vernon Jordan, was shot in 1983 in what appeared to be a racially motivated shooting, little press was given to the incident. These incidents are often not covered by the media unless they are even more unusual—e.g., the Jasper, Texas, incident of 1998 in which a black man was dragged by car to his death by a white man. Hernton, *Sex and Racism.*

42. R. T. Michael et al., *Sex in America: A Definitive Survey* (New York: Warner Books, 1994).

43. *Gallup Poll Monthly,* "For the first time, more Americans approve of interracial marriage than disapprove," no. 311: 60–64.

44. C. Astor, "Gallup Poll: Progress in Black/White Relations, But Race Is Still an Issue," *USIA Electronic Journal* 2 (August 1997).

45. Adams, *Interracial Marriage in Hawaii*.

46. M. B. Tucker and C. Mitchell-Kernan, "New Trends in Black American Interracial Marriage: The Social Structural Context," *Journal of Marriage and the Family* 52: 209–18.

47. Ralph Ellison wrote an insightful essay articulating the linkage between the prosperity of white America and African Americans: "What America Would Be Like without Blacks," in *Black on White*, ed. Roediger.

48. C. A. Fernandez, "Government Classification of Multiracial/Multiethnic People," in *The Multiracial Experience: Racial Borders As the New Frontier*, ed. M.P.P. Root (Thousand Oaks, Calif.: Sage Publications, 1996), pp. 15–36. Within the African American community, a class system was symbolized in part by colorism, discrimination based upon skin color with both preferential treatment for lighter skinned black persons and suspicion of lighter skinned black persons. See Daniel, "Passers and Pluralists."

49. A. W. Boykin, "The Triple Quandary and the Schooling of Afro-American Children," in *The School Achievement of Minority Children* (Hillsdale, N.J.: Lawrence Erlbaum, 1985).

50. P. vanden Berghe, *Race and Racism: A Comparative Perspective* (New York: John Wiley, 1967).

51. J. M. Jones, *Prejudice and Racism* (New York: McGraw Hill, 1997; 2d ed.).

52. In a system that is based on the imagined differences alleged to stem from differences in physical appearance, persons who are the product of inter-caste unions are deemed mistakes and, except for a period in the late nineteenth century in which the census enumerated the black-white mixed population, this slowly growing population has been relegated to the ranks of invisibility in much discourse on race. In order to have social standing, whether by class or caste, a person of mixed heritage has historically had to choose a single alliance and identity.

53. She constructs her daughter as naïve and innocent, a construction that was also used to justify cruelty against black men, as depicted in the 1915 film *Birth of a Nation*.

54. From the musical *South Pacific*.

55. Quoted in Ehrlich and De Bruhl, eds., *Thesaurus of Quotations*, p. 227.

56. T. W. Adorno et al., *The Authoritarian Personality* (New York: Norton, 1950; 1969; abridged ed.); M. Omi and H. Winant, *Racial Formation in the United States from the 1960s to the 1980s* (New York: Routledge & Kegan Paul, 1986); J. Salzman et al., eds., *Bridges and Boundaries: African Americans and American Jews* (New York: George Braziller and the Jewish Museum, 1992).

57. E. Goffman, *Stigma: Notes on the Management of Spoiled Identity* (New York: Simon and Schuster, 1963).

58. E. Said, *Orientalism* (New York: Random House, 1978); Young, *Colonial Desire;* see also Stoler, *Race and the Education of Desire.*

59. Ferber, *White Man Falling,* p. 102.

60. Harris, "Whiteness as Property," p. 107.

61. Hernton, *Sex and Racism.*

62. R. Frankenberg, *White Women, Race Matters: The Social Construction of Whiteness* (Minneapolis: University of Minnesota Press, 1993); F. W. Twine, "Heterosexual Alliances: The Romantic Management of Racial Identity," in *The Multiracial Experience,* ed. Root.

63. P. R. Spickard, "Injustice Compounded: Amerasians and Non-Japanese Americans in World War II Concentration Camps," in *Ethnic History* 5 (2): 5–22.

64. Ibid., p. 7.

65. Said, *Orientalism;* Ferber, *White Man Falling;* Young, *Colonial Desire.* It should also be noted that dominant nations are gendered as male, and specifically as white and heterosexual, which explains the political statement in Henry David Hwang's *M. Butterfly,* in which the Asian female object of white male desire turns out to be male. Countries to be dominated are cast as feminine and as needing the "protection" of the colonizer.

66. V. H. Houston, "To the Colonizer Go the Spoils: Amerasian Progeny in Vietnam War Films and Owning Up to the Gaze," *Amerasia Journal* 23 (1): 69–85.

67. Consider DuBois's list of the black intellectual elite referred to as the talented 10th—all but one of the people on this list was of mixed parentage, but all were identified as black. The black community has long accepted this convention as other historical figures portrayed solely as black were also of mixed heritage: W.E.B. DuBois, Frederick Douglass, Sojourner Truth, Crispus Attucks, Malcolm X.

68. F. J. Davis, *Who is Black? One Nation's Definition* (University Park: Pennsylvania State University Press, 1991).

69. This applied to Homer Plessy in the landmark case *Plessy v. Ferguson.* Plessy was deemed black by virtue of one great-grandparent's African heritage. Also see the politics of mixed race as it illustrates the power of one-drop rules in Daniel's "Passers and Pluralists" and J. Williamson's *New People: Miscegenation and Mulattoes in the United States* (New York: New York University Press, 1984).

70. M. L. King, Jr., *The Strength to Love* (New York: Harper & Row, 1963), p. 114.

Chapter Three

1. R. K. Merton, "Intermarriage and the Social Structure: Fact and Theory," *Psychiatry* 4: 362.

2. Ibid., 368.

3. Social class is defined as whatever is deemed relevant that defines someone outside the social group.

4. L. Berman, *Jews and Intermarriage* (New York: Thomas Yoseloff, 1968).

5. D. M. Heer, "Negro-White Marriages in the United States," *Journal of Marriage and the Family* 28: 262–73; D. M. Heer, "The Prevalence of Black-White Marriage in the United States, 1960 and 1970," *Journal of Marriage and the Family* 36: 246–58.

6. Johnson, through the longitudinal Hawaii Family Study of Cognitions, has extensively researched interracial families and the same conclusions on the mainland applied to interracial couples do not hold. This discrepancy is attributed to a different history and construction of race in Hawaii. See Ahern et al., "Personality Attributes"; C. T. Nagoshi, R. C. Johnson, and K.A.M. Honbo, "Assortative Mating for Cognitive Abilities, Personality, and Social Attitudes: Offspring from the Hawaii Family Study of Cognition," *Personality and Individual Differences* 13 (1992): 883–91; H. O., F. L., and R. C. Johnson, "Intraethnic and Interethnic Marriage and Divorce in Hawaii," *Social Biology* 37: 44–51; Adams, *Interracial Marriage;* Spickard, *Mixed Blood.*

7. R. C. Johnson, "On the Meaning of Being Local" (unpublished manuscript).

8. R. C. Johnson, "Group Income and Group Size as Influences on Marriage Patterns in Hawaii," *Social Biology* 31: 101–7.

9. Spickard, *Mixed Blood.*

10. R. E. Park, Foreword to Adams, *Interracial Marriage,* pp. xiii–xiv.

11. R. K. Merton, "Intermarriage and the Social Structure," 366–67.

12. J. Ogbu, "Black Education: A Cultural-Ecological Perspective," in *Black Families,* ed. H. P. McAdoo, 2d ed. (Thousand Oaks, Calif.: Sage Publications, 1988), pp. 169–84.

13. See E. Cose, *Rage of the Privileged Class* (New York: Harper Perennial, 1993).

14. Fujino, "Extending Exchange Theory."

15. Merton, "Intermarriage and the Social Structure," 367.

16. Ibid.

17. When Merton developed his theory in the late 1930s and early 1940s, there were few upper-class black people, and only a small black middle class existed.

18. Sung, *Chinese American Intermarriage*; C. Fernandez and L. Holscher, "Chicano-Anglo Intermarriage in Arizona, 1960–1980: An Exploratory Study of Eight Counties," *Hispanic Journal of Behavioral Sciences* 5 (3): 291–304.

19. K. Jester, "Analytic Essay: Intercultural and Interracial Marriage," in *Intermarriage in the United States,* ed G. Cretser and J. Leon (New York: Haworth Press, 1982).

20. C. J. Falicov, "Cross-Cultural Marriages," in *Clinical Handbook of Marital Therapy,* ed. N. S. Jacobson and A. S. Gurman (New York: Guilford), pp. 429–50.

21. Fujino, "Extending Exchange Theory."

22. Hernton, *Sex and Racism.*

23. Fanon, *Black Skin, White Masks,* p. 159.

24. Tenzer, *A Completely New Look.*

25. P. H. Collins, *Black Feminist Thought: Knowledge, Consciousness, and the Politics of Empowerment* (New York: Routledge, 1990), p. 77. This was one reason why black women were outraged by the Moynihan Report's depiction of black women. See P. Giddings, *When and Where I Enter: The Impact of Black Women on Race and Sex in America* (New York: Bantam Books, 1984).

26. V. H. Houston, "To the Colonizer Goes the Spoils: American Progeny in Vietnam War Films and Owning Up to the Gaze," *Amerasia Journal* 23 (1): 69–85; G. Marchetti, *Romance and the "Yellow Peril:" Race, Sex, and Discursive Strategies in Hollywood Fiction* (Berkeley: University of California Press, 1993).

27. Fanon, *Black Skin, White Masks,* 83–108.

28. Ibid., p. 93.

29. Ibid., p. 63.

30. E. Porterfield, "Black-American Intermarriage in the United States," *Marriage and Family Review* 5: 17–34.

31. An early example of this conclusion is found in E. Porterfield, *Black and White Mixed Marriages* (Chicago: Nelson-Hall, 1978). This study is based on ethnographic methodology. Empirical studies are provided by Ahern et al., "Personality Attributes"; Nagoshi et al., "Assortative Mating."

32. E. S. Bogardus, *Social Distance* (Yellow Springs, Ohio: Antioch Press, 1959).

33. M. M. Gordon, *Assimilation in American Life* (New York: Oxford University Press, 1964).

34. S. M. Lee and K. Yamanaka, "Patterns of Asian American Intermarriage and Marital Assimilation," *Journal of Comparative Family Studies* 21 (2): 287–305.

35. Fujino, "Extending Exchange Theory," p. 21.

36. R. D. Alba and R. M. Golden, "Patterns of Ethnic Marriage in the United States," *Social Forces* 65: 202–23.

37. Fernandez and Holscher, "Chicano-Anglo Intermarriage."

38. N. Salgado de Snyder and A. M. Padilla, "Interethnic Marriages of Mexican Americans after Nearly Two Decades," *Human Organization* 41: 359–62.

39. Nagoshi et al., "Assortative Mating."

40. Alba and Golden, "Patterns of Ethnic Marriage."

41. Blau et al. "Heterogeneity and Intermarriage."

42. T. C. Blum, "Racial Inequality and Salience: An Examination of Blau's Theory of Social Structure," *Social Forces* 62 (3): 607–17.

43. Blau et al., "Intersecting Social Affiliations and Intermarriage," *Social Forces* 62 (3): 585–606.

44. V. Garcia, "La Chicana, Chicano Movement and Women's Liberation," in *Chicana Feminist Thought: The Basic Historical Writings,* ed. A. M. Garcia (New York: Routledge, 1997), pp. 199–201.

45. Porterfield, *Black and White Mixed Marriages.*

46. See W. E. Cross, Jr., *Shades of Black: Diversity in African American Identity* (Philadelphia: Temple University Press, 1991); J. E. Helms, *Black and White Racial Identity: Theory, Research and Practice* (New York: Greenwood Press, 1990); and T. A. Parham and J. E. Helms, "Relation of Racial Identity Attitudes to Self-Actualization and Affective States of Black Students," *Journal of Counseling Psychology* 32 (2): 431–40.

47. Garcia, "La Chicano, Chicano Movement."

48. *Gallup Poll Monthly:* "More Americans approve," no. 311, pp. 60–64.

49. N. Kibria, "Vietnamese Families," in *Minority Families in the United States,* ed. R. L. Taylor, 2d ed., pp. 176–88.

50. N. Kibria, *Family Tightrope: The Changing Lives of Vietnamese Americans* (Princeton: Princeton University Press, 1993).

51. Staples, "Race and Marital Status."

52. Staples suggests that the greater number of black women in higher education was driven in part by the relative lack of job options available to black women, so that daughters were encouraged to attend college. Ibid; see also R. Staples, *The World of Black Singles* (Westport, Conn.: Greenwood Press, 1981).

53. Guttentag and Secord, *Too Many Women?*

54. Some prejudices may be suspended in order to satisfy sexual attraction and desire, but they can still remain just beneath the surface. Sometimes people rationalize that their lover is an "exception to the rule" for his or her race.

55. Spickard, *Mixed Blood.*

56. L. R. Gordon, "Race, Sex, and Matrices of Desire in an Antiblack World: An Essay in Phenomenology and Social Role," in *Race/Sex: Their Sameness, Difference, and Interplay* (New York: Routledge, 1997), pp. 119–32.

57. Guttentag and Secord, *Too Many Women?*

58. Ibid., p. 23.

59. Ibid., p. 190.

60. Ibid., p. 182.

61. Collins, *Black Feminist Thought.*

62. Ahern et al., "Personality Attributes"; Nagoshi et al., "Assortative Mating." These researchers found that a large cohort of intermarried Asian women in Hawaii tended to be more independent and essentially different in ways that facilitated their ability to make decisions to move outside the in-group for marriage. Anecdotally, this seems to be the case for many Filipina women who enter into correspondence marriages. Their independence is often overlooked or not understood by their husbands-to-be.

63. Guttentag and Secord, *Too Many Women?*

64. A. B. Chapman, "Male-Female Relations: How the Past Affects the Present," in *Black families,* ed. McAdoo.

65. Staples, *The World of Black Singles.*

66. J. Heiss, "Women's Values Regarding Marriage and the Family," in *Black Families,* ed. McAdoo.

Chapter Four

1. If we add to this figure the smaller number of interracial marriages between people of color not involving a black partner, the figures increase slightly and justify rounding up the numbers as I have done. U.S. Bureau of the Census, Current Population Reports, Series P20, "Household and Family Characteristics: March 1994," Fertility and Family Statistic Branch (303), 457-2465.

2. R. Sanjek, "Intermarriage and the Future of the Races in the United States," in *Race,* ed. S. Gregory and R. Sanjek (New Brunswick, N.J.: Rutgers University Press, 1994), p. 114.

3. C. Astor, Gallup Poll, 1997.

4. National Opinion Research Center (NORC-GSS).

5. Ibid.

6. Rosenblatt et al., *Multiracial Couples,* pp. 76–77.

7. P. C. Rosenblatt and T. A. Karis, "Family Distancing Following a Fatal Farm Accident," *Omega* 28: 183–200.

8. Porterfield, *Black and White Mixed Marriages*; M. Ramirez III, *Psychology of the Americas: Mestizo Perspectives and Mental Health* (New York: Pergamon Press, 1983); Rosenblatt et al., *Multiracial Couples;* Sung, *Chinese American Intermarriage.*

9. N. G. Brown and R. E. Douglass, "Making the Invisible Visible: The Growth of Community Network Organizations," in *The Multiracial Experience,* ed. Root, pp. 323–40.

10. *Seattle Post-Intelligencer* (July 8, 1998), "Race Advisory Board Rejects Idea of 'Colorblind' Society," C3.

Chapter Five

1. National Opinion Research Center (NORC), 1990.

2. J. Faulkner and G. K. Kich, "Assessment and Engagement Stages in Therapy with the Interracial Family," in *Cultural Perspectives in Family Therapy,* ed. J. C. Hansen and C. J. Falicov (Rockville, Md.: Aspen Systems Corp., 1983) pp. 78–90.

3. This group demonstrated how prejudices can be formed from one intense experience. None of the women had previously had much contact with non-white people. This intense contact with their ex-spouse and family resulted in conditioned fear and anger which subsequently generalized beyond the ex-partner or his family to other members of the same race. This overgeneralizing is symptomatic of a post-trauma response in which the individual is hyper-alert to a danger signal—some aspect of physical racial difference became the signal that turned on this alert and generated the fearful response. All of the women recognized that their fearful response was overgeneralized.

4. Adorno et al., *The Authoritarian Personality,* pp. 148–49.

5. D. Young-Ware and D. Ware, "An Interracial Developmental Model: A Thoughtful Presentation of the Components of Developing an Interracial Couple Relationship and Identity," *Interrace* 8 (3): 12–13.

6. Rosenblatt et al., *Multiracial Couples.* These authors indicated a similar finding in their study of black-white couples.

7. Frankenberg, *White Women, Race Matters;* Helms, *Black and White Racial Identity.*

8. Ibid.

9. C. Gallagher, "White Reconstruction in the University," *Socialist Review* 24 (1/2): 165–87.

10. Tucker and Mitchell-Kernan, "New Trends in Black American Interracial Marriage."

11. M. B. Tucker and C. Mitchell-Kernan, "New Trends in African American Interracial Marriage and Dating: Data from Southern California" (paper presented at the Nineteenth Annual Conference of the National Association for Ethnic Studies, Pomona, California, 1991).

Chapter Six

1. Faulkner and Kich, "Assessment and Engagement Stages in Therapy"; see also Crohn, *Mixed Matches*, which discusses the tensions in families and between couples and suggests ways to evaluate and work through major conflicts around these issues. Rosenblatt et al. in *Multiracial Couples* discuss how the opposition works and examine the issue of torn loyalties when conflicts arise. For a discussion of counseling, see Wehrly et al., *Counseling Multiracial Families.*

2. Harris, "Whiteness As Property."

3. Heer, "Negro-White Marriages in the United States."

4. G. Simmel, *Conflict and the Web of Group Affiliations* (New York: Free Press, 1908;1955). Simmel's work laid the foundation for Blau's work on macrostructural features that help account for intermarriage.

5. T. Monahan, "Interracial Marriage in a Southern Area: Maryland, Virginia, and the District of Columbia," *Journal of Comparative Family Studies* 8: 217–41.

6. Tucker and Mitchell-Kernan, "New Trends in Black American Interracial Marriage."

7. This 9 percent figure is a surprise because the Hispanic/Latino group in general has a high rate of intermarriage with Anglos.

8. N. Branden, "A Vision of Romantic Love," in *The Psychology of Love*, ed. R. J. Sternberg and M. L. Barnes (New Haven: Yale University Press), p. 220.

9. E. K. Rothman, *Hands and Hearts: A History of Courtship in America* (New York: Basic Books), p. 11.

10. R. J. Sternberg, *Love Is a Story: A New Theory of Relationships* (New York: Oxford University Press, 1998).

11. Branden, *A Vision of Romantic Love*, p. 224–25.

12. Heer, "The Prevalence of Black-White Marriage"; P. C. Glick, "Demographic Pictures of Black Families," in *Black Families*, ed. McAdoo.

13. Glick, "Demographic Pictures of Black Families."

14. R. C. Johnson and C. Nagoshi, "Intergroup Marriage in Hawaii," *Social Biology.*

15. See Berman, *Jews and Intermarriage;* Crohn, *Mixed Matches;* Prinzing

and Prinzing, *Mixed Messages;* Rosenblatt et al., *Multiracial Couples;* Spickard, *Mixed Blood;* Wehrly et al., *Counseling Multiracial Families.*

16. Quoted in Erlich and de Bruhl, eds., *Thesaurus of Quotations,* p. 143.

17. Quoted in ibid., p. 141.

Chapter Seven

1. D. Senna, *Caucasia* (New York: Riverhead Books, Penguin Putnam, 1998), pp. 335–36.

2. Few children of intermarriage were interviewed for the intermarriage study. To supplement their perspectives, I drew on interviews with more than sixty people who participated in the Biracial Sibling Project, which I conducted in Seattle from 1997 to 1998.

3. M. T. Reddy, *Crossing the Color Line: Race, Parenting, and Culture* (New Brunswick, N.J.: Rutgers University Press, 1994).

4. R. C. King, "Multiraciality Reigns Supreme?: Mixed Race Japanese Americans and the Cherry Blossom Queen Pageant," *Amerasia* 23 (1): 113–29.

5. Daniel, "Passers and Pluralists."

6. Frankenberg, *White Women, Race Matters;* Helms, *Black and White Racial Identity.*

7. See Root, ed., *Racially Mixed People in America* and *The Multiracial Experience.*

8. For a collective of narratives from young people of different racial combinations, see P. F. Gaskins, *What Are You? Voices of Mixed-Race Young People* (New York, Henry Holt, 1999). For young adult to early-middle-age black-white voices, see L. Funderburg, *Black, White, Other: Biracial Americans Talk about Race and Identity* (New York: William Morrow, 1994).

9. P. F. Gaskins, *What Are You?*

10. J. Jacobs, "Identity Development in Biracial Children," in *Racially Mixed People in America,* ed. Root, pp. 190–206.

11. See J. M. Dimas, "Psycho-Social Adjustment in Children of Inter-ethnic Families: The Relationship to Cultural Behavior and Ethnic Identity," Ph.D. diss., University of California, Berkeley; P. F. Gaskins, *What Are You?*; D. J. Johnson, "Developmental Pathways: Toward an Ecological Theoretical Formulation of Race Identity in Black-White children," in *Racially Mixed People in America,* ed. Root, pp. 37–49; R. L. Miller, "The Human Ecology of Multiracial Identity," in *Racially Mixed People in America,* ed. Root, pp. 24–36; M.P.P. Root, "The Biracial Baby Boom: Understanding Ecological Constructions of Racial Identity in the 21st Century," in *Racial and Ethnic Identity in School Practices: Aspects of Human Development,* ed. R. H. Sheets and E. R. Hollins (Mahwah, N.J.: Lawrence Erlbaum, 1999); C. W. Stephan, "Mixed-Heritage Individuals:

Ethnic Identity and Trait Characteristics," in *Racially Mixed People in America,* ed. Root, pp. 50–63; J. E. Trimble, "Social Psychological Perspectives on Changing Self-identification among American Indian and Alaska Natives," in *Handbook of Cross-Cultural/Multicultural Personality Assessment,* ed. R. H. Dana (Mahwah, N.J.: Lawrence Erlbaum, 1999).

12. P. F. Gaskins, *What Are You?* See also Root, "The Biracial Baby Boom"; N. Rodriguez et al., "The Transmission of Family Values across Generations of Mexican, Mexican American, and Anglo Amerian Families: Implications for Mental Health," in *Racial and Ethnic Identity in School Practices: Aspects of Human Development* (Mahwah, N.J.: Lawrence Erlbaum, 1999), pp. 141–56; W. E. Cross et al., "African American Identity Development across the Life Span: Educational Implications," in ibid., pp. 29–48; R. H. Sheets, "Human Development and Ethnic Identity," in ibid., pp. 91–105.

13. Ferber, *White Man Falling;* Frankenberg, *White Women, Race Matters.*

14. Some issues on parenting are touched upon by Crohn, *Mixed Matches;* Reddy, *Crossing the Colorline;* Rosenblatt et al., *Multiracial Couples;* and Wehrly et al., *Counseling Multiracial Families.*

15. G. K. Kich, "The Developmental Process of Asserting a Biracial, Bicultural Identity," in *Racially Mixed People in America,* ed. Root, pp. 304–17. See also N. Zack, ed., *American Mixed Race: The Culture of Microdiversity* (Lanham, Md.: Rowman & Littlefield); Reddy, *Crossing the Colorline;* K. Gay, *I Am Who I Am: Speaking Out about Multiracial Identity* (New York: Franklin Watts, 1995); G. Kaeser and P. Gillespie, *Of Many Colors: Portraits of Multiracial Families* (Amherst: University of Massachusetts Press, 1997).

16. M.P.P. Root, "Experiences and Processes Affecting Racial Identity Development: Preliminary Results from the Biracial Sibling Project," *Cultural Diversity and Mental Health* 4: 237–47.

17. M.P.P. Root, "Resolving 'Other' Status: Identity Development of Biracial Individuals," in *Diversity and Complexity in Feminist Therapy,* ed. L. S. Brown and M.P.P. Root (New York: Haworth Press, 1990), pp. 185–205.

18. M.P.P. Root, "Mixed-race Women," in *Women of Color: Integrating Ethnic and Gender Identities in Psychotherapy,* ed. L. Comas-Diaz and B. Greene (New York: Guilford Press), pp. 455–78.

19. Twine, "Heterosexual Alliances"; Frankenberg, *White Women, Race Matters.*

20. Root, "Resolving 'Other' Status."

21. Root, "Experiences and Processes Affecting Racial Identity Development."

22. M. C. Thornton et al., "Sociodemographic and Environmental Correlates of Racial Socialization by Black Parents," *Child Development* 61: 401–9. These authors found that racial socialization of black children by their

parents occurred more frequently with older parents, with mothers more often than with fathers, and with married parents more often than with single parents. They found that education and living in mixed-race neighborhoods was also associated with more overt socialization around race. The socialization was intended both to motivate children to work hard and to prepare them for oppressive environments.

23. Frankenberg, *White Women, Race Matters.*

24. Root, "Resolving 'Other' Status"; Root, "Mixed-race Women."

25. Root, "Experiences and Processes Affecting Racial Identity Development."

26. Root, "Resolving 'Other' Status"; see also Root, "Experiences and Processes Affecting Racial Identity Development."

27. There are numerous articles on this topic. Hair texture, hair color, eye shape, leg length, freckles, skin color, eye color, features that are typically used to gauge race, are often the object of change. See Root, "Resolving 'Other' Status."

28. See Root, *Racially Mixed People in America;* Root, *The Multiracial Experience;* Zack, *American Mixed Race;* C. Camper, *Miscegenation Blues: Voices of Mixed Race Women* (Toronto: Sister Vision Press, 1994); P. F. Gaskins, *What Are You?*

29. M.P.P. Root, "Factors Influencing the Variation in Racial and Ethnic Identity of Mixed Heritage Persons of Asian Ancestry," in *Reconfiguring Race, Re-articulating Ethnicity: Multiracial Identity and Asian America,* ed. T. K. Williams and C. Nakashima (Philadelphia: Temple University Press, forthcoming).

30. Waters, *Ethnic Options;* Root, "Variation in Racial and Ethnic Identity."

31. Waters, *Ethnic Options.*

32. Stephan found this in her Hawaii sample of mixed-heritage people; see her "Mixed-Heritage Individuals."

33. Root, "Experiences and Processes Affecting Racial Identity Development."

34. C.C.I. Hall, "The Ethnic Identity of Racially Mixed People: A Study of Black-Japanese," Ph.D. diss., University of California, Los Angeles; T. K. Williams, "Prism Lives: Identity of Binational Amerasians," in *Racially Mixed People in America,* ed. Root.

35. Root, *The Multiracial Experience;* M.P.P. Root, "A Bill of Rights for Racially Mixed People," in *The Multiracial Experience,* ed. Root, pp. 3–14.

36. Fernandez, "Government Classification of Multiracial/Multiethnic People."

37. D. A. Ramirez, "Multiracial Identity in a Color-Conscious World," in *The Multiracial Experience,* ed. Root, pp. 49–62. See also J. R. Goldstein and A. J. Morning, "The Multiple-Race Population of the United States: Issues

and Estimates," *PNAS* 97 (11): 6230–35. Based on results from the 1995 Current Population Survey, these researchers suggest that the number of people likely to identify themselves by more than one race will range from 3.1 to 6.6 percent of the U.S. population, tripling or quadrupling previous estimates of the number of people who will use the multiple check off option on the 2000 Census. This means between 8 and 18 million people identifying themselves as multiracial.

38. S. R. Graham, "The Real World," in ibid., pp. 37–48.

39. Root, "Resolving 'Other' Status."

40. Leonard, *Making Ethnic Choices*.

41. Stephan, "Mixed Heritage Individuals."

42. L. Comas-Diaz, "LatiNegra: Mental Health Issues of African Latinas," in *The Multiracial Experience*, ed. Root, pp. 167–90.

43. Root, "Resolving 'Other' Status."

44. J. R. Weisman, "An 'Other' Way of Life: The Empowerment of Alterity in the Interracial Individual," in *The Multiracial Experience*, ed. Root, pp. 152–64.

45. Quoted in Erlich and de Bruhl, eds., T*hesaurus of Quotations*, p. 563.

46. Quoted in Andrews, *Dictionary of Quotations*, p. 167.

Chapter Eight

1. A. Hurtado, *The Color of Privilege: Three Blasphemies on Race and Feminism* (Ann Arbor: The University of Michigan Press, 1996), p. 33.

2. Ferber, *White Man Falling*.

3. N. Zack, *Race/Sex" Their Sameness, Difference, and Interplay* (New York: Routledge, 1997).

4. Sanjek, "Intermarriage," p. 103.

5. H. L. Gates, Jr., *Thirteen Ways of Looking at a Black Man* (New York: Vintage Books, 1997), pp. 207–8.

6. *Seattle Post-Intelligencer,* "Race Advisory Board."

7. H. Ball, *A Defiant Life: Thurgood Marshall and the Persistence of Racism in America* (New York, Crown Publishers, 1998); I. Bernstein, *Guns or Butter: The Presidency of Lyndon Johnson* (New York: Oxford University Press, 1996).

8. Adorno et al., *The Authoritarian Personality*.

9. G. W. Allport, *The Nature of Prejudice* (Reading, Mass.: Addison-Wesley, 1954; 1979).

10. Ibid., p. 221.

11. hooks, "Representing Whiteness."

12. Spickard, *Mixed Blood*.

13. Ball, *A Defiant Life*.

14. Frankenburg, *White Women, Race Matters.*

15. Spickard, *Mixed Blood;* Wyatt, *Stolen Women.*

16. Waters, *Ethnic Options.*

17. b. hooks, *All about Love: New Visions* (New York, William Morrow, 2000).

18. Quoted in Erlich and de Bruhl, eds., *Thesaurus of Quotations*, p. 411.

19. Ibid., p. 143.

20. R. J. Sternberg, "A Triangular Theory of Love," *Psychological Review* 93: 119–35.

21. K. Prager, *The Psychology of Intimacy* (New York: Guilford Press, 1995), pp. 259–66.

22. Welwood, *Love and Awakening.*

23. Tucker and Mitchell-Kernan, "New Trends in Black American Interracial Marriage."

24. Nagoshi et al., "Assortative Mating"; see also Ahern et al., "Personality Attributes."

25. S. Peele, "Fools for Love: The Romantic Ideal, Psychological Theory, and Addictive Love," in *The Psychology of Love,* ed. R. J. Sternberg and M. L. Barnes (New Haven: Yale University Press, 1988), pp. 179–82, a review of some of the earlier work of Peele and Brodsky.

26. Earl of Harewood and Antony Peattie, eds., *The New Kobbe's Opera Book* (New York, Putnam, 1997), p. 610.

Appendix

1. U.S. Bureau of the Census, 1960, "Marital Status," PC (2) 4E.

2. M. C. Thornton, "The Quiet Immigration: Foreign Spouses of U.S. Citizens, 1945–1985," in *Racially Mixed People in America,* ed. Root, pp. 64–76.

3. Chan, *Asian Americans.*

4. A common Japanese saying is, "A light skin makes up for seven flaws." Colorism exists in many of the communities that have been exposed to colonization. In Asian countries, darker skin is associated with manual labor and exposure to the sun. This type of work is consider to be of a lower status and skin color becomes a code for assumed characteristics, including intelligence and refinement.

5. J. T. Fitzpatrick, *Puerto Rican Americans: The Meaning of Migration to the Mainland* (Englewood Cliffs, N.J.: Prentice-Hall, 1971).

6. Garcia, "La Chicana, Chicano Movement."

7. F. Mittelbach et al., "Intermarriage of Mexican Americans," *Mexican American Study Project Advance Report No. 6* (November) (Los Angeles: University of California, 1966).

8. J. N. Tinker, "Intermarriage and Assimilation in a Rural Society: Japanese Americans in the U.S.," in *Intermarriage in the United States*, ed. G. A. Cretser and J. J. Leon (New York: Haworth Press, 1982), pp. 61–74.

9. Kitano et al., "Interracial Marriages."

10. Ibid.

11. Thornton, "The Quiet Immigration," pp. 69–72, Tables 6.2 and 6.3.

12. U.S. Bureau of the Census, 1970; "Marital Status," PC (2) 4C, Table 12.

13. J. T. Fitzpatrick and D. T. Gurak, *Hispanic Intermarriage in New York City: 1975* (New York: Fordham University Hispanic Research Center).

14. Ibid.

15. L. Perez, "Cuban American families," in *Minority Families in the United States*, ed. R. L. Taylor, 2d ed. (Upper Saddle River, N.J.: Prentice Hall), pp. 108–24.

16. Kitano et al., "Interracial Marriages."

17. Ibid.

18. A. Kikumura and H. Kitano, "Interracial Marriage: A Picture of the Japanese Americans," *Journal of Social Issues* 29 (2): 67–81.

19. Tinker, "Intermarriage and Ethnic boundaries."

20. Kitano et al., "Interracial Marriages."

21. H. L. Kitano, *Race Relations* (Englewood Cliffs, N.J.: Prentice Hall, 1988).

22. Thornton, "The Quiet Immigration," pp. 69–72, Tables 6.2 and 6.3.

23. U.S. Bureau of the Census, 1980, "Marital Characteristics," PC80-2-4C.

24. Lee and Yamanaka, "Patterns of Asian American Intermarriage." Glick's analysis of the 1980 Census data suggests that 3.4 percent of marriages involving a black partner were black-white couples and .3 percent of white couples were involved in a black-white marriage. The difference might be attributed to higher percentages when first marriages are considered versus all marriages. Glick, "Demographic Pictures of Black Families," p. 123.

25. Glick, "Demographic Pictures of Black Families," p. 123.

26. M. Yellowbird and C. M. Snipp, "American Indian Families," in *Minority Families in the United States*, ed. Taylor.

27. Kitano et al., "Interracial Marriages."

28. H. L. Kitano and L. K. Yeung, "Chinese Interracial Marriage," in *Intermarriage in the United States*, ed. Cretser and Leon. These figures are higher than the rates for interracial marriage because they also include some interethnic marriage, e.g., Chinese married to Japanese, though these figures do not change the trend or the significance of the high percentage of intermarriage.

29. D. Y. Yuan, "Significant Demographic Characteristics of Chinese Who Intermarry in the United States," *California Sociologist* 3 (2): 184–96.

30. Sung, "Chinese American Intermarriage."

31. P. G. Min, "Korean Immigrants' Marital Patterns and Marital Adjustments," in *Family Ethnicity*, ed. McAdoo; H. L. Kitano and L. K. Chai, "Korean Interracial Marriage," *Marriage and Family Review* 5: 35–48.

32. E. Murguia, *Chicano Intermarriages: A Theoretical and Empirical Study* (San Antonio: Trinity University Press, 1982).

33. Fernandez and Holscher, "Chicano-Anglo Intermarriage."

34. L. M. Holscher, "Chicano Exogamous Marriages in New Mexico," paper presented at the annual meeting of the Pacific Sociological Association, Anaheim, California, 1979.

35. U.S. Bureau of the Census, 1990, "Characteristics of the Black Population," CP-3-6.

36. Besharov and Sullivan, "One Flesh."

37. Guttentag and Secord, *Too Many Women?* See also C. K. Cheng, and D. S. Yamamura, "Interracial Marriage and Divorce in Hawaii," *Social Forces* 36 (1): 77–84; Espiritu, *Asian American Women and Men*, pp. 95–98; A. Boyd-Franklin, *Black Families in Therapy: A Multisystem Approach* (New York: Guilford, 1989).

38. Besharov and Sullivan, "One Flesh," p. 21.

39. C. Astor, "Gallup Poll: Progress in Black/White Relations, but Race Is Still an Issue." *USIA Electronic Journal* 2 (1997).

40. U.S. Bureau of the Census, Current Population Reports, 1997.

41. Hayes-Bautista and Rodriguez, "L.A. County's Answer for Racial Tensions."

References

Adams, R. 1937. *Interracial Marriage in Hawaii*. New York: Macmillan.

Adorno, T. W., E. Frenkel-Brunswick, D. J. Levinson, and R. N. Sanford. 1950; 1969. *The Authoritarian Personality*. Abridged edition. New York: W. W. Norton.

Ahern, F. M., R. E. Cole, R. C. Johnson, and B. Wong. 1981. "Personality Attributes of Males and Females Marrying within vs. across Racial/Ethnic Groups." *Behavior Genetics* 11 (3): 181–94.

Alba, R. D., and R. M. Golden. 1986. "Patterns of Ethnic Marriage in the United States." *Social Forces* 65: 202–23.

Allman, K. M. 1996. "(Un)Natural Boundaries: Mixed Race, Gender, and Sexuality." In *The Multiracial Experience: Racial Borders As the New Frontier*, ed. M.P.P. Root, pp. 277–90. Thousand Oaks, Calif.: Sage Publications.

Allport, G. W. 1954; 1979. *The Nature of Prejudice*. Reading, Mass.: Addison-Wesley.

Andrews, R. 1987. *Concise Columbia Dictionary of Quotations*. New York: Avon Books.

Assembly of Bahai'is of the United States. 1991. *The Vision of Race Unity: America's Most Challenging Issue*. Wilmette, Ill: Baha'i Publishing Trust.

Astor, C. 1997. "Gallup Poll: Progress in Black/White Relations, but Race Is Still an Issue." *USIA Electronic Journal* 2 (3).

Ball, H. 1998. *A Defiant Life: Thurgood Marshall and the Persistence of Racism in America*. New York: Crown Publishers.

Berman, L. 1968. *Jews and Intermarriage*. New York: Thomas Yoseloff.

Bernstein, I. 1996. *Guns or Butter: The Presidency of Lyndon Johnson*. New York: Oxford University Press.

Besharov, D. J., and T. S. Sullivan. 1996. "One Flesh: America Is Experiencing an Unprecedented Increase in Black-White Intermarriage." *The New Democrat* (July/August): 19–21.

211

Blau, P. M., C. Beeker, and K. M. Fitzpatrick. 1984. "Intersecting Social Affiliations and Intermarriage." *Social Forces* 62 (3): 585–606.

Blau, P. M., T. C. Blum, and J. E. Schwartz. 1982. "Heterogeneity and Intermarriage." *American Sociological Review* 47: 45–62.

Blum, T. C. 1984. "Racial Inequality and Salience: An Examination of Blau's Theory of Social Structure." *Social Forces* 62 (3): 607–17.

Bogardus, E. S. 1959. *Social Distance.* Yellow Springs, Ohio: Antioch Press.

Bogle, D. 1996. *Toms, Coons, Mulattoes, Mammies, and Bucks.* New York: Continuum.

Booker, S. 1967. "Couple That Rocked the Courts." *Ebony,* 78–84.

Boyd-Franklin, N. 1989. *Black Families in Therapy: A Multisystem Approach.* New York: Guilford Press.

Boykin, A. W. 1985. "The Triple Quandary and the Schooling of Afro-American Children." In *The School Achievement of Minority Children,* ed. U. Neisser. Hillsdale, N.J.: Lawrence Erlbaum.

Boykin, A. W., and F. Toms. 1985. "Black Child Socialization Framework." In *Black Children: Social, Educational, and Parental Environments,* ed. H. P. McAdoo and J. L. McAdoo, pp. 33–51. Beverly Hills, Calif.: Sage Publications.

Branden, N. 1988. "A Vision of Romantic Love." In *The Psychology of Love,* ed. R. J. Sternberg and M. L. Barnes, pp. 218–31. New Haven: Yale University Press.

Brown, N. G., and R. E. Douglass. 1996. "Making the Invisible Visible: The Growth of Community Network Organizations." In *The Multiracial Experience: Racial Borders As the New Frontier,* ed. M.P.P. Root, pp. 323–40. Thousand Oaks, Calif.: Sage Publications.

Camper, C. 1994. *Miscegenation Blues: Voices of Mixed Race Women.* Toronto: Sister Vision Press.

Carrasquillo, H. 1998. "The Puerto Rican Family." In *Minority Families in the United States,* ed. R. L. Taylor, 2d. ed., pp. 95–107. Upper Saddle River, N.J.: Prentice Hall.

Chapman, A. B. 1988. "Male-Female Relations: How the Past Affects the Present." In *Black Families,* ed. M. P. McAdoo, 2d. ed., pp. 190–200. Thousand Oaks, Calif.: Sage Publications.

Chan, S. 1991. *Asian Americans: An Interpretive History.* Boston: Twayne Publishers.

Cheng, C. K., and D. S. Yamamura. 1957. "Interracial Marriage and Divorce in Hawaii." *Social Forces* 36 (1): 77–84.

Collins, P. H. 1990. *Black Feminist Thought: Knowledge, Consciousness, and the Politics of Empowerment.* New York: Routledge.

———. 1998. "It's All in the Family: Intersections of Gender, Race, and Nation." *Hypatia* 13 (3): 62–82.

Comas-Diaz, L. 1996. "LatiNegra: Mental Health Issues of African Latinas." In *The Multiracial Experience: Racial Borders As the New Frontier,* ed. M.P.P. Root, pp. 167–190. Thousand Oaks, Calif.: Sage Publications.

Cordova, F. 1983. *Filipinos: Forgotten Asian Americans.* Dubuque, Iowa: Kendall/Hunt Publishing Co.

Cose, E. 1993. *Rage of the Privileged Class.* New York: Harper Perennial.

Crohn, J. 1995. *Mixed Matches: How to Create Successful Interracial, Interethnic, and Interfaith Relationships.* New York: Fawcett Columbine.

Cross, W. E., Jr. 1991. *Shades of Black: Diversity in African American Identity.* Philadelphia: Temple University Press.

Cross, W. E., Jr., L. Strauss, and P. Fhagen-Smith. 1999. "African American Identity Development across the Life Span: Educational Implications." In *Racial and Ethnic Identity in School Practices: Aspects of Human Development,* ed. R. H. Sheets and E. Hollins, pp. 29–48. Mahwah, N.J.: Lawrence Erlbaum.

Daniel, G. R. 1992. "Passers and Pluralists: Subverting the Racial Divide." In *Racially Mixed People in America,* ed. M.P.P. Root, pp. 91–107. New York: Haworth Press.

Daniels, R. 1977. *The Politics of Prejudice: The Anti-Japanese Movement in California and the Struggle for Japanese Exclusion.* Berkeley: University of California Press.

Davidson, J. R. 1992. "Theories about Black-White Interracial Marriage: A Clinical Perspective." *Journal of Multicultural Counseling and Development* 20 (4): 150–57.

Davis, F. J. 1991. *Who Is Black? One Nation's Definition.* University Park: Pennsylvania State University Press.

Dimas, J. M. 1995. "Psycho-Social Adjustment in Children of Inter-ethnic Families: The Relationship to Cultural Behavior and Ethnic Identity." Ph.D. diss. University of California, Berkeley.

Ellison, R. 1970; 1998. "What America Would Be Like without Blacks." In *Black on White: Black Writers on What It Means to Be White,* ed. D. R. Roediger, pp. 160–67. New York: Shocken Books.

Encyclopaedia Britannica Online. 1998. "Women in American History: The Equal Rights Amendment."

Erlich, E., and M. de Bruhl, eds. 1996. *The International Thesaurus of Quotations.* New York: Harper Perennial.

Espiritu, Y. L. 1997. *Asian American Women and Men.* Thousand Oaks, Calif.: Sage Publications.

Falicov, C. J. 1986. Cross-Cultural Marriages. In *Clinical Handbook of Marital Therapy,* ed. N. S. Jacobson and A. S. Gurman, pp. 429–50. New York: Guilford.

Fanon, F. 1967. *Black Skin, White Masks.* New York: Grove.

Faulkner, J., and G. K. Kich. 1983. "Assessment and Engagement Stages in Therapy with the Interracial Family." In *Cultural Perspectives in Family Therapy,* ed. J. C. Hansen and C. J. Falicov, pp. 78–90. Rockville, Md.: Aspen Systems Corporation.

Ferber, A. L. 1998. *White Man Falling: Race, Gender, and White Supremacy.* Lanham, Md.: Rowman & Littlefield.

Fernandez, C. 1996. "Government Classification of Multiracial/Multiethnic People." In *The Multiracial Experience: Racial Borders As the New Frontier,* ed. M.P.P. Root, pp. 15–36. Thousand Oaks, Calif.: Sage Publications.

Fernandez, C., and L. Holscher. 1983. "Chicano-Anglo Intermarriage in Arizona, 1960–1980: An Exploratory Study of Eight Counties." *Hispanic Journal of Behavioral Sciences* 5 (3): 291–304.

Fishbein, M., I. and Ajzen. 1975. *Belief, Attitude, Intention and Behavior.* Reading, Mass.: Addison-Wesley.

Fitzpatrick, J. T. 1971. *Puerto Rican Americans: The Meaning of Migration to the Mainland.* Englewood Cliffs, N.J.: Prentice-Hall.

Fitzpatrick, J. T., and D. T. Gurak. 1979. *Hispanic Intermarriage in New York City: 1975.* New York: Fordham University Hispanic Research Center.

Forbes, J. D. 1988. *Black Africans and Native Americans.* New York: Basil Blackwell.

———. 1990. "The Manipulation of Race, Caste, and Identity: Classifying AfroAmericans, Native Americans, and Red-Black People." *Journal of Ethnic Studies* 17: 1–51.

Frankenberg, R. 1993. *White Women, Race Matters: The Social Construction of Whiteness.* Minneapolis: University of Minnesota Press.

Fromm, E. 1955. *The Sane Society.* New York: Rinehart.

Fujino, D. 1992. "Extending Exchange Theory: Effects of Ethnicity and Gender on Asian American Heterosexual Relationships. Ph.D. diss. University of California, Los Angeles.

Funderburg, L. 1994. *Black, White, Other: Biracial Americans Talk about Race and Identity.* New York: William Morrow.

Gallagher, C. 1995. "White Reconstruction in the University." *Socialist Review* 24 (1/2): 165–87.

Gallup Poll Monthly. August 1991. "For the first time, more Americans approve of interracial marriage than disapprove." No. 311: 60–64.

Garcia, V. 1997. "La Chicana, Chicano Movement, and Women's Liberation." In *Chicana Feminist Thought: The Basic Historical Writings,* ed. A. M. Garcia, pp. 199–201. New York: Routledge.

Gaskins, P. F. 1999. *What Are You?: Voices of Mixed-Race Young People.* New York: Henry Holt.

Gates, H. L., Jr. 1997. *Thirteen Ways of Looking at a Black Man.* New York: Vintage Books.

Gay, K. 1995. *I Am Who I Am: Speaking Out about Multiracial Identity.* New York: Franklin Watts.

Giddings, P. 1984. *When and Where I Enter: The Impact of Black Women on Race and Sex in America.* New York: Bantam Books.

Glick, P. C. 1988. "Demographic Pictures of Black Families." In *Black Families,* ed. H. P. McAdoo, 2d ed., pp. 111–32. Thousand Oaks, Calif.: Sage Publications.

Goffman, E. 1963. *Stigma: Notes on the Management of Spoiled Identity.* New York: Simon and Schuster.

Gold, S. J. 1993. "Migration and Family Adjustment: Continuity and Change among Vietnamese in the United States." In *Family Ethnicity: Strength in Diversity,* ed. H. P. McAdoo, pp. 300–314. Thousand Oaks, Calif.: Sage Publications.

Goldstein, J. R., and A. J. Morning. 2000. "The Multiple-Race Population of the United States: Issues and Estimates." *PNAS* 97 (11): 6230–35.

Gordon, L. R. 1997. "Race, Sex, and Matrices of Desire in an Antiblack World: An Essay in Phenomenology and Social Role." In *Race/Sex: Their Sameness, Difference, and Interplay,* ed. N. Zack, pp. 119–32. New York: Routledge.

Gordon, M. M. 1964. *Assimilation in American life.* New York: Oxford University Press.

Graham, S. R. 1996. "The Real World." In *The Multiracial Experience: Racial Borders As the New Frontier,* ed. M.P.P. Root, pp. 37–48. Thousand Oaks, Calif.: Sage Publications.

Guttentag, M., and P. F. Secord. 1983. *Too Many Women? The Sex Ratio Question.* Beverly Hills: Sage Publications.

Guthrie, R. V. 1976. *Even the Rat Was White.* New York: Harper and Row.

Hall, C.C.I. 1980. *The Ethnic Identity of Racially Mixed People: A Study of Black-Japanese.* Ph.D. diss. University of California, Los Angeles.

Harewood, Earl of, and A. Peattie, eds. 1997. *The New Kobbe's Opera Book.* New York: Putnam.

Hamilton, H.J.B. 1990. *Christmas and 33 Years Inside an Interracial Family.* Self-Published.

Harris, C. 1993; 1998. "Whiteness As Property." In *Black on White: Black Writers on What It Means to Be White,* ed. D. R. Roediger, pp. 103–18. New York: Shocken Books.

Hayes-Bautista, D. E., and Rodriguez, G. 1996. "L. A. County's Answer for Racial Tensions: Intermarriage." *Los Angeles Times,* May 5, p. M6.

Heer, D. M. 1966. "Negro-White Marriages in the United States." *Journal of Marriage and the Family* 28: 262–73.

————. 1974. "The Prevalence of Black-White Marriage in the United States, 1960 and 1970." *Journal of Marriage and the Family* 36: 246–58.

Heiss, J. 1988. "Women's Values Regarding Marriage and the Family." In *Black Families*, ed. H. P. McAdoo, 2d ed., pp. 201–14. Thousand Oaks, Calif.: Sage Publications.

Helms, J. E. 1990. *Black and White Racial Identity: Theory, Research, and Practice.* New York: Greenwood Press.

Hernton, C. C. 1965; 1988. *Sex and Racism in America.* New York: Doubleday.

Ho, F. C., and R. C. Johnson. 1990. "Intraethnic and Interethnic Marriage and Divorce in Hawaii." *Social Biology* 37: 44–51.

Holscher, L. M. 1979. "Chicano Exogamous Marriages in New Mexico." Paper presented at the annual meeting of the Pacific Sociological Association, Anaheim, California.

hooks, b. 1981. *Ain't I a Woman?: Black Women and Feminism.* Boston South End Press.

————. 1990. *Yearning: Race, Gender, and Cultural Politics.* Boston: South End Press.

————. 1998. "Representations of Whiteness in the Black Imagination." In *Black on White: Black Writers on What It Means to Be White*, ed. D. R. Roediger. New York: Schocken Books.

————. 2000. *All about Love: New Visions.* New York: William Morrow.

Houston, V. H. 1997. "To the Colonizer Goes the Spoils: American Progeny in Vietnam War Films and Owning Up to the Gaze." *Amerasia Journal* 23 (1): 69–85.

Hurtado, A. 1996. *The Color of Privilege: Three Blasphemies on Race and Feminism.* Ann Arbor: University of Michigan Press.

Hwang, S. S., R. Saenz, and B. E. Aguirre. 1997. "Structural and Assimilationist Explanations of Asian American Intermarriage." *Journal of Marriage and the Family* 59 (3): 758–72.

Ignatiev, N., and J. Garvey. 1996. *Race Traitor.* New York: Routledge.

Interrace Magazine (May/June 1992). Back cover.

Jacobs, J. H. 1992. "Identity Development in Biracial Children." In *Racially Mixed People in America*, ed. M.P.P. Root, pp. 190–206. Thousand Oaks, Calif.: Sage Publications.

Jester, K. 1982. "Analytic Essay: Intercultural and Interracial Marriage." In *Intermarriage in the United States*, ed G. Cretser and J. Leon. New York: Haworth Press.

Johnson, D. J. 1992. "Developmental Pathways: Toward an Ecological Theoretical Formulation of Race Identity in Black-White Biracial Children." In *Racially Mixed People in America*, ed. M.P.P. Root, pp. 37–49. Thousand Oaks, Calif.: Sage Publications.

Johnson, R. C. N.d. "On the Meaning of Being Local." Unpublished manuscript.

———. 1984. "Group Income and Group Size As Influences on Marriage Patterns in Hawaii." *Social Biology* 31: 101–7.

Johnson, R. C., and C. Nagoshi. 1990. "Intergroup Marriage in Hawaii." Unpublished manuscript.

Johnson, W. R., and D. M. Warren. 1994. *Inside the Mixed Marriage: Accounts of Changing Attitudes, Patterns, and Perceptions of Cross-cultural and Interracial Marriages.* Lanham, Md.: University Press of America.

Jones, J. M. 1997. *Prejudice and Race.* 2d ed. New York: McGraw Hill.

Kaeser, G., and P. Gillespie. 1997. *Of Many Colors: Portraits of Multiracial Families.* Amherst: University of Massachusetts Press.

Katz, W. L. 1986. *Black Indians.* New York: Atheneum.

Kibria, N. 1993. *Family Tightrope: The Changing Lives of Vietnamese Americans.* Princeton: Princeton University Press.

———. 1998. "Vietnamese Families." In *Minority Families in the United States,* ed. R. L. Taylor, 2d ed., pp. 176–88. Upper Saddle River, N.J.: Prentice Hall.

Kich, G. K. 1992. "The Developmental Process of Asserting a Biracial, Bicultural Identity." In *Racially Mixed People in America,* ed. M.P.P. Root, pp. 304–17. Thousand Oaks, Calif.: Sage Publications.

Kikumura, A., and H. Kitano. 1973. "Interracial Marriage: A Picture of the Japanese Americans." *Journal of Social Issues* 29 (2), 67–81.

King, M. L., Jr. 1963. *Strength to love.* New York: Harper & Row.

King, R. C. 1997. "Multiraciality Reigns Supreme?: Mixed Race Japanese Americans and the Cherry Blossom Queen Pageant." *Amerasia* 23 (1): 113–30.

Kitano, H. L. 1988. *Race relations.* Englewood Cliffs, N.J.: Prentice Hall.

Kitano, H. L., and L. K. Chai. 1982. "Korean Interracial Marriage." *Marriage and Family Review* 5: 35–48.

Kitano, H. L., and L. K. Yeung. 1982. "Chinese Interracial Marriage." In *Intermarriage in the United States,* ed. G. Cretser and J. Leon, pp. 35–48. New York: Haworth Press.

Kitano, H. L., D. C. Fujino, and J. T. Sato. 1998. "Interracial Marriages: Where Are the Asian Americans and Where Are They Going?" In *Handbook of Asian American Psychology,* ed. L. C. Lee and N. W. Zane, pp. 233–60. Thousand Oaks, Calif.: Sage Publications.

Lang, R. L., ed. 1994. *The Birth of a Nation.* New Brunswick, N.J.: Rutgers University Press.

Lee, S. M., and K. Yamanaka. 1990. "Patterns of Asian American Intermarriage and Marital Assimilation." *Journal of Comparative Family Studies* 21 (2): 287–305.

Leonard, K. I. 1992. *Making Ethnic Choices: California's Punjabi Mexican Americans*. Philadelphia: Temple University Press.

Lerner, G. 1986. *The Creation of Patriarchy*. New York: Oxford University Press.

Lewis, A. 1987. "What Does the Bible Say about Mixed Marriage? *The Standard* (June): 8.

Liska, A. E. 1984. "A Critical Examination of the Causal Structure of the Fishbein/Ajzen Attitude-Behavior Model." *Social Psychology Quarterly* 47: 61–74.

Loewen, J. W. 1971. *Mississippi Chinese: Between Black and White*. Cambridge: Harvard University Press.

Macdonald, A. 1978; 1996. *The Turner Diaries*. New York: Barricade Books.

Marchetti, G. 1993. *Romance and the "Yellow Peril": Race, Sex, and Discursive Strategies in Hollywood Fiction*. Berkeley: University of California Press.

McClintock, A. 1995. *Imperial Leather: Race, Gender and Sexuality in the Colonial Contest*. New York: Routledge.

McCunn, R. L. 1995. *Wooden Fish Songs*. New York: Dutton.

McDonald, L. 1977. *Racial Equality*. Skokie, Ill. and New York: National Textbook Company and American Civil Liberties Union.

McGlen, N. E., and K. O'Connor. 1995. *Women, Politics and American Society*. Englewood Cliffs, N.J.: Prentice-Hall.

Merton, R. K. 1938. "Social Structure and Anomie." *American Sociological Review* 3: 672–82.

———. 1941. "Intermarriage and the Social Structure: Fact and Theory." *Psychiatry* 4: 361–74.

Michael, R. T., J. H. Gagnon, E. O. Laumann, and G. Kolata. 1994. *Sex in America: A Definitive Survey*. New York: Warner Books.

Miller, R. L. 1992. "The Human Ecology of Multiracial Identity. In *Racially Mixed People in America*, ed. M.P.P. Root, pp. 24–36. Thousand Oaks, Calif.: Sage Publications.

Min, P. G. 1993. "Korean Immigrants' Marital Patterns and Marital Adjustment." In *Family Ethnicity: Strength in Diversity*, ed. H. P. McAdoo, pp. 287–99. Thousand Oaks, Calif.: Sage Publications.

Mittelbach, F., J. W. Moore, and R. McDaniel. 1966. "Intermarriage of Mexican Americans." *Mexican American Study Project Advance Report No. 6* (November). Los Angeles: University of California.

Monahan, T. 1977. "Interracial Marriage in a Southern Area: Maryland, Virginia, and the District of Columbia." *Journal of Comparative Family Studies* 8: 217–41.

Murguia, E. 1982. *Chicano Intermarriages: A Theoretical and Empirical Study*. San Antonio: Trinity University Press.

Myrdal, G. 1944; 1964. *An American Dilemma: The Negro Problem and Modern Democracy*. New York: McGraw-Hill.

Nagoshi, C. T., R. C. Johnson, and K.A.M. Honbo. 1992. "Assortative Mating for Cognitive Abilities, Personality, and Attitudes: Offspring from the Hawaii Family Study of Cognition. *Personality and Individual Differences* 13: 883–91.

National Opinion Research Center. 1990. USNORC.GSS91.R125A.

Nicolay, J. G., and J. Hay, J., eds. 1894. *Abraham Lincoln, Complete Works.* New York: The Century Company.

Ogbu, J. U. 1988. "Black Education: A Cultural-Ecological Perspective." In *Black Families,* ed. H. P. McAdoo, 2d ed., pp. 169–84. Thousand Oaks, Calif.: Sage Publications.

Omi, M., and H. Winant. 1986. *Racial Formation in the United States from the 1960s to the 1980s.* New York: Routledge & Kegan Paul.

Ordonez, R. 1997. "Mail-order Brides: An Emerging Community." In *Filipino Americans: Transformation and Identity,* ed. M.P.P. Root, pp. 121–42. Thousand Oaks, Calif.: Sage Publications.

Page, S. 1997. "Little Rock Nine Welcomed Back as Heroes." *USA Today,* September 26, 6A.

Pagnini, D. L., and S. P. Morgan. 1990. "Intermarriage and Social Distance among U.S. Immigrants at the Turn of the Century." *American Journal of Sociology* 96 (2): 405–32.

Parham, T. A., and J. E. Helms. 1985. "Relation of Racial Identity Attitudes to Self-Actualization and Affective States of Black Students." *Journal of Counseling Psychology* 32 (2): 431–40.

Peele, S. 1988. "Fools for Love: The Romantic Ideal, Psychological Theory, and Addictive Love." In *The Psychology of Love,* ed. R. J. Sternberg and M. L. Barnes, pp. 159–88. New Haven: Yale University Press.

Peele, S., and A. Brodsky. 1976. *Love and Addiction.* New York: NAL.

Perez, L. 1998. "Cuban American Families." In *Minority Families in the United States,* ed. R. L. Taylor, 2d ed., pp. 108–24. Upper Saddle River, N.J.: Prentice Hall.

Peterson, K. S. 1997. "For Today's Teens, Race 'Not an Issue Anymore.'" *USA Today,* November 23, 1A.

Porterfield, E. 1978. *Black and White Mixed Marriages.* Chicago: Nelson-Hall.

———. 1982. "Black-American Intermarriage in the United States." *Marriage and Family Review* 5: 17–34.

Prager, K. J. 1995. *The Psychology of Intimacy.* New York: Guilford Press.

Prinzing, F., and A. Prinzing. 1991. *Mixed Messages: Responding to Interracial Marriage.* Chicago: Moody Press.

Quian, Z. 1997. "Breaking the Racial Barriers: Variations in Interracial Marriage between 1980 and 1990." *Demography 34:* 263–76.

Ramirez, D. A. 1996. "Multiracial Identity in a Color-Conscious World." In

The Multiracial Experience: Racial Borders As the New Frontier, ed. M.P.P. Root, pp. 49–62. Thousand Oaks, Calif.: Sage Publications.

Ramirez, M., III. 1983. *Psychology of the Americas: Mestizo Perspectives on Personality and Mental Health.* New York: Pergamon Press.

Reddy, M. T. 1994. *Crossing the Colorline: Race, Parenting, and Culture.* New Brunswick, N.J.: Rutgers University Press.

Rodriguez, N., M. Ramirez III, and M. Korman. 1999. "The Transmission of Family Values across Generations of Mexican, Mexican American, and Anglo American Families: Implications for Mental Health." In *Racial and Ethnic Identity in School Practices: Aspects of Human Development,* ed. R. H. Sheets and E. Hollins, pp. 141–56. Mahwah, N.J.: Lawrence Erlbaum.

Root, M.P.P. 1990. "Resolving 'Other' Status: Identity Development of Biracial Individuals." In Diversity and *Complexity in Feminist Therapy,* ed. L. S. Brown and M.P.P. Root, pp. 185–205. New York: Haworth Press.

———, ed. 1992. *Racially Mixed People in America.* Thousand Oaks, Calif.: Sage Publications.

———. 1994. "Mixed-race Women." In *Women of Color: Integrating Ethnic and Gender Identities in Psychotherapy,* ed. L. Comas-Diaz and B. Greene, pp. 455–78. New York: Guilford Press.

———, ed. 1996. *The Multiracial Experience: Racial Borders As the New Frontier.* Thousand Oaks, Calif.: Sage Publications.

———. 1997. "Multiracial Asians: Models of Ethnic Identity." *Amerasia* 23 (1): 29–42.

———. 1998. "Experiences and Processes Affecting Racial Identity Development: Preliminary Results from the Biracial Sibling Project." *Cultural Diversity and Mental Health* 4: 237–47.

———. 1999. "The Biracial Baby Boom: Understanding Ecological Constructions of Racial Identity in the 21st Century." In *Racial and Ethnic Identity in School Practices: Aspects of Human Development,* ed. R. H. Sheets and E. Hollins, pp. 67–90. Mahwah, N.J.: Lawrence Erlbaum.

———. Forthcoming. "Factors Influencing the Variation in Racial and Ethnic Identity of Mixed Heritage Persons of Asian Ancestry." In *Reconfiguring Race, Re-articulating Ethnicity: Multiracial Identity and Asian America,* ed. T. K. Williams and C. Nakashima. Philadelphia: Temple University Press.

Rosenblatt, P. C., and T. A. Karis. 1993–1994. "Family Distancing Following a Fatal Farm Accident." *Omega* 28: 183–200.

Rosenblatt, P. C., T. A. Karis, and R. D. Powell. 1995. *Multiracial Couples: Black and White Voices.* Thousand Oaks, Calif.: Sage Publications.

Rothman, E. K. 1984. *Hands and Hearts: A History of Courtship in America.* New York: Basic Books.

Said, E. 1978. *Orientalism.* New York: Random House.

Sailer, S. 1997. "Is Love Colorblind?" *National Review,* July 14, pp. 30–33.

Salgado de Snyder, N., and A. M. Padilla. 1982. "Interethnic Marriages of Mexican Americans after Nearly Two Decades." *Human Organization* 41: 359–62.

Salzman, J., A. Back, and G. S. Sorin, eds. 1992. *Bridges and Boundaries: African Americans and American Jews.* New York: George Braziller and the Jewish Museum.

Sanjek, R. 1994. "Intermarriage and the Future of Races in the United States." In *Race,* ed. S. Gregory and R. Sanjek, pp. 103–30. New Brunswick, N.J.: Rutgers University Press.

Seattle Post-Intelligencer. 1998. "Race Advisory Board Rejects Idea of 'Colorblind' Society." July 8, C3.

Sheets, R. H. 1999. "Human Development and Ethnic Identity." In *Racial and Ethnic Identity in School Practices: Aspects of Human Development,* ed. R. H. Sheets and E. Hollins, pp. 91–101. Mahwah, N.J.: Lawrence Erlbaum.

Senna, D. 1998. *Caucasia.* New York: Riverhead Books, Penguin Putnam, Inc.

Shinagawa, L. H., and G. Y. Pang. 1988. "Intraethnic, Interethnic, and Interracial Marriages among Asian Americans in California, 1980." *Berkeley Journal of Sociology* 33: 95–114.

Simmel, G. 1908; 1955. *Conflict and the Web of Group Affiliations.* New York: Free Press.

Southern Poverty Law Center. 1999. "All in the Family." *Intelligence Report* 95: 12–19.

Spaights, E., and H. E. Dixon. 1984. "Socio-psychological Dynamics in Pathological Black-White Romantic Alliances." *Journal of Instructional Psychology* 11 (3): 132–38.

Spickard, P. R. 1989. *Mixed Blood: Intermarriage and Ethnic Identity in Twentieth-Century America.* Madison: University of Wisconsin Press.

———. 1989. "Injustice Compounded: Amerasians and Non-Japanese Americans in World War II Concentration Camps." *Journal of Ethnic History* 5 (2): 5–22.

Staples, R. 1981. *The World of Black Singles.* Westport, Conn.: Greenwood Press.

———. 1988. "An Overview of Race and Marital Status." In *Black Families,* ed. H. P. McAdoo, 2d ed., pp. 187–89. Thousand Oaks, Calif.: Sage Publications.

Stephan, C. W. 1992. Mixed-Heritage Individuals: Ethnic Identity and Trait Characteristics." In *Racially Mixed People in America,* ed. M.P.P. Root, pp. 50–63. Thousand Oaks, Calif.: Sage Publications.

Sternberg, R. J. 1986. "A Triangular Theory of Love." *Psychological Review* 93: 119–35.

———. 1998. *Love Is a Story: A New Theory of Relationships.* New York: Oxford University Press.

Stoler, L. A. 1995. *Race and the Education of Desire: Foucault's History of Sexuality and the Colonial Order of Things.* Durham: Duke University Press.

Sue, S., and J. K. Morishima. 1982. *The Mental Health of Asian Americans.* San Francisco: Jossey-Bass.

Sung, B. L. 1990. *Chinese American Intermarriage.* New York: Center for Migration Studies.

Taylor, P. L., M. B. Tucker, and C. Mitchell-Kernan. 1998. "Interethnic Marital Attitudes and Dating Patterns in Twenty-One Cities." Unpublished manuscript.

Tenzer, L. R. 1990. *A Completely New Look at Interracial Sexuality: Public Opinion and Select Commentaries.* Manahawkin, N.J.: Scholars' Publishing House.

Thibaut, J. W., and H. H. Kelley. 1959. *The Social Psychology of Groups.* New York: Wiley.

Thornton, M. C. 1992. "The Quiet Immigration: Foreign Spouses of U.S. Citizens, 1945–1985." In *Racially Mixed People in America,* ed. M.P.P. Root, pp. 64–76. Thousand Oaks, Calif.: Sage Publications.

Thornton, M. C., L. M. Chatters, R. J. Taylor, and W. R. Allen. 1990. "Sociodemographic and Environmental Correlates of Racial Socialization by Black Parents." *Child Development* 61: 401–9.

Time Magazine. 1993. Special Issue, fall.

Tinker, J. N. 1982. "Intermarriage and Assimilation in a Rural Society: Japanese Americans in the U.S." In *Intermarriage in the United States,* ed. G. A. Cretser and J. J. Leon (New York: Haworth Press), pp. 61–74.

Trimble, J. E. 1999. "Social Psychological Perspectives on Changing Self-identification among American Indian and Alaska Natives." In *Handbook of Cross-Cultural/Multicultural Personality Assessment,* ed. R. H. Dana. Mahwah, N.J.: Lawrence Erlbaum.

Trinh, T. M-h. 1989. *Woman, Native, Other.* Bloomington: Indiana University Press.

Tucker, M. B., and C. Mitchell-Kernan. 1990. "New Trends in Black American Interracial Marriage: The Social Structural Context." *Journal of Marriage and the Family* 52: 209–18.

———. 1991. "New Trends in African American Interracial Marriage and Dating: Data from Southern California." Paper presented at the Nineteenth Annual Conference of the National Association for Ethnic Studies.

———. 1995. *The Decline in Marriage among African Americans.* New York: Russell Sage Foundation.

Twine, F. W. 1996. "Heterosexual Alliances: The Romantic Management of

Racial Identity. In *The Multiracial Experience: Racial Borders As the New Frontier,* ed. M.P.P. Root, pp. 291–304. Thousand Oaks, Calif.: Sage Publications.

U.S. Bureau of the Census. 1960. Population Reports. *Marital Status,* PC (2) 4E.

U.S. Bureau of the Census. 1970. Population Reports. *Marital Status,* PC (2) 4C, Table 12.

U.S. Bureau of the Census. 1980. Population Reports. *Marital Status,* PC80 (2) 4C.

U.S. Bureau of the Census. 1990. Population Reports. *Characteristics of the Black Population,* CP (3) 6.

U.S. Bureau of the Census. 1990. Population Reports. *Household and family characteristics,* P20, March 1994.

vanden Berghe, P. 1967. *Race and Racism: A Comparative Perspective.* New York: John Wiley.

Waters, M. C. 1990. *Ethnic Options: Choosing Identities in America.* Berkeley: University of California Press.

Weathers, D. 1997. "Corporate race wars." *Essence,* October, pp. 80–84, 156–58, 160.

Wehrly, B., K. R. Kenney, and M. E. Kenney. 1999. *Counseling Multiracial Families.* Thousand Oaks, Calif.: Sage Publications.

Weisman, J. R. 1996. "An 'Other' Way of Life: The Empowerment of Alterity in the Interracial Individual. In *The Multiracial Experience: Racial Borders As the New Frontier,* ed. M.P.P. Root, pp. 152–64.

Welwood, J. 1996. *Love and Awakening: Discovering the Sacred Path of Intimate Relationship.* New York: Harper Collins.

Whitfield, S. J. 1988. *A Death in the Delta: The Story of Emmett Till.* New York: Free Press.

Williams, T. K. 1992. "Prism Lives: Identity of Binational Amerasians." In *Racially Mixed People in America,* ed. M.P.P. Root, pp. 280–303. Thousand Oaks, Calif.: Sage Publications.

———. 1996. "Race as Process: Reassessing the 'What Are You?' Encounters of Biracial Individuals." In *The Multiracial Experience: Racial Borders As the New Frontier,* ed. M.P.P. Root, pp. 191–210. Thousand Oaks, Calif.: Sage Publications.

Williamson, J. 1984. *New People: Miscegenation and Mulattoes in the United States.* New York: New York University Press.

Wilson, T. P. 1992. "Blood Quantum: Native American Mixed Bloods." In *Racially Mixed People in America,* ed. M.P.P. Root, pp. 108–25. New York: Haworth Press.

Wong, M. L. 1994. "An Act of Revenge: Toying with Race, Passions, Desire, and Danger." Paper presented at the annual meeting of the American Psychological Association, Toronto, Canada.

Wyatt, G. E. 1997. *Stolen Women: Reclaiming Our Sexuality, Taking Back Our Lives.* New York: John Wiley.

Yellowbird, M., and C. M. Snipp. 1998. "American Indian Families." In *Minority Families in the United States,* ed. R. L. Taylor, pp. 226–48. Upper Saddle River, N.J.: Prentice Hall.

Young, R.J.C. 1995. *Colonial Desire: Hybridity in Theory, Culture, and Race.* New York: Routledge.

Young-Ware, D., and D. Ware. 1998. "An Interracial Developmental Model: A Thoughtful Presentation of the Components of Developing an Interracial Couple Relationship and Identity." *Interrace* 8 (3): 12–13.

Yuan, D. Y. 1980. "Significant Demographic Characteristics of Chinese Who Intermarry in the United States." *California Sociologist* 3 (2): 184–96.

Zack, N., ed. 1995. *American Mixed Race: The Culture of Microdiversity.* Lanham, Md.: Rowman & Littlefield.

———. 1997. *Race/Sex: Their Sameness, Difference, and Interplay.* New York: Routledge.

Index